INVISIBLE

WHAT TO DO WHEN AI ERASES YOUR BUSINESS

MICHAEL J. GOLDRICH

ISBN: 979-8-89079-414-7 (hardcover)
ISBN: 979-8-89079-415-4 (paperback)
ISBN: 979-8-89079-416-1 (ebook)

Printed in the United States of America

To my family.

IMPORTANT DISCLAIMER AND LIMITATION OF LIABILITY

This book provides educational insights and strategic frameworks only. It does not constitute legal, financial, or professional consulting advice, nor does it guarantee specific outcomes such as revenue growth, market share gains, or ROI improvements. Readers must evaluate applicability to their own operations, conduct independent testing, and seek qualified professional guidance before making business decisions.

Because AI platforms evolve rapidly, specific tactics described here may become outdated as systems change their retrieval, ranking, or citation processes. The author and publisher disclaim responsibility for any losses or outcomes arising from reliance on this material. Readers assume full responsibility for how frameworks are applied and accept inherent risks related to emerging technologies and evolving data environments.

Portions of this work were developed with assistance from generative AI and reviewed by the author for accuracy and intent. By continuing past this page, you acknowledge and accept these terms in full.

CONTENTS

PROLOGUE
WHAT YOU WILL FIND HERE

The Shift That Changes Every Industry

Something fundamental broke in how people find businesses.

For twenty-five years, discovery worked the same way. A person typed words into a search engine. The search engine returned a list of links. The person clicked through to websites, compared options, and made a decision. Every business built its digital strategy around earning a position on that list.

That model is breaking apart. The fractures are already visible.

AI systems increasingly answer the question directly. The customer asks what to buy, where to stay, which product to choose. The AI responds with a specific recommendation, a specific reason, and a specific set of facts supporting the choice. The customer never sees a list of links. The customer may visit a website later to complete a transaction, but the discovery decision already happened. The customer never encounters your brand unless the AI decided you were the answer.

That is what invisible means. Your business still exists. Your website still works. Your reviews still shine. None of it matters if the AI does not know you are there. The shift from search results to AI-generated answers created a new form of competitive exclusion. Businesses that appear in AI recommendations get considered. Businesses that do not get skipped. There is no second page of results to scroll to. There is no list at all.

This transformation affects every industry that depends on search-driven discovery. Retail, financial services, legal, healthcare, SaaS, real estate. Any business that a potential customer might research before purchasing faces the same structural shift. Algorithms are replacing search results. The question of whether your business appears in AI-generated answers is becoming as consequential as whether your business appeared on the first page of Google a decade ago.

Why Hospitality, and Why It Matters for Every Industry

I focus deeply on the hospitality industry in these pages. I use hotel examples, cite travel data, and discuss guest booking journeys. I do this for a specific reason.

Hotels sell perishable inventory. A room unsold on Tuesday night cannot be resold on Wednesday. Once the date passes, that revenue is gone permanently. This makes discovery failures uniquely punishing. A retail brand that loses visibility can discount inventory next month. A professional services firm can ramp up outreach next quarter. A hotel that fails to fill rooms tonight absorbs a loss that compounds every night it continues.

That economic pressure makes hospitality the clearest case study for what happens when AI reshapes discovery. The stakes are immediate. The consequences are measurable. The patterns that emerge here will repeat across every service industry in the years that follow. Wynter's 2026 survey of B2B buyers found that 84 percent now use AI for vendor discovery, with 68 percent starting their research in AI tools before opening Google. The pattern crosses industries. AI evaluates. Google verifies. The click that analytics records is not where the decision formed.

The principles, however, are universal. Whether you sell software, manage a retail brand, or run a professional services firm, the mechanics of the shift are identical. If you are not in hospitality, swap "guest" for "customer" and "booking" for "conversion." Schema markup applies identically regardless of industry. Citation network strategy works the same way for a law firm as it does for a resort. The Visibility Score testing protocol in Chapter 8 requires changing only the prompt wording to match your business category. The Answer Spiral describes how consumers research any considered purchase, not only hotel stays. The concepts most specific to hospitality are OTA (online travel agency) dynamics, Google Business Profile optimization for lodging, and the property-level risk assessment in Chapter 1. Read "property" as "business," "amenity" as "feature," and "rate" as "price." The frameworks hold.

Consider how the translation works in practice. A law firm's "bridge entity" (a contextual anchor that connects a business to a landmark, event, or concept the AI already recognizes) is the courthouse, the business district, or the specialized practice area that links the firm to what a client is actually searching for. When someone asks an AI platform for an estate planning attorney near a specific neighborhood, the AI performs the same retrieval process described in Chapter 6. It searches for structured data, cross-references citations from legal directories and bar association profiles, and synthesizes a recommendation from multiple sources. The firm that appears has schema markup on its practice area pages, consistent NAP data across Avvo, Martindale-Hubbell, and Google Business Profile, and published articles that third-party sources reference. The firm that remains invisible has a well-designed website that no AI platform can parse.

A retailer faces the same dynamics at product scale. When a shopper asks an AI for running shoes that work on wet pavement, the AI retrieves product specifications, aggregates review sentiment, and compares options across merchant listings. The retailer with structured product data, detailed specifications, and consistent information across shopping platforms earns the recommendation. The retailer relying on brand awareness and paid search placement does not appear in the conversation. Google's Universal Commerce Protocol, announced alongside retail industry partners in early 2026, signals how quickly AI-mediated product discovery will formalize.

A SaaS company loses enterprise deals when the procurement team asks an AI to shortlist project management platforms with specific integration requirements. The AI consults G2 reviews, analyst reports, comparison articles, and product documentation. The vendor with detailed feature specifications structured for extraction appears in the shortlist. The vendor with marketing language describing "powerful, flexible solutions" does not. The citation tier framework in Chapter 7 applies directly. G2 and Gartner function as Tier 2 sources. Product directories function as Tier 3.

LinkedIn published its own guide applying these same principles to B2B marketing content. Their internal analysis found traffic declines of up to 60 percent on non-brand keywords when AI Overviews launched. Their response mirrors every recommendation in this book: answer-first formatting, descriptive heading hierarchies, FAQ schema, structured data, and content architecture designed for AI extraction. The platform that dominates professional networking optimizes its own content using the same techniques this book recommends for hotels. The frameworks are not hospitality-specific. They are AI-retrieval-specific.

The Three Pillars of This Strategy

The strategy presented here rests on three distinct foundations:

The evidence. AI-mediated discovery is replacing traditional search. The traffic collapse is real and measured. DMG Media reported an 89% publisher click-through rate drop when AI Overviews appeared. Zero-click searches jumped from 56% to 69% in 12 months before stabilizing at that elevated level. Similarweb tracked 357% year-over-year growth in AI referrals to travel sites, growth that has since normalized into a persistent structural shift rather than an accelerating curve.

The numbers require context, and "A Note on the Numbers" later in this prologue explains why seemingly contradictory statistics actually measure different things. The headline finding holds across every study: zero-click behavior reached elevated levels and stayed there. Traditional search retains 95% market share. It also delivers fewer clicks. ChatGPT reached 37% of U.S. desktop users by September 2025, growing from a base of nearly zero 24 months earlier. These patterns document transformation, not replacement. AI platforms operate alongside traditional search, not instead of it.

Your response must address both channels because customers now use both.

The industry recognizes AI matters. It has not yet recognized where AI matters most. Wyndham's 2026 Hotel Owner Trends Report, surveying 325 hotel owners and developers across North America, found that 98% have already incorporated AI into their businesses. The adoption concentrates on operational efficiency (64%), energy management (54%), and revenue optimization (53%). Guest experience personalization registered at 9%. AI-mediated discovery, the subject of this book, does not appear among measured categories at all. Meanwhile, 73% of those same owners report feeling overwhelmed and unsure where to begin with further AI integration. The industry adopted AI for operations. It has not yet confronted the discovery crisis.

The technical analysis. The frameworks in this book come from studying how AI platforms function. Platform documentation, testing, and developer guidelines reveal what these systems need to accurately surface your business. The technical requirements (schema markup, rendering accessibility, and content structure) derive from documented platform behaviors.

The pattern recognition. I have been in this room before.

In 2013, I sat in boardrooms where executives argued that "serious business travelers" would never book luxury suites on a four-inch iPhone screen. They delayed mobile investment. Two years later, mobile bookings were climbing past 15% and accelerating quarter over quarter. I watched those same properties panic-spend six figures to catch up with a shift they had dismissed as irrelevant.

In 2016, I heard GMs dismiss Instagram as a "teenager's toy," only to watch them lose their high-margin wedding business to a competitor across the street who understood that brides plan weddings on visual platforms, not in brochures.

I saw the industry treat OTAs as "cheap billboards" rather than data-hungry rivals, waking up only after they were locked into paying 25% commissions to buy back their own guests.

The implementation timelines and organizational roadmaps in this book are extrapolated from the price hotels paid the last three times they waited for "perfect evidence" before acting. Every industry has its own version of these stories. The details differ. The pattern does not.

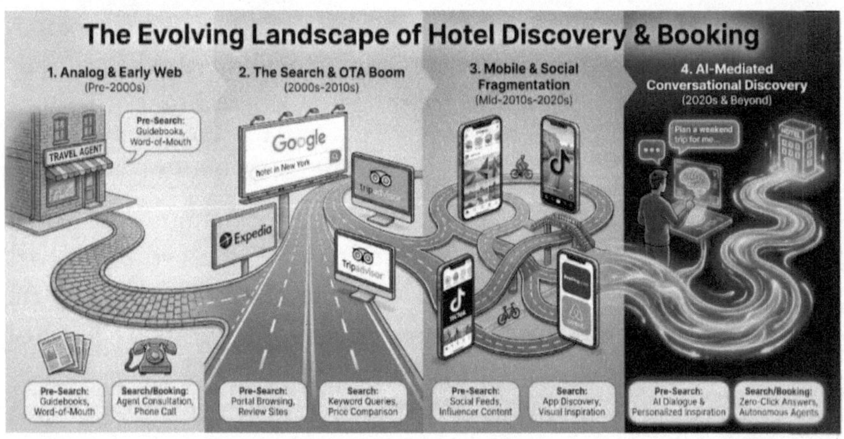

Here is What That Means

These frameworks combine what we know about how AI platforms work with what we have learned about how organizations successfully navigate digital transformation. The technical guidance stands on solid ground. The timelines represent informed projections from limited data.

Early implementations show promise. You should expect to adjust these approaches based on what you learn during execution.

What This Book Provides

The Visibility Score framework in Chapter 8 gives you measurement capability where none existed: testing methodology, component-level analysis, and trend tracking despite attribution limitations. You can measure whether you are improving, declining, or stuck, even without perfect analytics.

Strategic frameworks for navigating uncertainty. The maturity curve in Chapter 5 helps you assess current capabilities and plan progression. The risk segmentation in Chapter 1 helps you determine urgency. The market tier analysis in Chapter 7 sets realistic expectations about what you can achieve.

Implementation guidance based on how organizations actually work. The roadmaps in Chapter 9 reflect organizational realities I have observed across hundreds of properties and businesses. How decisions get made. How budgets get allocated. How resistance manifests. How initiatives succeed or fail based on factors unrelated to the technology itself.

The schema markup guidance in Chapter 6, citation network strategies in Chapter 7, and content strategy in Chapter 3 provide technical foundations that outlast any single platform. Structured code that helps AI systems understand your website content delivers durable value regardless of which AI platforms dominate in six months or two years.

Honest acknowledgment of what we do not know. Chapter 2 addresses the measurement gap. I do not pretend you can calculate a precise ROI. I will show you how to make evidence-based decisions despite attribution limitations.

The Companion Implementation Site

As organizations implement these frameworks, I will document real outcomes at www.vivanderadvisors.com/AI-Visibility. You will find case studies of complete implementations, refined Visibility Score weights based on actual correlation data, adjusted timelines reflecting real implementation experiences, and platform evolution updates as AI systems change.

This book provides the initial framework. The companion site provides evolving evidence.

How to Use This Book

If you need a guaranteed ROI before acting, close the book now. Wait for comprehensive industry research. Accept that you are choosing invisibility by default while you wait for certainty that may arrive after competitors have already claimed their advantages.

If you can invest in infrastructure during platform transformation despite measurement limitations, this book provides the structure you need.

Start with Chapter 1. Assess your risk level. Understand your competitive urgency. Read Chapter 2 next. Understand the measurement gap before you commit resources. Accept the attribution limitations.

Work through Chapters 3 through 7 to understand the transformation's technical and strategic dimensions. Then use Chapter 8 to establish baseline measurement and Chapter 9 to select your implementation roadmap.

Execute methodically. Measure monthly. Adjust quarterly. Maintain discipline through the plateau periods when visible progress slows despite continued effort. The compounding benefits emerge later for organizations that sustain commitment through early uncertainty.

A Note on the Numbers

You will encounter statistics throughout this book that appear contradictory. Zero-click searches at 69%. Also at 27%. Traffic declines of 89%. Also 20%. ChatGPT reaching 37% of users. Also 43%.

These numbers do not contradict each other. They measure different things.

Start with zero-click. The 69% figure comes from SparkToro and Datos research tracking global behavior across all devices. Mobile drives the number up. A person who asks their phone for a business's hours, reads the answer, and puts the phone away registered a zero-click search. That happens billions of times daily. The 27% figure comes from the same Datos report but isolates U.S. desktop behavior, where the gap narrows because desktop users research more deliberately, click more often, and complete more transactions. Desktop is where businesses generate most direct revenue. Both numbers matter. The 69% tells you the overall scale of the shift. The 27% tells you how much of your highest-value search traffic disappears without a click.

The traffic decline numbers split the same way. The 89% figure reflects publisher click-through rates when AI Overviews appear in specific search results. The 20% figure measures year-over-year referral traffic decline to travel sites across all searches. One captures the severity when AI answers appear. The other captures the cumulative drag over time.

Regional adoption varies significantly. Europe reached 43% ChatGPT penetration by September 2025. The U.S. reached 37%. Businesses in different markets face different competitive timelines.

I could have smoothed these numbers into a single clean narrative. I chose not to. The transformation happening in AI-mediated discovery defies simple characterization. Different research methodologies reveal different dimensions of the same underlying shift. Presenting only the numbers that support a tidy story would misrepresent reality.

What matters is directional agreement. Every credible study points in the same direction. According to the Q4 State of Search Report by Datos, zero-click behavior persists at elevated levels. AI platform adoption normalized into sustained use rather than continued vertical growth. Traditional search traffic declines. The volume of searches people conduct is also shrinking. Both the queries and the clicks are moving in the same direction. The specific percentages matter less than the trajectory they document.

When you encounter seemingly conflicting statistics in later chapters, remember this context. The researchers measured different populations, different timeframes, and different behaviors. The apparent contradictions reveal the complexity of transformation rather than unreliable evidence.

Read for direction, not precision. The direction is clear. Where this book offers specific operational targets or scoring thresholds, those reflect practitioner frameworks applied to the available evidence, not standalone empirical findings.

The Question This Book Answers

The question is not, "Can you prove this works?"

The question is, "How do I respond to a transformation that has already happened despite incomplete measurement and limited validated best practices?"

This book answers that question through frameworks.

The transformation is real. The evidence proves it through documented traffic collapse, measured platform adoption, and observed user behavior shifts. What remains uncertain is which specific optimization tactics deliver the best outcomes.

That uncertainty does not eliminate the need for a response. It changes what response looks like.

You cannot optimize for perfect ROI. You can build capabilities enabling directional measurement. You can establish technical foundations that serve you regardless of how the platforms change. You can develop organizational structures that ensure this work continues beyond the initial enthusiasm.

Organizations establishing competitive advantages through 2026 and 2027 will not have perfect evidence. They will act despite uncertainty, measure progress despite attribution gaps, and sustain commitment despite organizational challenges.

This book shows you how to become one of them. Not by guaranteeing specific outcomes. By providing frameworks built on two decades of pattern recognition from similar digital evolutions.

You will still have to measure and adjust. But you will have a map. That is more than most of your competitors have right now.

1
THE DISCOVERY CRISIS

I NEED TO show you some numbers.

A majority of the Google searches that matter for hotel discovery now surface some form of AI-generated answer. Pew Research Center's July 2025 study found that 18% of all Google searches triggered full AI summaries, with that rate climbing to 53% for queries containing ten or more words and 60% for question-based searches. Hotel research queries skew toward exactly these longer, question-based patterns. When a traveler types 'best pet-friendly hotels near downtown Austin with parking,' that query triggers an AI-generated answer more often than not. Pew's October 2025 survey confirmed the behavioral shift: 65% of U.S. adults now encounter AI summaries in their search results regularly, and the pattern persists. It did not retreat after the novelty faded.

The downstream effects compound from there. McKinsey projects that $750 billion in U.S. consumer spending will flow through AI-powered search by 2028. They estimate that roughly half of Google searches now surface some form of AI-enhanced result, including featured snippets, knowledge panels, and AI Overviews. McKinsey expects that percentage to exceed 75% within three years.

Those numbers describe the structural shift. Here is what it looks like in practice.

How Discovery Actually Works Now

A woman opens ChatGPT at 10:00 PM to plan a conference trip to Austin. She types: "Best hotels near the convention center for business travelers."

ChatGPT lists five properties. Your hotel does not appear among them.

She asks a follow-up: "Which of these has the quietest rooms?" ChatGPT pulls details from reviews, website descriptions, and blog posts. Engineers call this process query fan-out. When the traveler asked about quietest rooms, the AI did not look up a single answer. It generated and executed multiple distinct background searches:

"Austin convention hotels soundproofing reviews."

"Quietest luxury hotels Austin forum discussions."

"Hotel noise complaints Austin downtown."

The platform read the results of those searches, synthesized the findings, and delivered a confident recommendation. The AI performed the research clicks so the traveler never had to.

The system compares soundproofing mentions and recommends two properties.

She drills down on the two properties: "Does the JW Marriott Austin have good conference facilities?" She gets detailed responses about meeting room sizes, AV capabilities, and catering options.

Your property is three blocks from the convention center. You renovated your meeting rooms last year. Your soundproofing scores higher on TripAdvisor than the JW Marriott. None of that mattered. The AI never surfaced your hotel as an option.

She never visits your website. She never sees your Google ranking. She never clicks an ad. She books the JW Marriott because the AI conversation gave her confidence in the choice.

Your analytics show nothing. No session exists. No impression appears. You have no awareness that you lost a booking.

This scenario plays out across your market right now. The frequency increases every month as AI adoption embeds deeper into traveler behavior.

Notice the pattern. She did not move through a marketing funnel. She spiraled through iterative questions, each answer generating the next query, awareness and consideration and conversion collapsing into a single conversation. Chapter 3 defines this as the Answer Spiral. It replaces the funnel as the organizing model for how travelers research.

Who Uses AI Search and How They Use It

McKinsey research found that among AI-powered search users, 44% call it their primary and preferred information source. That tops traditional search at 31%, brand websites at 9%, and review sites at 6%.

The adoption pattern defies expectations. AI search use spans all age groups, not younger travelers alone. McKinsey documented that half of consumers across every demographic now intentionally seek out AI-powered search engines, including baby boomers. The typical technology adoption curve, where younger users lead and older segments lag years behind, did not materialize. This shift moved fast across the entire market.

More than 70% of AI-powered search users ask questions to learn about categories, brands, products, or services. Between 40% and 55% of consumers in travel, consumer electronics, grocery, wellness, apparel, beauty, and financial services use AI-based search to make purchasing decisions.

Traditional search frustrations accelerate this migration. A report from Eight Oh Two, an SEO and PPC marketing agency, documents that consumers increasingly use AI tools rather than Google as their first source of information, driven by dissatisfaction with traditional search results and rising expectations for AI-powered alternatives.

The Traffic Collapse

When AI answers appear, travelers behave differently than they did with traditional search results. Research shows only 8% of users click through to traditional results after viewing an AI-generated response. The rest either get their answer directly from the AI summary or abandon the search entirely. This pattern produces traffic reductions approaching 47% compared to searches without AI features.

The decline shows up across multiple measurements. Digital Content Next reported that median referral traffic from Google Search dropped 10% year-over-year in May and June 2025, with some publishers experiencing declines as steep as 25%. Chartbeat data shows organic Google search traffic down 33% globally from November 2024 to November 2025, with U.S. traffic down 38% over the same period. The Wikimedia Foundation documented that Wikipedia page views from human users declined 8% year-over-year between March and August 2025.

Across U.S. travel sites specifically, Similarweb data shows an approximately 20% year-over-year decline in search referrals in May 2025, with news and media sites declining approximately 17%.

DMG Media filed reports with UK regulators documenting exactly what happened when Google's AI Overviews appeared in search results. Publisher click-through rates dropped from 25.23% to 2.79%, an 89% decline. This represents measured traffic destruction across 18 months, not a projection or model.

These percentages vary because they measure different things. Publisher traffic behaves differently from travel site traffic. Global patterns differ from U.S. patterns. Desktop users research differently from mobile users. Every credible measurement confirms the same trajectory: traffic from traditional search declines.

The Alligator Mouth Effect

You can see this pattern in your own data. Open Google Search Console for any property that has maintained consistent rankings over the past 18 months. The impressions line trends upward or holds steady. Google still shows your pages. More queries than ever trigger results that include your listings. The clicks line diverges downward. Fewer travelers click through to your site despite those stable or rising impressions. SEO practitioners call this the "alligator mouth effect" because the two lines spread apart over time like opening jaws. Impressions above, clicks below, the gap widening quarter after quarter.

The pattern reveals what aggregate industry statistics cannot. Your rankings did not drop. Your content did not deteriorate. Your SEO team did nothing wrong. The search results page itself changed. AI Overviews now answer the question your listing used to answer. The traveler reads the AI-generated summary, gets enough information to form an opinion, and never clicks through to your website. Your impression counted. Your click did not. Multiply that interaction across thousands of queries per month and the alligator mouth opens wider.

This matters because it exposes a dangerous blind spot in traditional SEO reporting. A team that reports on rankings and impressions can present a dashboard showing stability or growth. The property looks healthy. The underlying reality is that each impression generates less traffic than it did 12 months ago. Properties that track only rankings or only impressions will miss the structural erosion until revenue shifts become impossible to ignore.

The **Alligator** Graph

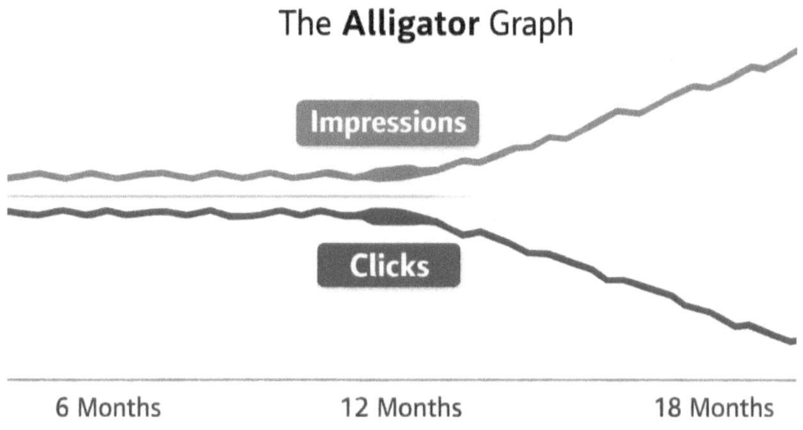

A Structural Decline, Not a Vertical Spike

Data from Milestone, analyzing over 3,500 websites, puts a timeline on this shift. AI referral share climbed from under 1% to between 2% and 3% before growth began to slow in November and December 2025. In a February 2026 conversation, Milestone's Anil Aggarwal noted that accurate projections remain difficult because Google does not split out Gemini traffic from traditional search. The real volume of AI-mediated discovery may already exceed what standard analytics capture, because queries handled by Gemini within the Google ecosystem never register as AI referrals. Aggarwal projected AI referral share reaching 10% to 15% by the end of 2026, a trajectory that reflects sustained adoption rather than the exponential spike many in the industry anticipated.

For two years, the industry watched the adoption curves of ChatGPT and Gemini with held breath, waiting for the vertical takeover.

It did not arrive the way most people expected.

Q4 2025 data from Datos reveals what the shift actually looks like. In the United States, the number of Google searches per searcher dropped by nearly 20% year-over-year. AI search visits grew 81% year over year. Traditional search visits declined 0.5%.

Those trajectories require careful reading. Overall desktop search volume held relatively stable at 90 to 100 searches per user monthly through Q3 2025. The decline measured by Datos reflects search intensity per session contracting as AI answers resolve queries that previously required multiple searches. Travelers still open Google. They conduct fewer follow-up searches once they arrive because AI-generated answers satisfy more of their initial questions.

Semrush research adds a counterintuitive finding: users who adopted ChatGPT actually increased their Google sessions from 10.5 to 12.6 per week. AI did not replace their search behavior. It expanded their total research activity while changing what they searched for.

The crisis for hoteliers extends beyond AI platforms claiming clicks from your search listings. It now includes the transformed searcher, the traveler who still uses Google but whose queries look different, run longer, and require different content to satisfy.

The Blurring Boundary Between Traditional and AI Search

The boundary between traditional and AI search blurs further every month. Semrush data from April 2024 through March 2025 shows that traditional search engines received 1,863 billion visits globally. AI search platforms received 55.2 billion visits during that same period. That is a 34 to 1 ratio.

The gap between these two ecosystems runs deeper than traffic volume. Ahrefs research found that 80% of sources cited by AI search platforms do not appear in Google's results at all. Only 12% overlap with Google's top 10 organic rankings. Ranking well in traditional search provides no guarantee of appearing in AI-generated answers. The two systems draw from fundamentally different source pools.

Measuring visits to ChatGPT alone misses the larger picture. The industry is moving toward agentic discovery, where AI agents on phones and desktops perform searches autonomously. A single user interaction with an AI agent might trigger fifty background searches to Google. The traffic volume to the AI interface represents a fraction of the actual search activity. The far larger volume sits underneath: billions of automated queries these agents perform across the web. Your hotel must be able to answer those queries to earn a recommendation.

The Semrush data does not count queries answered by AI within Google and Bing themselves. Zero-click behavior stabilized at 69% globally and 27% on U.S. desktops, as detailed in the Prologue. Those numbers did not keep climbing. The threat is no longer accelerating. It is persistent, locked into the architecture of how search results display.

That distinction matters. A growing threat invites urgency arguments. A persistent threat demands infrastructure arguments.

Zero-click behavior is not a wave you can wait out. It settled into the foundation of how Google and Bing deliver results. Google integrated Gemini across Search, Maps, and its entire product ecosystem, generating AI Overviews that answer queries before the user reaches any organic listing. Bing uses ChatGPT and its proprietary Copilot AI to provide conversational search results directly in its interface. The platforms converged. Travelers interact with AI whether they realize it or not.

This means the actual AI-mediated search volume runs substantially higher than the 55.2 billion figure suggests. You cannot cleanly separate "traditional" from "AI" search anymore. The zero-click rates documented in the Prologue persist because AI-generated answers resolve queries within the search interface itself. Users do not click to your site. They do not visit booking platforms. They read an AI-generated answer, form an impression, and move on. Your analytics capture nothing from that interaction.

Hotels do not face problems unique to their industry. This evolution affects every sector that depends on organic search traffic. Hotels face a particular vulnerability because discovery decisions happen during research sessions that you cannot track at all.

This decoupling creates a measurement problem unlike anything the industry has faced. For twenty years, the industry relied on a simple feedback loop. You ranked. You got clicks. You measured success. The AI era breaks that loop. Platform-side data is beginning to emerge, but no tool yet reconstructs the full path from AI recommendation to booking.

A travel agent AI might recommend your hotel fifty times a day to high-intent travelers who then book through a third-party platform or call you directly. Your Google Analytics will show zero sessions. Your SEO rank tracker will show no movement. You are being found constantly, but your dashboard says you are invisible.

You are no longer fighting for visibility alone. You are fighting to measure it.

The Cross-Industry Pattern

This traffic collapse extends beyond hospitality. Tank's 2025 Google AI Search Shift Report analyzed 800 companies across 16 UK industries, measuring organic traffic before and after Google launched AI Overviews. The findings apply globally.

Before AI search, organic traffic grew 26.3% on average across all sectors. After AI search launched, growth slowed to 3.7%. That is a 22.6 percentage-point decline in the growth rate. Every sector felt the impact. None escaped.

Hospitality absorbed the steepest decline of any industry measured. Organic traffic swung from 47.9% growth to negative 6.7%, a total reversal of 54.6 percentage points. Fashion followed at 36.6 points. Travel and tourism dropped 36.3 points. Finance fell 14.5 points. Manufacturing went from 2.5% growth to a 3.8% decline.

A handful of sectors held up better. IT slowed by only 0.6 percentage points. Charity and nonprofit organizations slowed by 2.5 points. Healthcare dropped 3.6 points. These sectors share a characteristic that hospitality does not: their content resists easy summarization. IT queries require technical depth that AI compresses poorly. Charity searches involve trust and emotional connection. Healthcare queries demand authoritative sources that users verify independently.

Hotel searches produce the opposite pattern. Location, amenities, policies, pricing. AI platforms summarize these facts well enough to satisfy the traveler without sending them to your website. That structural vulnerability explains why hospitality leads the decline and why AI visibility optimization carries more urgency for hotels than for most other industries.

The pattern should look familiar. Properties that delayed adopting direct booking technology watched as OTAs captured relationship ownership. Those that ignored mobile optimization lost bookings to competitors. Others dismissed social media and missed brand-building opportunities during the platform's emergence. Early adopters establish advantages that late movers struggle to replicate. You face that same dynamic now.

The Parallel Surface of Visibility

Recent research from Conductor, analyzing over 17 million AI-generated responses and 100 million citations across 10 industries, quantifies what this transformation looks like in practice. AI referral traffic currently accounts for roughly 1% of total website visits. That number grows approximately 1% month over month. ChatGPT dominated AI referral traffic through mid-2025, driving 87% across industries in Conductor's measurement period.

These percentages sound small until you recognize what they represent: millions of brand interactions happening before travelers ever reach your website. The customer journey now begins inside AI experiences that answer questions, guide intent, and shape perception in real time. If your property does not appear in those answers, you remain invisible during the moments that increasingly determine which hotels travelers consider.

The research reveals something counterintuitive about who wins in AI visibility. Financial publishers like NerdWallet capture more AI citations than traditional banks. Video content on YouTube earns top citation rates across industries. Reddit discussions get referenced for authentic user experiences. The domains AI platforms cite most frequently are not always the brands you would expect. Authority in AI search follows different patterns than authority in traditional search. Properties that understand these patterns can position themselves where AI platforms actually look for information. Properties that assume traditional SEO success translates automatically to AI visibility discover otherwise.

Google's AI Overviews add another dimension. Conductor's analysis of nearly 22 million Google searches found that over 25% now trigger AI Overview results. Health care queries trigger AI Overviews almost 49% of the time. The content types most frequently cited in these overviews include blogs, videos, articles, and news content. This shift extends beyond text. Multimodal search through tools like Google Lens means travelers now search by pointing their cameras at a hotel facade. They ask voice assistants complex questions while driving. In every format, the traditional list of links gives way to a direct answer or visual overlay. Product pages appear less often.

This pattern reinforces what the technical foundations chapter explains: AI platforms reward comprehensive, authoritative content that answers questions directly. Properties creating that content appear in the AI-generated summaries now dominating the top of search results. Properties lacking that content get bypassed entirely, even when they rank well in traditional organic results below.

One more layer matters. Google launched AI Mode as a dedicated conversational search experience alongside AI Overviews. In late 2025, AI Mode represented a fraction of total search activity. That changed fast. Google upgraded AI Mode to Gemini 3 in January 2026 and began merging the two experiences: tapping "Show more" on any AI Overview now flows directly into AI Mode's conversational interface. Google found that users prefer this integrated transition and rolled it out globally on mobile. AI Overviews already trigger on roughly 21% of Google searches, with informational queries appearing at significantly higher rates. Searches containing seven or more words trigger an AI Overview 46% of the time. The convergence is clear. AI Overviews are becoming the entry point, and AI Mode is becoming the conversation that follows. Meanwhile, 75% of AI Mode sessions end without the user clicking an external link. Properties that dismiss these features because traditional search revenue continues to grow will find themselves optimizing retroactively once the conversational experience becomes the default.

Three Paths Forward

You face a strategic choice right now. Three options exist. Each creates a different future.

Path One: Lead the transformation. You commit resources despite measurement limitations. You execute baseline testing this month. You secure budget and team capacity for optimization. You sustain effort through the full timeline, even when visible progress slows during plateau periods. You build capabilities while competitors wait for perfect evidence.

This path demands courage. You invest without guaranteed returns. You measure despite attribution gaps. You defend the initiative when stakeholders question spending on channels that do not appear in your conversion reports.

Path Two: Follow the market. You wait for more evidence. You monitor competitors. You demand proof of ROI before committing. You treat AI visibility as experimental rather than strategic. You allocate modest resources for testing but not implementation.

This path feels prudent. You avoid premature investment in unproven channels. You maintain budget flexibility. You wait until best practices emerge through industry consensus.

Citation networks and algorithmic momentum accumulate for competitors who moved earlier. By the time you have perfect evidence, competitive positioning may have already stratified. Compression cannot accelerate the 18-month timeline for citation building. You pay premium prices for rushed execution that delivers inferior outcomes.

Path Three: Accept invisibility. You focus exclusively on traditional channels with clear attribution. You optimize website conversion. You increase paid search spending. You pursue OTA partnerships. You maintain marketing approaches that you can precisely measure.

This path provides familiar comfort. You execute established processes. You calculate ROI using proven formulas. You avoid organizational disruption from new initiatives.

You progressively lose market share to properties building AI visibility. Your traditional channels deliver diminishing returns as AI adoption persists and compounds. When you finally recognize the urgency, competitive positions have already hardened. Recovery requires exponential effort compared to early adaptation.

Here is what makes urgency hard to calibrate. Traditional search still commands 95% market share. Google's dominance has not collapsed. Your current traffic sources remain intact. This creates a dangerous comfort. Properties watching stable Google Analytics dashboards convince themselves the transformation has not reached their markets yet. Meanwhile, AI platforms add discovery capacity that your analytics never capture. Travelers research on ChatGPT, validate on Google, and book direct. You see the conversion but miss the discovery shift. The urgency is about building AI visibility before competitors claim the available positioning.

Understanding Your Specific Risk

Not every property faces equal urgency. You need to assess your situation because response timing depends on your competitive context.

These risk categories and associated timelines reflect patterns from mobile optimization and OTA response initiatives. The extreme urgency for high-risk properties mirrors the compressed timelines that proved necessary when properties faced immediate competitive threats during those transformations. Your actual urgency may vary based on how deeply AI adoption penetrates your specific markets.

Some hotels face aggressive timelines. Others can plan further out. The difference comes down to two factors: how quickly you could lose competitive positioning and what structural advantages you possess.

Let me walk you through the assessment.

You operate in the high-risk category if:

Your bookings depend primarily on discovery. When 60% or more of your reservations originate from travelers finding you through online research, you face severe vulnerability. Boutique hotels without established repeat business fall into this category. New properties without loyal guest bases face this risk. Properties targeting transient leisure travelers operate with this vulnerability. These properties depend critically on discovery channels.

When discovery shifts to AI platforms and you remain invisible there, you lose a primary guest acquisition channel.

You compete in the mid-tier range. Properties positioned between budget and luxury face pressure from both directions. Budget travelers use AI platforms extensively for price comparison. Luxury travelers use AI for initial research before direct contact. Mid-tier properties lack both the repeat business that protects luxury hotels and the price advantage that protects budget options.

You compete for high-volume search terms. Convention center hotels face this challenge. Properties near airports confront this reality. Hotels offering major attraction access operate in this space. These queries generate substantial research volume among travelers. AI platforms recommend properties with strong citation networks and accurate information. Invisibility in high-volume query responses means losing consideration despite proximity advantages.

If you operate in this category, you need to act quickly. Execute baseline testing within two weeks to understand your current position. If you appear in fewer than 30% of relevant queries while competitors appear in more than 50%, you face an urgent competitive disadvantage that requires an immediate response.

You operate in the medium-risk category if:

You have loyal repeat guests providing a buffer. Resort and destination properties where 40-60% of bookings come from returning guests possess protection against immediate discovery channel collapse. Repeat guests book directly without requiring AI discovery. New guest acquisition still depends on discovery channels. You experience gradual erosion rather than an immediate crisis.

You have strong local or regional brand recognition. Hotels deeply embedded in communities through decades of presence benefit from brand awareness transcending platform algorithms. Locals recommend you through word of mouth. Regional travelers know your property without requiring AI discovery. Brand recognition provides partial protection, as younger travelers and out-of-region guests increasingly rely on AI platforms.

You serve niche segments with limited competition. Pet-friendly resorts, extended-stay properties, accessible hotels, and wellness retreats face less competitive intensity than broad-market hotels. Lower competitive pressure reduces urgency while still requiring eventual response.

If you operate in this category, act within the next few quarters. Execute baseline testing within 30 to 60 days to establish the current position and competitive context. Implement programs that enable quality execution without emergency compression. You have breathing room for deliberate capability building.

You operate in the lower-risk category if:

You derive substantial revenue from corporate contracts. Extended-stay properties where 60-80% of bookings come through negotiated corporate rates depend less on transient traveler discovery. Corporate travel managers select properties through RFP processes, considering factors beyond AI visibility. Contract business provides insulation from discovery channel shifts affecting leisure and individual business travelers.

Location dominates choice. Airport hotels within perimeters or offering shuttle service compete primarily on convenience rather than discovery positioning. Travelers book airport hotels for functional proximity, not through research comparing alternatives.

You operate at ultra-luxury levels. Hotels at the highest tier operate through travel advisors, concierge relationships, and personal referrals rather than online discovery. Guests at this level work with luxury travel specialists, maintaining property knowledge independent of AI platforms.

You focus on group and meeting business. Hotels deriving substantial revenue from conferences, meetings, and group events depend less on individual traveler discovery. Event planners and meeting professionals select properties through specialized channels, considering capacity, facilities, and service levels.

If you operate in this category, monitor and act within the next year. Execute baseline testing within 90 to 180 days. Monitor quarterly how AI adoption develops among your core segments.

Lower risk means you have time for quality execution without emergency timelines. This does not mean you should ignore transformation until circumstances force a crisis response.

Capabilities build most effectively when urgency allows deliberate execution. Programs launched during lower-pressure periods achieve superior results because quality takes priority over speed. Waiting until urgency develops means paying premium prices for emergency execution that delivers inferior outcomes.

Hotel AI Risk Assessment Matrix

Risk Level	Property Characteristics	Competitive Urgency & Action Timing
HIGH RISK	• 60%+ bookings from online discovery • Boutique/New properties without loyal base • Transient leisure focus • Compete for high-volume search terms (e.g., convention center, airport)	Severe vulnerability. Immediate response required. Execute baseline testing within 2 weeks. If visible in <30% of queries, act now.
MEDIUM RISK	• 40-60% repeat guest base (resorts) • Strong local/regional brand recognition • Serve niche segments with less competition (e.g., pet-friendly, wellness)	Gradual erosion. Act within next few quarters. Execute baseline testing within 30-60 days. Deliberate capability building.
LOW RISK	• 60-80% corporate contract bookings • Location dominates choice (airport perimeter) • Ultra-luxury (travel advisor reliance) • Group/meeting business focus	Monitor and act within next year. Execute baseline testing within 90-180 days. Quarterly monitoring of AI adoption.

The Market Tier Reality

Your risk level determines when you act. Your market tier determines what you are fighting for and why you might already be losing.

Chapter 7 details the complete framework, but you need to understand the stakes right now because they define your strategy.

In Major Metros (NYC, LA, Chicago), you face an asymmetric fight. Independent properties here face structural disadvantages against brands with citation networks decades in the making. You cannot out-shout Marriott or Hilton on broad terms. This disadvantage is structural. AI models were trained on the open internet as it existed over the past twenty years. They carry a statistical preference for the brands that dominated that era. Researchers call this frequency bias. The more often a brand appeared in training data, the more readily the model retrieves it. This book calls it Primary Bias: the built-in advantage large brands carry before any optimization begins. Marriott, Hilton, and IHG appear billions of times across two decades of web content. Independent properties do not. The AI does not dislike your hotel. It has never learned enough about your hotel to form a preference at all.

Ahrefs data quantifies the scale of this advantage. Brands in the top 25% for web mentions earn more than ten times the AI Overview mentions of brands in the next quartile. The gap between established and emerging brands in AI visibility is not incremental. It is an order of magnitude.

If your independent property was not prominent enough to be encoded into the model's long-term memory, you face a more fundamental challenge than search rankings. You are fighting to be recognized as a valid option at all.

Every month you wait, you lose the chance to own the specific, high-value niches (pet-friendly luxury, design-focused, heritage) where AI still prefers unique independents. Waiting will not keep you small. It will make you generic inventory.

In Regional Hubs (Austin, Nashville, Denver), you are in a race for parity. This is currently a fair fight. You can match brand visibility, but only if you build your citation network *before* the major chains turn their massive SEO machinery toward AI optimization in your specific market. The window to establish parity is open, but it is closing.

In Emerging Markets, you have a first-mover opening. In smaller cities and resort destinations, brand penetration is low. The first property to build a serious AI footprint becomes the default answer for the entire destination. If you act now, you establish a position that takes competitors years to match. If you wait, you hand that advantage to the first competitor who reads this book.

Your market tier shapes your realistic ceiling. Your risk level shapes your deadline. Both inform which implementation roadmap you must choose in Chapter 9.

THREE PRINCIPLES THAT DETERMINE VISIBILITY

The frameworks in this book rest on three foundational principles. These principles transcend specific platforms, survive algorithm changes, and explain why some properties appear in AI recommendations while competitors remain invisible.

Principle One: AI-Friendly Content Wins

The old playbook rewarded keyword density. Match words on a page to words in a search bar. That approach fails with AI platforms.

Computer scientists describe the change as a shift from strings to things. Old search engines matched strings of text. Type "luxury hotel," and the engine scanned pages for those letters. AI models operate on a fundamentally different principle. They think in entities. They understand that The Ritz-Carlton is an entity associated with concepts like luxury, high service, and premium pricing, even if those exact words never appear on the page.

The technical mechanism behind this matters. Large Language Models convert your content into mathematical coordinates called embeddings. When a traveler asks a question, the AI maps their intent to a specific location in vector space and looks for content with coordinates nearby. This is semantic proximity. Content stuffed with keywords but lacking semantic meaning lands far from the traveler's intent in that mathematical space. The AI ignores it.

When a traveler asks ChatGPT for hotel recommendations, the platform synthesizes information from across the web. Properties with clear, comprehensive content that answers actual traveler questions appear in those synthesized answers. Properties packed with keywords but lacking substance get overlooked entirely.

If the AI's internal map does not connect your hotel as an entity to the concept of family friendly as an attribute, no amount of keyword optimization will change the outcome. You are no longer optimizing for words. You are training the machine's understanding of who you are.

This shift favors properties that communicate well over properties that optimize aggressively. Write for the answer, not the visit. The algorithms follow. The traveler might never reach your site. You need to win the answer to earn the recommendation, the brand recall, or the eventual booking, even when the transaction happens elsewhere.

Principle Two: Technical Consistency Shapes Understanding

AI platforms cannot guess what you mean. They parse structured data, cross-reference information sources, and build understanding from technical signals.

Schema markup tells platforms what your content represents. Consistent NAP information across citations enables entity recognition. Server-side rendering ensures platforms can access your content at all.

These technical foundations matter more now than during the traditional search era. Search engines could index imperfect pages and rank them based on link authority. AI platforms synthesize information into direct answers. Ambiguity in your technical implementation produces ambiguity in how platforms describe your property. Inconsistency in your data produces inconsistency in AI recommendations.

Technical excellence creates the conditions for visibility. Technical mediocrity creates the conditions for confusion.

Principle Three: Visibility Requires Thinking Like an Algorithm

The industry calls the technical work behind this shift Generative Engine Optimization, or GEO. Where SEO optimized for ranking URLs in a list, GEO optimizes for inclusion in AI-synthesized answers. The distinction matters. SEO rewarded keyword matching. GEO rewards entity recognition, intent alignment, and authority signals that answer the questions travelers actually ask.

Many marketers want to call this SEO. Chapter 5 explains why that framing obscures the strategic challenge and what to call it instead.

Success requires understanding three things. First, the questions travelers actually ask. Not the keywords you wish they searched, but the conversational queries they type into AI platforms. Second, the sources AI platforms trust. Not every citation carries equal weight. Authority hierarchies determine which information platforms believe. Third, the patterns of AI-generated answers. How platforms structure recommendations, which details they include, and what triggers favorable positioning.

Properties that understand how AI platforms think can optimize for how AI platforms behave. Properties that treat AI visibility as traditional SEO with a new label miss the fundamental differences in how these systems operate.

What This Means for You

Open a Temporary Chat in ChatGPT or Gemini right now. Type "best hotels in [your specific neighborhood]." Check whether your property appears.

Try five different variations:

- "Where should I stay in [your neighborhood] for business travel"
- "Pet-friendly hotels near [your closest landmark]"
- "Hotels with [your key amenity] in [your area]"
- "[Your city] hotels near [major venue]"
- "Romantic hotels in [your neighborhood]"

Document what you see. Which properties appear? What position do they occupy? What do the AI platforms say about them? What do they say about you, if you appear at all? Are you being mentioned, or are you being recommended? That is your baseline reality right now.

Next month, your competitors who remain invisible today might start building citation networks. In three months, they might implement comprehensive technical foundations. Next quarter, they might secure their first regional media placements.

By next year, they might appear in 60% of AI recommendations, while you still appear in 15%.

I am trying to show you reality clearly enough that you can make informed decisions about timing and investment.

Your choice: lead transformation, follow the market, or accept invisibility.

Each creates a different future.

Choose deliberately rather than defaulting to Path Three.

Discovery has moved. This book shows you how to move with it.

2
THE MEASUREMENT GAP

YOU ALREADY KNEW Google Analytics told an incomplete story. Privacy restrictions blocked data. Technical failures created gaps. Last-click attribution distorted reality.

A guest discovers your hotel through Instagram, validates it on TripAdvisor, compares prices on Google, and then clicks a branded search ad to book. Analytics credits the ad with 100% of the conversion. Instagram, which drove initial discovery, appears nowhere.

You lived with this imperfection because partial measurement enabled directional optimization. You could not prove Instagram drove the booking, but you observed a correlation between Instagram engagement and increases in branded search. This directional evidence justified continued investment despite the limitations of attribution.

AI-mediated discovery makes these problems exponentially worse.

Watch what actually happens now. A conference organizer opens Perplexity during a lunch break. He searches for hotel room blocks near the venue. Perplexity mentions five properties. He watches YouTube room tours for two of them. He checks Instagram for photos of one. He reads TripAdvisor reviews for all five. He asks ChatGPT which hotel has the best meeting facilities. He compares group rates on Google Hotels. He returns to Perplexity with refined questions about parking capacity. He texts colleagues for opinions. He checks the hotel website for ballroom configurations. He books through Booking.com because the rate matches.

Twelve touchpoints across eight platforms. No single dashboard tracks this full path. No attribution model captures which touchpoint drove the decision. The AI recommendation that started the journey remains invisible in your analytics, even as platform-side measurement tools begin to surface fragments of it.

You cannot optimize what you cannot measure. You cannot budget effectively when most influence happens in blind spots you did not know existed.

The Invisible Research Session

Entire research sessions now happen where you have zero measurement capability.

That scenario assumed your property appeared somewhere in the journey. The worse version: a traveler asks ChatGPT for hotel recommendations. ChatGPT suggests five properties. Yours does not appear among them. He books a competitor the next morning.

Your analytics show nothing. No session started. No page loaded. You had no awareness that the opportunity existed. You lost a booking and have no idea it happened.

This differs fundamentally from traditional attribution problems. With Instagram or TripAdvisor, you at least knew the touchpoint existed, even if you could not measure its precise contribution. With AI platforms, the entire discovery conversation happens privately. You do not know which travelers researched your market. You do not know which properties they compared. You do not know what information influenced their decisions.

The measurement gap creates real tension. You need numbers. Leadership demands ROI calculations. Traditional attribution cannot exist when travelers research privately across walled AI platforms.

This creates a choice. Wait for attribution tools that arrive incrementally and incompletely. Or invest based on the directional signals you can track right now.

The Signal in the Noise: Server Logs as Input Metrics

You cannot track the traveler's private conversation with ChatGPT. You can track when ChatGPT reads your website to prepare for that conversation.

This distinction matters. Output metrics measure what happens after the answer is generated, like a click. Input metrics measure what happens before. Your server logs contain your input metrics. Most marketing teams ignore this data source entirely.

Ask your IT team to filter server logs for specific user agents, the digital identification that bots present when they visit your site. Three signatures matter most:

ChatGPT-User signals that OpenAI is fetching your pages in real time to answer a user's question. GPTBot signals that OpenAI is crawling your site for model training. PerplexityBot signals that Perplexity is indexing your content for live answers.

Gemini retrieves your content through Google's standard search index, so Googlebot activity serves as your proxy for Gemini visibility. Your existing Google Search Console data already tracks this.

The metric to watch is crawl frequency. If these bots visit your site regularly, you are in the active retrieval set. A sudden drop in bot activity functions as a warning light. It means your technical infrastructure may be blocking the very systems you are trying to reach. High bot activity proves you are in play, even when Google Analytics shows zero clicks.

One caveat: newer AI agents do not always identify themselves in server logs. ChatGPT's Atlas browser uses a standard Chrome user agent string indistinguishable from regular visitors. Copilot draws from Bing's index, so Bingbot activity serves as your proxy, but the conversational interface itself leaves no separate footprint.

Bing Webmaster Tools now supplements this passive signal with platform-reported citation data, described later in this chapter.

What You Can Actually Measure

The strongest measurement signals for AI visibility differ from traditional SEO metrics. You need proxy indicators that reveal whether your optimization works despite attribution limitations.

Track branded search volume as a lagging indicator. Monitor direct traffic patterns. Measure channel mix shifts. If multiple signals move in a consistent positive direction as your Visibility Scores improve (Chapter 8), the pattern indicates a relationship, despite lacking perfect attribution.

Focus on four measurement layers.

First: Branded search volume. Your brand's search volume relative to competitors over a 90-day rolling period. Use Google Trends for broad demand. Triangulate with Semrush for search volume. Watch the trend line, not the weekly spikes.

When an LLM recommends your property (linked or not), travelers often open a new tab and Google your brand. Recommendation sparks curiosity. Curiosity drives search. Search provides the signal you can measure.

Rising branded search means your brand's availability increases inside generative engines and the surrounding culture. Declining search means competitors gain ground.

Second: Non-branded commercial traffic. Of your non-branded search clicks from Google Search Console, how many show clear commercial intent versus informational queries? How does your share of buyer intent traffic compare to competitors?

If branded search stays flat but buyer intent share rises, you harvest demand without creating enough of it. If branded search rises but buyer intent share does not, you have conversion problems. Your AI visibility sparks curiosity, but your site fails to convert that into qualified traffic. If both metrics rise, allocate more resources. If both decline, fix your positioning before adjusting technical optimization.

One more behavioral signal worth tracking: pages per session by referral source. Not engagement rate percentages. Actual page depth.

Seer Interactive's analysis found ChatGPT visitors exploring significantly more pages per session than other channels. Gemini visitors showed lower exploration patterns. Both channels showed similar engagement rates around 60%, identical to Google Organic. Surface metrics suggested equivalence.

Page depth told a different story. ChatGPT sends curious researchers who explore multiple pages. Gemini sends task-focused visitors who find what they need and convert quickly. Both behaviors convert well. They need different content strategies to maximize performance.

Track both dimensions. Engagement rate alone masks which platforms send explorers versus converters. You need to know the difference because your content optimization depends on understanding what each platform's visitors actually do on your site.

Third: Conversational query performance. In Google Search Console, filter for long natural-language queries of six to ten or more words that read like sentences. These are often the artifacts of Query Fan-Out. When a user asks an AI a complex question, the AI breaks it down into multiple sub-searches to find facts. Those specific, long-tail searches frequently hit your site.

If impressions for queries starting with "How," "What," "Where," and "Best" are climbing, your content aligns with the conversational patterns AI platforms use during research. Some of those impressions come from AI-triggered background searches. Others come from travelers typing longer, more natural queries influenced by their AI interactions.

Are commercial conversational queries rising as a share of the total? If not, your AI visibility represents a cost center, not a growth driver. If 70% of your clicks come from informational queries ("what is a resort fee?"), you are not marketing. You are donating free training data to the LLMs.

This commercial intent focus matters more than most properties realize. Seer Interactive analyzed seven months of traffic for a client and found striking patterns. ChatGPT visitors converted at

16%. Google Organic visitors converted at 1.8%. The AI channel converted nine times better despite representing only 0.07% of traffic volume.

That pattern creates exactly the measurement tension this chapter addresses. The channel converting best shows up as noise in traditional dashboards. A separate 12-month analysis by Visibility Labs across 94 ecommerce sites found ChatGPT traffic converting 31 percent higher than non-branded organic search, with higher revenue per session despite lower average order value, consistent with visitors who have already narrowed their choices before clicking. Leadership dismisses channels under 1% of traffic. When a channel outperforms your primary traffic source by nearly nine times, volume becomes the wrong metric entirely.

The dollar math matters here. Take your average booking value. Multiply it by the number of AI-referred conversions you can identify in the past quarter. That absolute dollar figure is how you present this to leadership, not as a traffic percentage. A property averaging $250 per night for a two-night stay that captures even 200 AI-driven bookings per quarter generates $100,000 in direct revenue from a channel that does not appear on any standard dashboard. Your number will differ. Calculate it. The exercise transforms an abstract traffic percentage into a concrete revenue figure that demands attention.

Watch commercial intent signals alongside volume metrics. Growing AI traffic with declining conversion rates means visibility without qualification. Flat AI traffic with rising conversions means you attract the right visitors despite limited reach. Both signals matter. Track both monthly.

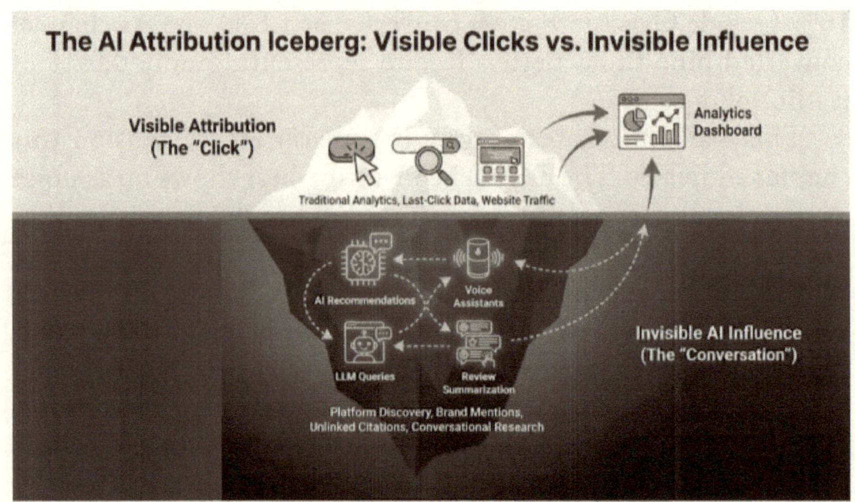

Fourth: The analog signal through guest validation. When digital attribution goes dark, operational data becomes your source of truth. Add AI Recommendation as a specific option on your check-in survey or post-stay questionnaire.

The responses will surprise you. Guests will say they asked ChatGPT for a quiet hotel near the convention center. Your analytics attributed that booking to Direct or Organic Search. This qualitative data calibrates your confidence in the quantitative proxies. It closes the gap between what your dashboard reports and what actually drove the booking decision.

An Emerging Signal: Paid Placement as a Measurement Proxy

In February 2026, OpenAI began testing advertising placements inside ChatGPT for logged-in users on its Free and Go subscription tiers. The ads appear as clearly labeled sponsored content, visually separated from ChatGPT's organic answers. OpenAI states that advertising does not influence the responses ChatGPT generates.

The advertising itself matters less to this chapter than what it reveals about measurement. A hotel can now place a paid ad inside an AI conversation and receive performance data back. Impression counts tell you whether travelers are discussing your market inside ChatGPT. Click-through rates tell you whether your property compels action when it appears in that context. Neither metric existed before. Both create a direct measurement signal from inside an ecosystem that resisted observation until now.

You are not buying ads. You are buying data.

Run a 30-day test at controlled spend. The goal is not conversion. The goal is intelligence. Early trigger analysis by Adthena across 1,500 prompts found that commercial intent modifiers, particularly "best" and "new," carry significant weight in activating ad placements, with most ads appearing on the first prompt rather than requiring repeated queries. Structure your test prompts accordingly: "best hotel near [landmark]" and "new hotel in [destination]" will give you the clearest signal on whether your market generates commercial activity inside the platform. If impressions appear when ChatGPT matches your ad to trip-planning conversations in your market, you have confirmed that travelers research hotels in your destination inside the platform. If those impressions generate clicks, your positioning resonates enough to pull travelers out of an AI conversation and onto your property page. If impressions run low or zero, your market may not yet generate enough ChatGPT travel activity to warrant organic optimization urgency at the levels this book describes. Each of those outcomes tells you something your analytics cannot.

The data sharpens your organic strategy. High impressions with low clicks suggest travelers find your market inside ChatGPT but your property description fails to differentiate. That points to a content problem you can fix with the FAQ and answer-unit work in Chapter 6. Strong clicks on specific query topics reveal which traveler needs ChatGPT associates with your property, giving you a prioritization signal for citation building in Chapter 7. Low overall impressions in your market tell you the organic urgency timeline from Chapter 1 may extend further than the national averages suggest for your specific destination.

Think about what this test gives the leadership conversation. The four measurement layers above rely on proxy signals and directional evidence. A 30-day ChatGPT ad test produces concrete numbers: impressions served, clicks generated, cost per interaction. Those numbers will not capture the full picture of AI visibility. They do provide the first verifiable data point from inside an AI platform that you can present to a general manager who demands proof that travelers research hotels through these channels.

The pilot has boundaries worth noting. Plus, Pro, Business, Enterprise, and Education subscribers do not see ads. Targeting relies on conversation topic matching rather than traditional demographic segmentation. Performance data remains aggregated. OpenAI does not share individual chat content with advertisers. Your test measures a subset of ChatGPT activity, not all of it.

Perplexity launched sponsored follow-up questions in late 2024, then paused the program by late 2025. Google monetizes AI Overviews through its existing ad infrastructure. For platforms relying on consumer freemium models, advertising represents a direct path to revenue that subscriptions alone may not sustain. The format and timing will differ across platforms.

This development does not replace the organic visibility strategies throughout this book. Properties with no organic presence will pay premium rates for paid placement that stronger competitors earn through citation authority. The organic foundation becomes the baseline that paid amplifies. Properties without it face the same dynamic that made Google Ads expensive for hotels without strong SEO: paying more to reach travelers your competitors attract through earned authority.

Platform-Side Measurement: The First Dashboard

The ChatGPT ad test gives you measurement through paid spend. Microsoft introduced a different path in February 2026: free measurement through Bing Webmaster Tools.

The new AI Performance dashboard shows how your content appears as a cited source across Microsoft Copilot, AI-generated summaries in Bing, and select partner integrations. The dashboard reports total citations, average cited pages per day, grounding queries (the phrases the AI used when retrieving your content), and page-level citation activity. A platform operator published the data that this entire chapter argues you cannot access.

The significance extends beyond Microsoft's ecosystem. Bing provides the search infrastructure behind ChatGPT. Copilot serves as Microsoft's conversational AI interface across Windows, Edge, and Office. When Bing Webmaster Tools reports that your property page received 47 citations across AI-generated answers last month, that number reflects activity across multiple AI surfaces drawing from the same index. Bing also supports IndexNow, a protocol that notifies participating search engines whenever you add, update, or remove content. For properties that update rates, packages, or seasonal information frequently, IndexNow reduces the lag between publishing a change and having AI systems reference the current version.

Three implications matter for your measurement strategy.

First, the data validates or contradicts your manual testing. If your Visibility Score testing (Chapter 8) shows strong performance on ChatGPT and Bing-powered surfaces, the AI Performance dashboard should reflect corresponding citation activity. Discrepancies between your manual scores and the platform's reported citations reveal blind spots in either methodology. Use both signals together.

Second, the grounding queries metric shows you which phrases trigger AI retrieval of your content. These phrases function differently from traditional search queries. They represent the internal search the AI performs when constructing an answer, not the words the traveler typed. Comparing grounding queries to your prompt library from Chapter 8 reveals whether the AI retrieves your content for the queries travelers actually ask or for tangential topics that generate citations without generating bookings.

Third, Microsoft's decision to release this data creates competitive pressure on Google and Anthropic. Google already provides extensive search performance data through Search Console. Extending that reporting to cover AI Overviews and Gemini-generated answers follows a logical path. Anthropic, which operates Claude, has no comparable webmaster toolset today. The precedent now exists. Publishers will expect equivalent transparency from every major platform.

By the time you read this, the measurement environment may have shifted further. Google faces clear pressure to extend Search Console reporting into AI Overviews and Gemini. OpenAI may offer publishers visibility into how ChatGPT retrieves and cites their content. If new reporting tools exist when you pick up this book, apply the same integration approach described above: use platform data to validate your Visibility Score testing, compare grounding queries against your prompt library, and treat platform-reported citations as one signal among several rather than a complete picture. The strategic guidance in every chapter remains valid regardless of which platforms provide data, because the core challenge was never the absence of dashboards. The core challenge is that AI-mediated discovery operates through pathways too fragmented and too private for any single data source to capture fully.

Monitor the AI Performance dashboard monthly alongside your Visibility Score testing. The platform-reported data measures different signals than your manual protocol. Your testing captures qualitative dimensions like description quality and positioning. The dashboard captures quantitative dimensions like citation volume and retrieval patterns. Neither replaces the other. Together, they provide the most complete measurement picture available at this stage of the transformation.

The Measurement Reality Check

Recent industry analysis from Chatoptic reveals a fundamental truth about AI visibility measurement that most vendors obscure in their pitch decks. Unlike traditional search engines that produce largely deterministic results by ranking indexed pages, large language models generate answers probabilistically.

Each response emerges on the fly based on likelihood, not fixed rankings. The same prompt delivered to the same platform by different users can produce entirely different brand recommendations. This variability creates a measurement challenge that no current tool has fully solved. Most platforms build estimates using third-party datasets, clickstream panels, and extrapolation models to forecast relative popularity. That approach provides directional guidance, but treating these numbers as precise metrics leads to flawed strategic decisions.

A January 2026 study by SparkToro and Gumshoe.ai put harder numbers on this variability. Across 2,961 tests of 12 prompts through ChatGPT, Claude, and Google AI, fewer than 1 in 100 responses contained the same list of brands. The odds of seeing that list in the same order dropped below 1 in 1,000. The conclusion aligns with the framework in this chapter: ranking position in AI responses is too variable to serve as a reliable metric. Frequency of appearance across many prompt runs is the meaningful signal. This is why Citation Rate carries the heaviest weight in the Visibility Score, and why position scores belong to multi-month trend analysis rather than single-session reporting. The question then becomes what does correlate with AI visibility.

The correlation data tells a more nuanced story about what actually drives AI visibility. An Ahrefs analysis found that third-party mentions of a brand show the strongest correlation with AI Overview visibility, with a correlation coefficient of 0.664. This suggests models rely far more on off-site context than on what appears on a brand's own website. A separate Semrush study found that Reddit and LinkedIn rank among the top five most-cited domains across ChatGPT, Google's AI Overviews, and Perplexity.

Most of what AI platforms reference when making recommendations comes from sources outside your website. Citation networks, review platforms, and third-party publications you influence but do not control carry the majority of the weight. Chapter 3 quantifies this split. Properties focused on on-site optimization alone miss the fundamental shift in how authority signals accumulate.

The Unlinked Citation Problem

Airlines tested 376 flight-search prompts across AI platforms. ChatGPT mentioned airlines in 42% of responses without linking to the airline's website. The unlinked rate for airlines reached 74.6%, more than 9 times higher than for online travel agencies.

Hotels face identical dynamics.

A traveler asks about pet-friendly hotels. ChatGPT mentions your property: "The Riverside Hotel welcomes dogs under 50 pounds." Then it provides links to Booking.com and Expedia for comparison. The traveler books through the OTA.

For hotels, the unlinked citation is a direct donation to Expedia. The AI sells you. The OTA captures the booking commission because they secured the link you did not get. You appear in the answer without appearing in the attribution.

Think about what this means. No platform yet provides hotel operators with full visibility into how the algorithm describes their properties. Microsoft cracked the door in February 2026 with citation data across Copilot and Bing AI surfaces. Other platforms may follow with their own reporting tools. Even when they do, each dashboard will reveal activity within one ecosystem. No single data source will show you how your property is described across all AI conversations, which attributes get emphasized, which competitors appear alongside you, or whether the AI recommends you or merely mentions you. The measurement gap narrows with each new tool. The structural gap persists because AI-mediated discovery happens across fragmented platforms, private conversations, and probabilistic responses that no dashboard can fully reconstruct.

Near-zero visibility into the channels driving discovery.

As discussed in Chapter 2, OpenAI launched advertising inside ChatGPT in early 2026, giving hotels their first opportunity to place paid content directly within AI trip-planning conversations. The ad data flows one direction only. Advertisers receive aggregated impression and click counts. They do not see chat content, user identities, or conversation history.

The Infrastructure Mindset

Stop thinking about AI visibility as a marketing campaign. Start thinking about it as an infrastructure investment.

Roads enable commerce without generating revenue themselves. Plumbing enables every function of a hotel without appearing on any guest's booking criteria. AI visibility infrastructure enables discovery that leads to bookings through pathways too complex to precisely measure.

Infrastructure investments require longer time horizons than campaigns. Campaign budgets expect results within weeks or months. Infrastructure budgets plan for value delivery over quarters or years. Expecting campaign-speed returns from infrastructure investment creates frustration and premature abandonment before compounding benefits materialize.

This reframing matters because your leadership team will ask for ROI calculations. You need to explain honestly why traditional ROI does not apply here while showing that the investment still makes strategic sense.

Cross-industry research confirms the gap. McKinsey documented that only 16% of brands systematically track AI search performance. The remaining 84% see their traffic declining and suspect AI search plays a role, but have no measurement systems in place to confirm it or respond.

This creates an early-mover advantage window. When most competitors lack measurement capability, any systematic approach provides competitive intelligence they do not have. You identify pattern changes months before they appear in occupancy reports. You spot competitive threats while competitors wonder why bookings softened.

That 16% figure will not last. As AI search impact becomes undeniable, measurement adoption will accelerate across the market. The strategic question is whether you establish measurement discipline while most competitors still lack measurement systems, or wait until measurement becomes standard practice and the advantage disappears.

Tank's 2025 Google AI Search Shift Report attempted to isolate the impact of AI search by comparing yearly growth rates before and after Google's AI features launched. The problem: their "after AI" period combined 12 months of AI Overviews with only one month of AI Mode. Which feature drove which changes? Unknown. This methodological limitation does not invalidate their findings. Hospitality still showed a 54.6 percentage point decline. It illustrates why precise ROI calculations remain impossible. The variables change too fast. The platforms evolve too quickly. The attribution pathways stay hidden.

What This Means for Your Decision

You cannot calculate a precise ROI for AI visibility investment. Accept that limitation explicitly right now, because demanding traditional ROI calculations will paralyze you into inaction while competitors build advantages.

You can measure whether optimization correlates with improved business performance through proxy metrics and competitive positioning. Chapter 8 provides the complete Visibility Score framework and testing protocol, with monthly testing across 20 prompts on four platforms (ChatGPT, Gemini, Perplexity, Claude) organized across four query categories. Appendix C expands the available prompts and adds a fifth category for multi-criteria compound queries.

For now, understand the philosophical shift required.

The ROI conversation with leadership needs reframing. Calculate your average booking value. Multiply by the AI-driven conversions you can identify. Present that absolute dollar figure, not a traffic percentage.

The Seer data tells the story: a channel that converts at nine times the rate of Google Organic does not appear on any standard dashboard. Run the same calculation against your own numbers.

A concrete revenue figure changes the conversation in ways that "0.07% of traffic" never will.

Same data. Different frame. Different decision.

Stop defending AI visibility using traffic percentages. Start presenting dollar values generated by channels that leadership never tracked. AI traffic at sub-1% volume sounds irrelevant. AI conversions generating meaningful direct revenue demand attention and resources.

This reframing works because it shifts the threshold question. Not "when will AI represent 5% of traffic" but "when does the absolute revenue justify dedicated optimization." For properties with high average booking values, that threshold may have already passed. For others, it approaches faster than volume metrics suggest.

Consider this scenario: A marketing manager could not tell their GM that AI visibility optimization led to a 6-point increase in occupancy. They could show six months of visibility improvements correlating with branded search increases, direct traffic growth, and channel mix shifts toward direct bookings.

They secured continued investment based on directional evidence rather than perfect attribution.

Leadership will raise the confounding variable problem. A property that improves its Visibility Score from 28 to 55 over six months while also launching renovated rooms and benefiting from a citywide event will face leadership attributing improvement to those other factors. Isolating AI visibility's contribution from concurrent initiatives is genuinely difficult. The component-level analysis from Chapter 8 provides the closest approximation to controlled measurement. When your Positioning Quality improves three weeks after content restructuring while other components remain flat, the connection is specific enough to defend. Track which dimensions respond to which actions. The correlation between specific initiatives and specific component improvements builds the evidence base that aggregate metrics cannot.

Six months later, their visibility reached competitive parity. Occupancy stabilized at healthy levels. Competitors who waited for perfect measurement spent those 12 months falling further behind.

You face the same choice. Demand perfect measurement and wait. Or accept directional evidence as sufficient for infrastructure investment during platform transformation.

The transformation already occurred. The measurement gap is narrowing, not closing. Your decision about whether to act determines everything that follows.

A Note on Terminology

You will encounter different terms for measuring AI visibility across the industry. Share of voice. Share of answer. Topical authority. Share of search. These terms describe related but distinct concepts.

Share of voice (traditional marketing) measures your brand's mentions relative to competitors in media coverage. Share of answer (AI-specific) measures how often AI platforms recommend you versus competitors. Topical authority (SEO) measures your content's perceived expertise on specific topics. Share of search measures branded search volume relative to competitors. This book uses this term when discussing the proxy metric, which you can track in Google Trends and Semrush.

The Visibility Score framework in Chapter 8 provides the measurement approach for AI visibility. Citation Rate (30% weight) measures the frequency of mentions. Platform Spread (25% weight) measures cross-platform presence. Positioning Quality (20% weight) measures sentiment and recommendation. Information Accuracy (15% weight) measures correctness. Competitive Context (10% weight) measures relative performance.

Different terminology serves different purposes. Search share provides a lagging indicator of whether your brand grows or shrinks. The Visibility Score provides an operational metric indicating whether your AI optimization works.

You now understand why you cannot measure this perfectly. Next, we need to examine why the structure of the traveler's research process itself has broken. The marketing funnel you learned served you well for decades. It no longer describes reality.

3
THE ANSWER SPIRAL REDEFINES DISCOVERY

THE MARKETING FUNNEL is not dead. I know you have heard people claim otherwise. Every few years, someone announces the death of some foundational marketing concept. Usually, the claims are exaggerated. This time, the evidence suggests genuine transformation. Awareness, consideration, and conversion still happen. They no longer happen in the order the funnel assumed, on the platforms the funnel measured, across the timelines the funnel required.

Let me show you what I mean.

What the Funnel Got Wrong

For decades, we organized marketing around the conversion funnel. Travelers moved through predictable stages. Awareness at the top, consideration in the middle, conversion at the bottom. We allocated budgets across funnel stages. Brand advertising for awareness. Content marketing for consideration. Retargeting for conversion.

The funnel offered comforting clarity. You measured progress through each stage. You optimized transitions between stages. You calculated conversion rates at each level.

The funnel was always a simplification, but a useful one for resource allocation and strategic thinking. Buyer journeys never followed neat funnels. They never will. What changed is that AI platforms compress the entire journey into single conversational interfaces where the stages overlap, repeat, and collapse into minutes. The sequence broke. The stages remain.

From Pinball to Spiral

Rand Fishkin, who built SparkToro after years running Moz, describes the modern buyer journey accurately: "This classic buyer journey, as imagined by marketers, has the top of the funnel where your audience learns about the problems you solve, then potential customers engage with your brand, then they decide whether they're going to buy from you. I admit it's kind of a terrible metaphor today because buyer journeys don't look like this. They look like a pinball machine."

Fishkin accurately describes the pinball chaos. His model captures what happened before AI platforms collapsed that chaos into single conversations.

Here is what actually happens now. A traveler opens Gemini on a Sunday afternoon to plan a weekend trip to Austin during a music festival. He types: "Best hotels in Austin for a music festival weekend."

Gemini synthesizes information from across the web and responds with recommendations. Several properties. Details about each. Positioning statements pulled from reviews, websites, and blog posts.

He refines immediately: "Which has the quietest rooms? I need good soundproofing."

Gemini responds with specifics about soundproofing mentioned in reviews. The conversation continues. Each answer triggers new questions. He asks about parking, room service, and proximity to venues. Gemini pulls answers from hotel websites, OTA listings, reviews, and blog posts.

The entire journey takes place in a single chat window. No platform bouncing. No visible touchpoints. No measurable attribution.

He conducted awareness, consideration, and conversion research without ever leaving Gemini. The funnel's sequential stages and the pinball machine's platform chaos both collapsed into conversational iterations within a single AI interface.

How the Spiral Actually Works

Watch this pattern emerge from analyzing platform behavior:

Initial query: "Best hotels in Austin for a music festival weekend."

AI answer mentions several properties. The traveler researches two on YouTube and discovers that both lack late-night food options.

Refined query: "Austin hotels near music venues with 24-hour room service."

AI answer mentions different properties. The traveler checks reviews and finds noise complaints at one.

Refined query: "Quiet Austin hotels near music venues with room service and good soundproofing."

AI answer narrows to two properties. The traveler compares prices, checks availability, reviews photos, reads policies, and books.

Each answer generates new questions. Each platform visit reveals new information requiring additional research. The traveler spirals through multiple platforms and multiple AI interactions before reaching a booking decision.

This is the Answer Spiral. Travelers research through iterative AI conversations where each answer generates the next question, discovery and evaluation and decision-making happen simultaneously rather than sequentially, and the journey cycles across platforms until the traveler reaches sufficient confidence to book. The spiral represents a new organizing model for how travelers research considered purchases.

The spiral compresses what the funnel spread across weeks into minutes. Awareness, consideration, and conversion still happen.

They no longer happen in predictable sequence across measurable touchpoints. A single AI response can introduce a property, establish its credibility, and move the traveler toward booking in one paragraph. The stages overlap, repeat, and collapse into conversational turns that your analytics never capture.

You can still optimize for discovery, consideration, and comparison. You can no longer assume they happen in that order, on separate platforms, across a timeline you can track.

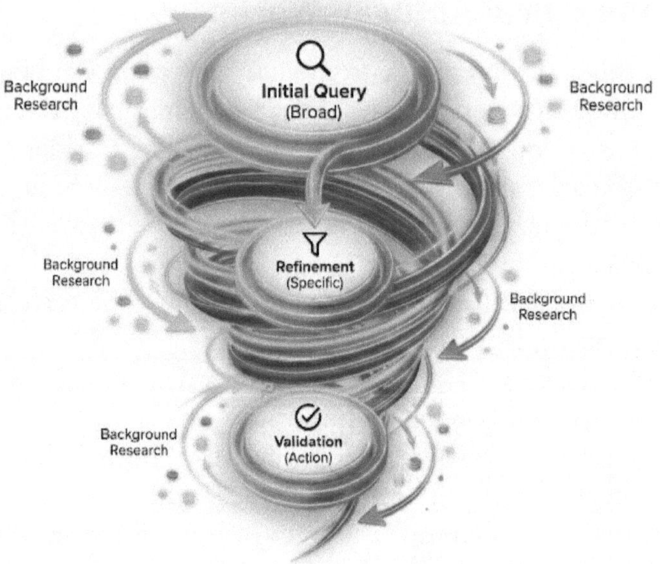

Google Confirms the Spiral

In October 2025, Google's VP of Product Robby Stein described what he calls the "next generation" of search. His description validates the answer spiral.

Stein explained that Google is converging three AI capabilities into one unified experience: AI Overviews for quick answers, multimodal search through visual discovery with Lens, and AI Mode for conversational turn-based discovery. He describes AI

Mode as "a brain that is effectively this way to talk to Google and get at this knowledge."

Not a search engine. A brain. A conversational partner for information discovery.

Stein describes how this works: "You can go back and forth. You can have a conversation. And it taps into 50 billion products in the Google Shopping Graph, 250 million places in maps, all of the finance information, the entire context of the web."

Users can now enter multi-sentence questions directly into Google's search box. Complex queries automatically trigger AI Mode previews with options to go deeper into conversational search. Take a photo through Google Lens, and it connects you to the same conversational system.

The numbers prove that travelers use AI Mode differently than they use traditional search. By October 2025, data showed that the average length of questions in AI Mode ran three times longer than traditional search queries. Q4 2025 data from Datos sharpens that observation into specific brackets. The fastest-growing query categories are 6-to-9-word searches and long-form questions of 15 words or more.

That granularity matters. The industry optimized for two decades around queries like "hotel Miami" or "Austin hotels pet-friendly parking." Two words. Four words. Shorthand that forced the search engine to guess intent. Those queries still exist. They no longer represent where growth occurs.

The growth sits in questions like: "What are the best hotels in downtown Austin that allow medium-sized dogs and have secure parking within walking distance of the convention center?" That query contains 23 words. It specifies location, pet policy, parking type, and proximity requirement in a single sentence. The traveler is not searching. The traveler is prompting. The brevity of the keyword era gave way to the specificity of the conversation era. Q4 data confirms this is not a behavioral experiment. It is the new default.

Your content must answer these compound questions at the passage level. A page optimized for "pet-friendly hotels Austin" will not surface when the AI decomposes a 15-word query into sub-searches about dog size policies, parking security, and walking distances. Each sub-query demands a self-contained answer block on your site. Chapter 6 details the technical implementation.

In January 2026, Google introduced Personal Intelligence into AI Mode, meaning search results now incorporate individual user preferences, history, and context. A traveler who previously researched pet-friendly hotels receives AI Mode answers that weigh pet policies more heavily. A business traveler who books conference hotels regularly sees convention center proximity emphasized in recommendations. This personalization layer compounds the answer spiral. Each interaction teaches the system more about the traveler's priorities, and future answers reflect that accumulated understanding. Properties with detailed, structured data about specific amenities and policies give the AI more material to match against individual traveler profiles. Generic content provides nothing for the personalization engine to work with.

The platform distinctions blur. Speaking, typing, or photographing all connect to the same underlying process: deciding how to respond. Users do not choose between "search" and "AI chat." Google detects intent and automatically serves the appropriate experience.

This convergence matters because it confirms the spiral is not a user behavior pattern platforms will resist. The spiral is the experience platforms are deliberately building. When Google's VP says users "shouldn't have to think about" which interface they are using because "it should feel like a consistent, simple product experience," he describes a world where the answer spiral becomes the default discovery mechanism. Google is building the spiral to keep users on Google.

Your hotel either appears in these conversational flows, or it does not. The traditional funnel assumed you could allocate separate budgets and separate content to awareness, consideration, and conversion as distinct, sequential stages. The spiral, now architected into the platforms themselves, demands that your content serve all three at once. A single FAQ answer may need to introduce your property, differentiate it from competitors, and provide the booking details that close the decision.

How Different Platforms Shape the Spiral

Different AI platforms send travelers with different behaviors and expectations. ChatGPT visitors averaged 2.3 pages per session in measured traffic analysis. Google Organic visitors averaged 1.2 pages. The ChatGPT visitor has already eliminated alternatives through the AI conversation. They click through to explore details, confirm information, and validate the recommendation. They navigate deeper because they arrive with clearer intent.

Gemini traffic concentrated on calculator pages and practical tools. Those visitors came for specific tasks, not exploration. Perplexity showed similar focused behavior. The differences matter because you cannot optimize for generic "AI traffic." Each platform sends travelers at different research stages, expecting different content experiences.

Properties treating all AI traffic identically miss these behavioral patterns. Your ChatGPT optimization needs depth. Your Gemini optimization needs utility. The platforms differ in what they send and what those visitors need when they arrive.

Clickstream data from Datos confirms this pattern. YouTube, Reddit, Amazon, Wikipedia, and Facebook remained the top five destinations from search. Their rankings barely shifted year over year. ChatGPT entered at position nine, joining the ecosystem rather than replacing it. Reddit overtook Facebook in U.S. desktop visits during this period. Platform diversity intensified instead of consolidating. Travelers did not abandon multi-platform research. They added AI platforms to their existing discovery patterns. The answer spiral describes what happens within AI interactions, not the elimination of platform bouncing that still characterizes most research journeys.

AI platforms do not entirely eliminate platform bouncing. They change which platforms serve which functions.

AI platforms drive initial discovery and iterative refinement. ChatGPT, Gemini, and Perplexity answer questions, provide recommendations, and facilitate comparison across options. They function simultaneously as discovery engines and research assistants.

Video platforms enable visual validation. YouTube room tours, TikTok hotel reviews, and Instagram stories provide visual evidence that written descriptions cannot match. Travelers want to see actual rooms, not marketing photos. AI platforms might recommend your property, but travelers still validate through video before booking.

Review platforms provide social proof and risk mitigation. TripAdvisor, Google Reviews, Booking.com, Yelp, Reddit, and booking site reviews validate AI recommendations through peer experiences. Travelers trust other travelers more than they trust hotels or automated systems.

Social platforms enable peer consultation. Travelers ask friends on Instagram, post questions in Reddit travel communities, and consult Facebook groups dedicated to specific destinations. These social validations often prove decisive in final booking decisions.

Booking platforms facilitate price comparison and transaction. Google Hotels, OTAs, and metasearch engines enable quick comparisons across properties and booking channels. They function as transaction facilitators rather than discovery drivers.

Hotel and brand websites provide property-specific depth. Travelers who receive an AI recommendation often visit the property website to browse photos, explore room types, read amenity details, and get a feel for the experience. The website validates the AI recommendation through visual and informational richness that no third-party platform replicates.

You must maintain presence across all these platform types. Optimizing for one while neglecting others creates vulnerability.

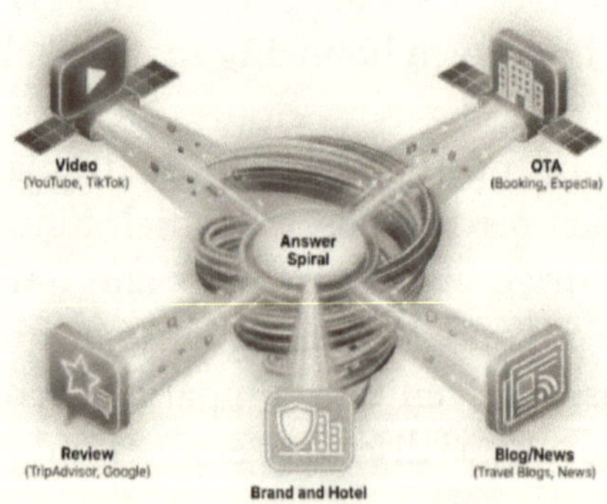

Why Citation Networks Matter More Than You Think

The data on where AI platforms source their information challenges website-centric thinking. Research from Cloudbeds and VertoDigital, detailed in Chapter 7, reveals that own-site content accounts for roughly 25% of the answer text in AI-generated responses. The remaining 75% comes from external citations: OTA listings, review platforms, YouTube videos, travel blogs, industry publications, and directory listings. Not a single hotel website ranked among the top ten most-cited sources in travel AI overviews.

Your website provides the authoritative foundation that AI platforms check against other sources. The website alone cannot drive AI visibility the way it drove search rankings. Chapter 7 details how to build the citation networks that supply three-quarters of the information AI systems use when recommending hotels.

What This Means for Your Content Strategy

The answer spiral requires different content strategies than the funnel demanded.

Funnel-optimized content targeted specific stages. Awareness content was broad and inspirational. Consideration content was detailed and comparative. Conversion content was urgent and transactional. Each stage received specialized content designed to move travelers to the next stage.

That approach assumed travelers would encounter your content in the right order. They will not.

Spiral-optimized content must be modular. AI systems rarely retrieve entire pages. They retrieve passages, sometimes called fraggles. They look for a specific paragraph that answers a specific sub-query within the fan-out process.

Profound's analysis of over 730,000 ChatGPT conversations containing web citations found that citation behavior concentrates heavily in the opening question. The first turn of a conversation was 2.5 times more likely to trigger web citations than Turn 10 and nearly four times more likely than Turn 20. Only 18 percent of all ChatGPT conversations triggered a web search at all. When searches did occur, they clustered at the start of the research process, not during follow-up refinements. The implication for content strategy is direct. The broad discovery query ("best hotels in downtown Austin") triggers the heaviest web research. Follow-up turns ("which of those has a rooftop pool?") rely more on sources the model already retrieved. If your content does not surface during that initial retrieval, later conversational turns rarely introduce new sources that include you. Your content must answer the question that starts the research, not the question that continues it.

Your content strategy cannot rely on one long page. It must function as a collection of clear, self-contained blocks. A paragraph on soundproofing. A table on parking fees. A list of pet amenities. Each block must stand alone as a complete answer when the AI extracts it from your page to construct its response.

These platforms pull from your website to answer questions ranging from broad awareness queries to specific operational details. A passage written for initial discovery may surface during a final booking decision. A granular policy detail may appear in a broad recommendation. You cannot predict which questions AI platforms will answer with which content pieces.

This multi-purpose requirement demands comprehensive content that addresses questions at all levels of specificity. Your website needs both broad positioning and granular details. AI systems might use either piece of information to answer queries, and you cannot predict which information will prove decisive for any particular traveler.

Marriott's restructured destination content provides one documented example. They restructured pages to answer natural questions about locations and amenities. The restructured content achieved a 6.6-point lift in keyword performance for long-tail conversational queries. The lift was specific to their context, but the principle applies broadly. Spiral-optimized content can deliver measurable results, though comprehensive validation across diverse properties remains limited.

Content must also achieve platform portability. AI systems synthesize information from your website. YouTube requires video content. Instagram demands visual content. TikTok needs short-form video. Review platforms aggregate guest feedback. Each platform has different content requirements, yet all contribute to the answer spiral. You cannot optimize for one content format without neglecting platforms requiring different formats.

The Competitive Reality

A property with strong AI visibility but weak reviews loses during validation. Strong reviews without AI visibility means never entering consideration. The competitive requirement: baseline competence everywhere while developing excellence in platforms most important to your target segments.

A business hotel might prioritize AI visibility and review scores over Instagram presence. A lifestyle hotel might emphasize Instagram and YouTube over business traveler platforms. Neither can completely neglect any platform where target travelers might research.

Platform dynamics vary by traveler segment and property tier. Budget accommodations receive OTA links in 50% or more of AI recommendations, according to HotelRank's testing of thousands of prompts across advanced model variants. Luxury resorts receive direct links almost exclusively. Understanding these patterns for your segment helps you determine where to invest resources.

What This Means for Your Strategy

The answer spiral requires strategic reorientation. These recommendations synthesize technical requirements (how AI platforms work) with strategic patterns (how digital transformations succeed). The technical requirements rest on documented platform behavior. The strategic recommendations extrapolate from transformation patterns. Both should be tested and refined based on what you learn during implementation.

Stop optimizing for sequence. Awareness, consideration, and conversion still matter as concepts. They no longer happen in a predictable order you can target with stage-specific content. Your strategy must address all three simultaneously because a single AI response can accomplish all three in one paragraph.

Prioritize platform diversity. No single platform dominates all aspects of discovery. Your visibility must span the full platform ecosystem relevant to your target segments. A traveler who starts on Gemini may validate on ChatGPT and compare prices through Perplexity before booking. Your property needs to appear across that entire path.

Optimize for influence, not control. You cannot control traveler journeys. You can increase the probability of favorable outcomes through visibility optimization. The goal shifts from guiding travelers through predetermined paths to achieving visibility wherever travelers choose to research.

Invest in infrastructure, not campaigns. Campaign-based marketing assumes you can time interventions to match funnel stages. The spiral demands sustained optimization. Your investment must build lasting capabilities rather than temporary campaign bursts. Chapter 2 frames this as an infrastructure mindset. The same principle applies here.

The properties that adapt fastest are not necessarily the ones with the biggest budgets or the most sophisticated teams. They are the ones that recognize how discovery changed and commit to building visibility across the spiral. They stop asking "Which funnel stage does this serve?" and start asking "Does this content answer the question a traveler will ask, regardless of where they are in their research?"

Content strategy alone cannot solve the visibility challenge. Each AI platform operates as an independent ecosystem with different rules, different data sources, and different competitive dynamics. Success on one platform transfers nothing to another.

4
THE WALLED GARDEN PROBLEM

YOUR INSTAGRAM SUCCESS means nothing for AI visibility, at least not directly. Fifty thousand engaged followers do not help you appear in ChatGPT recommendations. Each platform operates as an independent silo, and capabilities do not transfer between them. This creates a strategic vulnerability that most hotels do not recognize until occupancy starts declining for reasons they cannot explain.

How the Walls Actually Work

The term "walled garden" describes exactly what is happening. These platforms deliberately build walls, keeping users inside their ecosystems. They control the data, the experience, and every interaction that happens within their boundaries.

Facebook serves roughly 3.07 billion monthly active users, and Instagram reached 3 billion MAUs as of September 2025. Amazon controls purchase intent data. TikTok users spend over an hour a day on the app, with heavy users spending four or more hours. Each platform creates what industry research calls "a unique, rich experience to keep users engaged within the platform."

The business model depends on containment. And the containment runs deeper than most marketers realize.

Meta explicitly documents how Instagram decides what you see. Instagram's Feed AI system orders posts by predicting what a user will find "most valuable and relevant." The signals it uses include your activity inside Instagram (likes, saves, comments), post metadata from within Instagram, and your relationship history with other Instagram accounts. Meta's "Instagram Ranking Explained" blog confirms that the platform uses multiple algorithms and classifiers for Feed, Stories, Explore, and Search, each tracking thousands of ranking signals from user history, content metadata, and post popularity. All measured within the app.

What is missing from those ranking signals? External web authority. Links from authoritative sites. Citations from respected sources. Schema markup. Any signal from outside Instagram's walls. Meta's documentation confirms the absence. The platform emphasizes in-app behavioral, relationship, and content signals. It does not cite external web authority signals for Instagram ranking.

Even massive follower counts only feed into Instagram's internal algorithm. They create zero advantage for AI visibility outside Instagram's ecosystem. Viral fame might drive a temporary spike in brand searches. The AI itself cannot value the content that caused the spike. It registers the search volume increase without connecting it to the social media performance that generated it.

The containment extends to how users spend their time. Studies tracking U.S. mobile internet behavior show that 88% to 90% of mobile time happens inside apps. Not on the open web through browsers. Inside apps with walls. AI systems rely on web citations and discovery patterns to determine authority. When audiences stay inside apps, those signals never generate.

Social platforms do more than passively contain users. They actively suppress content that tries to send users elsewhere.

Facebook's algorithm updates over the past several years have consistently favored content that keeps users inside conversations while de-prioritizing external link posts. Meta published "system cards" disclosing how different ranking surfaces work for Feed, Stories, and Reels. These cards show that interaction history, content popularity, format preferences, and user relationship signals sit at the center of ranking logic. External links are allowed. They rarely receive an algorithmic boost. The system favors native content that keeps users interacting within the app rather than content that sends them elsewhere.

The walls are not psychological. They constitute architectural features preventing the kind of open web behavior that feeds AI visibility.

When Platforms Do Not Talk to Each Other

It would be concerning enough if this dynamic were limited to social media. The architecture of containment has spread beyond social platforms. The AI platforms you are trying to reach have replicated the exact same fractured logic, creating a second layer of walls that isolates your content even further.

Think about what you have built over the past decade. You optimized for Google search. You earned hundreds of TripAdvisor reviews. You grew your social media following. You assumed these capabilities would transfer, that strength on one platform would at least partially benefit you on others.

That assumption breaks down.

ChatGPT does not care about your Instagram followers. Gemini does not factor in your TikTok engagement. Each AI platform makes independent decisions about which hotels to recommend, based on distinct signals.

Your social media success lives in one walled garden. Your search visibility lives in another. Your AI visibility lives in yet another set of gardens with different rules, different gatekeepers, and different currencies of trust.

The walls between platforms prevent capability transfer by design. Instagram's internal ranking systems use in-app signals. Your web authority does not register in their algorithms. In-app browser instrumentation wraps even external clicks in platform tracking, obscuring clean referral signals. Mobile attention concentration in apps means less traffic flows to open web pages where AI systems can observe authority patterns. Algorithmic de-emphasis of external links means social reach does not drive the external discovery that builds AI visibility.

These represent documented platform behaviors that prevent social success from translating into AI visibility.

How Different AI Platforms Retrieve Information

Each AI platform runs on its own retrieval architecture. They do not share data sources, citation indexes, or quality signals. Performance on one platform does not predict performance on another.

ChatGPT combines trained knowledge with active web research. Nectiv's analysis of 8,500 prompts found that ChatGPT triggered background searches in 31% of all commercial queries, but for prompts with local intent, that rate nearly doubled to 59%, generating multiple queries per prompt at an average length of 5.48 words. It favors structured data, verified facts, and machine-readable details. Hotels with accurate schema and consistent information across the web earn higher visibility because ChatGPT can verify their claims during these background searches.

Perplexity performs real-time web retrieval on every query, functioning as a conversational search engine. It favors freshness, link authority, and citation density. Online travel agencies often appear more frequently because their data is standardized, their pages run deep, and their content updates continuously. Properties competing against OTAs on Perplexity need strong external citations from sources the platform already indexes.

Gemini integrates conversational AI with Google's search index, Maps, and Shopping Graph. Its rankings follow the same logic that governs traditional SEO: reputation, relevance, and structured accuracy. Hotels already optimized for Google benefit disproportionately because Gemini draws on those existing signals across every Google surface. For hospitality specifically, Gemini carries outsized strategic weight because recommendations surface in Maps, Hotels, and AI Overviews simultaneously.

Claude's retrieval behavior is less documented than the other three platforms. Early testing suggests it favors readable, well-organized content with clear factual density. Detailed FAQ pages, property guides, and long-form answers appear to perform well. Anthropic has not published the kind of architectural detail that Google, OpenAI, and Perplexity have made available, so optimization strategies for Claude remain more observational than empirical.

This fragmentation is permanent. Each platform develops and updates in isolation, guided by its own data, users, and business model. ChatGPT, Gemini, Perplexity, Claude, and emerging competitors update their models, ranking logic, and features on schedules ranging from weeks to months. No coordination exists between them.

Competition drives this constant evolution. Platforms adopt and adapt successful features from rivals to attract and retain users. What works today could become irrelevant next quarter when a platform copies a competitor's retrieval approach or restructures how it weights source authority. This creates persistent instability for anyone trying to maintain visibility across multiple systems at once.

Building Resilience Despite the Walls

The strategic response starts with accepting reality. Platform independence is not a temporary problem that will be solved. These companies compete with each other. They have no incentive to make your multi-platform optimization easier. Their business model depends on keeping everything inside their walls.

So you diversify. Build visibility across multiple AI platforms. Diversification protects against platform-specific algorithm changes and shifts in market share. Properties with strong performance across four platforms maintain discovery even if one platform changes algorithms overnight.

One category of work does transfer across every platform. Accurate structured data, consistent business information, and comprehensive FAQ content serve all four AI platforms simultaneously because every platform, despite different architectures, needs to parse the same underlying facts about your property. The technical foundation described in Chapter 6 is not platform-specific work. It is the shared infrastructure that makes platform-specific optimization possible. Build it once. Every platform benefits.

Diversification requires platform-specific capabilities. Each platform needs specialized optimization. You cannot copy-paste your ChatGPT strategy to Gemini and expect it to work. Generic approaches perform poorly everywhere.

Assign team members to become platform specialists who understand specific dynamics. These are roles, not necessarily different people. One person might own ChatGPT optimization while also monitoring Gemini. Another tracks Perplexity and Claude. In smaller teams, one individual often manages multiple platforms. The specific accountability for each ecosystem must remain distinct.

Maintain information consistency across the platform landscape. Implement processes ensuring accurate information across all platforms. When check-in time changes, processes update your website, Google Business Profile, Bing Places, OTA listings, review platforms, and social profiles simultaneously. Single-point content management prevents the drift that erodes entity recognition.

Monitor platform evolution. Track algorithm changes and feature updates across platforms. Monthly scanning of platform announcements, combined with performance checks, enables early detection and a proactive response before competitive positioning erodes.

Build durable foundations that serve you across platform evolution: accurate information, comprehensive content, strong citation networks, and technical excellence. Reserve tactical resources for platform-specific optimization, accepting that some work will become obsolete when platforms change. That is not wasted investment. That is the cost of participating in dynamic channels. Chapter 9 details the specific resource requirements and implementation timelines for properties at different competitive levels.

Where the Walls Are Heading

End-to-end hotel booking is not yet broadly completed inside social feeds or AI chat interfaces. The direction is clear. These platforms are building toward transactional capability. Saved preferences. Embedded checkout. Authenticated identities. Agent-assisted actions. In this model, the platform becomes the decision broker, even when the final transaction still technically happens elsewhere.

Breaking through these walls is no longer about producing more content optimized for clicks. It is about eligibility, verification, and interoperability. Platforms increasingly privilege structured, trusted data over narrative content because data is what allows them to compare, rank, recommend, and eventually transact. For hotels, that means accurate, continuously updated inventory, pricing, amenities, policies, and metadata flowing into the systems each platform relies on. Whether that system is Google Hotel Center, a social commerce catalog, or an AI-accessible partner API, the requirement stays constant.

Google's announcement of a Universal Commerce Protocol alongside retail industry partners signals how quickly this trajectory is materializing. UCP creates an open standard for AI agents to discover products, compare options, and complete purchases through structured machine-readable interfaces. For hotels, this means AI systems could interact directly with booking engines without navigating human-designed websites. The protocol remains early. Its existence confirms that the shift from recommendation to transaction is being actively engineered, not theorized. The Epilogue examines UCP's implications in detail.

Content still matters for brand perception and differentiation. Data determines whether a hotel can enter the consideration set at all. As interfaces evolve into storefronts, structured data becomes the admission requirement. The walled garden blocks traditional traffic. It opens selectively to products it can confidently understand, verify, and sell.

The real risk for hotels is not any single platform becoming an OTA. It is the cumulative effect of many platforms quietly repositioning themselves as intermediaries between intent and action. Visibility without data readiness amounts to presence without influence.

The Emerging Fragmentation Within Platforms

The walled garden problem described in this chapter addresses fragmentation between platforms. A second layer of fragmentation is emerging within them.

AI platforms are beginning to incorporate personal data into their recommendation logic. Signals such as location, language, device context, stated preferences, and limited account history increasingly filter the results the AI delivers.

Google's AI extends long-standing account-based personalization in search to its AI responses for logged-in users, primarily using context signals such as location and inferred intent. ChatGPT's memory features retain user-stated preferences and conversational context across sessions when enabled. Apple's AI integration prioritizes on-device personal data, routing queries through private local context before generating responses. Each platform implements personalization differently, using different data sources, different weighting, and different privacy boundaries.

This creates a layer of visibility variation that no amount of optimization can fully standardize or control across users. A traveler whose past behavior signals preference for boutique hotels will see different AI recommendations than one whose history skews toward extended-stay properties. Both asked the same question. The AI answered differently because relevance is now calculated against the traveler, not the query alone.

The strategic implications for properties are threefold.

Content specificity becomes more valuable as personalization matures. Properties with rich, detailed content describing specific traveler scenarios create more surface area for personalization algorithms to match against. A property whose content addresses business travelers, family vacationers, wedding groups, and wellness seekers separately gives the AI more precise material to serve to each traveler profile. Generic content that describes the property the same way regardless of audience provides fewer personalization signals for the AI to work with.

Traveler segmentation in your content strategy now serves a dual purpose. Segmented content has always helped human visitors find relevant information. It now helps AI platforms match your property to specific traveler profiles during personalized retrieval. The content architecture from Chapter 6, particularly the FAQ page strategy and modular answer units, provides the structural foundation for this matching.

Measurement becomes harder to standardize. The testing protocol in Appendix C uses fresh browser sessions, incognito mode, and disabled AI memory features to prevent personalization from skewing results. This produces consistent benchmarks for competitive comparison. It does not capture how personalized results differ from standardized ones. Properties at Integrated and Optimized maturity levels should consider supplemental testing from logged-in accounts representing different traveler profiles to understand how personalization affects their visibility. This supplemental testing adds complexity. It also reveals dynamics that standardized testing cannot detect.

Personalization remains in early deployment across most platforms. The trajectory points toward increasingly individualized recommendations based on behavioral data that accumulates over time. Properties building rich, segmented, specific content today position themselves to benefit as this layer matures. Properties maintaining generic, undifferentiated content will be systematically deprioritized in personalized recommendations, even when their citation networks and technical foundations are otherwise strong.

The walls exist at three levels. Platforms operate as independent silos requiring separate optimization. Transaction layers are forming behind those silos, demanding structured data readiness that goes beyond content quality. Personalization algorithms are adding a third variable that no amount of standardized optimization can fully control.

The work ahead addresses all three. Chapters 6 and 7 provide the technical and citation strategies that build resilience across fragmented ecosystems. The measurement framework in Chapter 8 gives you a way to track progress despite personalization variability.

Chapter 5 shows you exactly where your property stands and what capabilities you need to build.

5
KNOWING WHERE YOU STAND

What to Call This Transformation

THE INDUSTRY HAS fractured the conversation about AI discovery into technical subspecialties. Technical SEO addresses crawlability, structured data, and rendering. AEO (Answer Engine Optimization) and GEO (Generative Engine Optimization) are often used interchangeably across the industry. Both describe optimizing for citation and recommendation within AI-generated responses. This book uses GEO throughout.

In February 2026, Microsoft formalized the term in its rewritten Bing Webmaster Guidelines, making it the first major platform to adopt GEO as a named optimization category in published policy. The guidelines define GEO as focused on content eligibility for grounding and reference in AI-generated answers, and note that GEO does not guarantee citations any more than SEO guarantees rankings. That framing should anchor expectations throughout the practical work in Chapters 6, 7, and 8.

Then we layer on measurement frameworks. Share of voice tracks brand mentions. Share of answer quantifies AI recommendation rates. These distinctions matter operationally. Your technical team needs to know that schema markup differs from meta descriptions. Your analytics lead needs measurement approaches that work despite attribution gaps.

The problem is that despite all these emerging subspecialties, many marketers still want to call the entire discipline SEO. They argue that since AI systems often retrieve information through search mechanisms, this is all an evolution of search engine optimization. They are comfortable with SEO. They have SEO teams, SEO budgets, and SEO reporting structures. Calling everything SEO feels easier than acknowledging a fundamental shift.

That comparison deserves more examination than dismissal. The core tactics do share DNA with traditional SEO. Structured data, clean content architecture, authoritative backlinks, answering questions clearly and concisely. Practitioners who have built strong SEO programs for years will recognize most of the building blocks. Google themselves have said that good SEO produces good GEO results. Content published with solid SEO fundamentals appears across AI platforms within hours.

LinkedIn's own internal analysis confirms this alignment. After studying how LLMs processed and ranked their web content, the platform identified three factors driving AI retrieval performance: structure, relevance, and clarity. Those same factors have driven traditional search performance for years. The overlap is real. The divergence comes in how you optimize for each. LinkedIn warns that focusing solely on LLM optimization while ignoring site performance, crawlability, or content depth can damage Google ranking. The disciplines reinforce each other when implemented together. They undermine each other when treated as separate priorities.

The recognition is accurate. The conclusion drawn from it is not.

Insisting that GEO is SEO is like insisting the automobile is a horseless carriage. The name acknowledges that something changed while clinging to the old frame of reference. It obscures what actually happened. The underlying mechanics shifted. Ranking selects pages from a list. Retrieval selects fragments of meaning from across the web, synthesizes them, and presents a single constructed answer. Your property can hold position one on Google for a target query while producing weak results when an AI system parses that same page into segments and evaluates them for recommendation worthiness. A ranking metric will never reveal a retrieval failure. An SEO dashboard will never show you that ChatGPT described your competitor favorably and omitted your property entirely.

Yes, traditional SEO fundamentals still matter. Crawlability, structured data, and content quality remain essential. Properties that treat GEO as a label swap for existing SEO budgets will underperform those that recognize where the systems diverge.

The real shift is not about search versus AI search. It is about visibility. Visibility in search engines. Visibility in AI answer engines. Visibility on social platforms. Visibility across review sites. Visibility wherever travelers look for hotels, regardless of which technology mediates that discovery.

For two decades, visibility and SEO meant the same thing because search engines dominated discovery. The terms became interchangeable. Now that discovery happens across fragmented platforms using completely different mechanisms, we need language that describes the actual strategic challenge rather than anchoring us to frameworks designed for a world that no longer exists.

This book uses AI visibility to describe presence in AI-mediated discovery channels and visibility as the broader strategic framework encompassing all discovery platforms. The technical subspecialties appear when discussing specific implementation tactics. The organizing principle throughout is visibility: the fundamental business challenge of being discovered by travelers, regardless of platform or technology.

Stop calling everything SEO because it is familiar. The discipline evolved. The name needs to evolve with it.

Where Properties Actually Stand

Once you accept that visibility is the real challenge, the next question becomes practical. Where does your property stand right now? What does progress look like from here?

Properties fall across five capability stages. These are not rungs on a ladder that everyone climbs from the bottom. A property with strong schema markup, consistent business data, and a well-maintained Google Business Profile might already operate at a Structured level without having done any deliberate AI optimization. Good digital hygiene produces a head start. The framework exists to help you identify where you are now, understand why you landed there, and see what the next stage requires.

Most hotels currently operate at the first or second level. Properties advancing to levels three and four gain significant competitive advantages that compound over time.

The stages are sequential in their requirements, not necessarily in how you experience them. A property cannot execute advanced citation network strategies without first having accurate structured data for those citations to reference. A property cannot measure visibility improvement without baseline content that AI platforms can retrieve. The foundations of each stage support the capabilities of the next. Attempting advanced optimization without those foundations wastes resources and creates problems that require expensive corrections later.

Some properties will discover they already cleared the early stages through years of disciplined SEO and content management. Others will find that a strong website masks serious gaps in citation consistency or platform coverage. The assessment tells you what you have. The maturity levels tell you what you need.

These levels synthesize patterns from digital transformation assessment frameworks applied to AI visibility requirements. The specific point ranges and progression timelines represent informed estimates based on observed patterns. Use them as directional guidance and refine the thresholds based on what you observe during implementation.

Properties that want precise scores should complete the full testing protocol in Chapter 8. The Visibility Score methodology measures five weighted components: Citation Rate (30%), Platform Spread (25%), Positioning Quality (20%), Information Accuracy (15%), and Competitive Context (10%). The combined weighted score places you within one of the five maturity levels. If you need your exact position right now, skip ahead to Chapter 8, complete the baseline testing, then return here to understand what your score means for capability development.

Level 0: Invisible (0 to 19 Points)

Hotels at this level appear rarely or never in AI recommendations. When platforms mention them, the information appears incomplete or wrong. Some properties land here because they never prioritized digital infrastructure. Others arrive because a website redesign broke their schema, or because a management transition left their Google Business Profile unclaimed for years. The cause matters less than the diagnosis.

Picture a 120-room independent hotel operating at this level. Their website has no schema markup. JavaScript dependencies prevent AI systems from accessing half their content. The property may have FAQ content on the website. Some Invisible properties have dozens of questions scattered across service pages or buried inside accordion elements that collapse content behind JavaScript clicks. The volume does not matter if AI platforms cannot retrieve it. Common problems at this level include FAQ content hidden inside click-to-expand elements that AI crawlers cannot execute, questions answered with marketing language rather than specific operational details, content distributed across multiple pages without FAQPage schema connecting the questions to structured answers, and no answer-first formatting that allows AI systems to extract a usable response from each entry. A property with 50 questions behind JavaScript accordions is invisible for the same reason a property with eight questions is invisible. The AI cannot reach the content.

Their Google Business Profile sits unclaimed. Their address appears differently across five major platforms. OTA listings contain conflicting check-in times and pet policies. They have no media coverage beyond a single chamber of commerce listing from years ago.

Nobody owns AI visibility as a responsibility. Marketing, operations, and IT never coordinate. Leadership has no awareness that the transformation is happening. When you ask the general manager when they last tested whether travelers could find them through AI platforms, you get blank looks. "We rank fine on Google. That matters most, right?"

Meanwhile, competitors scoring above 50 points capture bookings before this property enters travelers' consideration.

Level 1: Reactive (20 to 39 Points)

Properties at this level achieve sporadic AI mentions through minimal, unsystematic efforts. They respond to problems after they occur rather than prevent them through systematic processes.

Some properties start here because their existing SEO discipline and OTA management produced incidental AI visibility without deliberate effort. That foundation has value. The gap is not effort. It is intentionality.

Technical implementation shows partial schema markup. The Hotel type exists on the homepage, but room Product schemas and FAQ schemas are missing. The website renders inconsistently across pages. Some content remains accessible while other content gets blocked by JavaScript.

Content addresses only obvious questions. FAQ content exists, typically covering 20 to 30 common inquiries. The quantity may appear adequate. The format often undermines it. At this level, properties commonly have some but not all of the following problems resolved: FAQ content may be visible on the page but lack FAQPage schema, meaning AI platforms read the text without recognizing the question-and-answer structure. Answers may address the right topics without answer-first formatting, burying the specific detail inside a paragraph of context. Some content may remain trapped inside accordion elements or JavaScript-dependent displays on certain pages while other pages render correctly. The inconsistency means AI platforms can extract answers from some questions and not others.

Beyond the FAQ, other content pages show similar patterns. Room descriptions use marketing language without specific dimensions, bed configurations, or quantified amenities. Amenity pages list features without operational details like hours, fees, or seasonal availability. Policy pages may exist but use legal formatting that AI systems struggle to parse into direct answers. The content structure problem at this level is not limited to the FAQ page. It runs through every page type that AI platforms retrieve when constructing responses.

Properties at this level have content. They do not have content architecture. The distinction matters because AI retrieval depends on structure as much as substance. A property with 25 questions in proper FAQPage schema with answer-first formatting outperforms a property with 40 questions that lack markup and lead with marketing language.

Citation presence achieves the bare minimum. The Google Business Profile is claimed and partially completed but not optimized. Major OTA listings maintain reasonable accuracy with inconsistency across platforms. Review responses happen sporadically without monitoring systems.

Properties at this level appear in some AI recommendations for broad queries. Specific, high-intent searches miss them completely. Information accuracy remains inconsistent. Sometimes AI platforms help their case. Sometimes the platforms actively hurt it.

Properties at this level know they should do more with AI visibility. They have not determined what that actually means.

Level 2: Structured (40 to 59 Points)

Properties with years of disciplined SEO, comprehensive Google Business Profiles, and consistent citation management sometimes discover they already operate at this level before any deliberate AI optimization. Their existing digital infrastructure created a head start. The work ahead shifts from building foundations to refining them for AI-specific retrieval.

Properties at this level implement processes that deliver consistent baseline performance. Operational capabilities support sustained optimization.

Technical implementation reaches full coverage. Complete schema markup spans all key page types: Hotel, multiple Product schemas for room types, FAQPage, and Review aggregation. The website renders perfectly in reader mode across all content pages. Page speed optimization delivers sub-2-second loads.

Content structure serves AI comprehension. FAQ content addresses 30 to 60 questions covering traveler research needs across reservations, policies, amenities, location, and accessibility categories. At this level, the structural problems that limit Reactive properties are resolved. FAQPage schema marks up every question-answer pair. Every answer follows answer-first formatting with specific, quantified details. The content renders as static text on a crawlable, dedicated FAQ page rather than hiding behind accordions or distributing across multiple service pages. Natural language optimization uses conversational phrasing that mirrors how travelers ask AI platforms for recommendations. Policy documentation remains thorough and transparent.

The difference between Reactive and Structured is not primarily the number of questions. It is the architecture. A Structured property's FAQ page functions as a retrieval asset. A single page load during Query Fan-Out gives the AI enough structured, schema-marked, answer-first content to satisfy multiple sub-queries without additional retrieval cycles. The content is findable, parseable, and extractable. All three conditions must hold for the FAQ to produce visibility value.

The same three conditions apply beyond the FAQ page. Room pages carry Product schema with specific pricing, bed types, square footage, and occupancy limits. Amenity pages document operational hours, fees, seasonal restrictions, and capacity details in plain language rather than marketing copy. Policy documentation states cancellation terms, pet fees, parking costs, and check-in procedures with the same answer-first specificity the FAQ uses. At Structured maturity, the content architecture is consistent across page types. The AI retrieves a room page and finds structured, extractable facts. It retrieves an amenity page and finds the same. No page type reverts to the vague marketing language that characterizes Reactive content.

Citation presence achieves coverage. The Google Business Profile operates with complete information, regular posts, photo updates, and review responses. Initial success in editorial placement produces 2 to 5 placements in regional media or trade publications.

Measurement capability establishes itself. Monthly Visibility Score testing uses standardized protocols. Quarterly competitive benchmarking occurs. Documentation enables trend analysis.

The Marriott case study from Chapter 3 validates what this level delivers. Their restructured content achieved a 6.6-point lift in keyword performance for conversational queries. Structured-level implementation produces measurable results.

Properties reaching this level typically appear in a meaningful share of relevant AI queries with high information accuracy. The specific citation rate varies depending on how the other four Visibility Score components perform. A property with strong Platform Spread and Positioning Quality might reach Structured maturity with a citation rate in the low 30s. A property with weaker spread across platforms might need citation rates above 50% to compensate. The composite score determines the level, not any single component.

Competitive positioning achieves parity with similar properties. Differentiation from stronger competitors remains limited.

You built the foundation. Now you can improve.

Level 3: Integrated (60 to 79 Points)

Hotels at this level embed AI visibility across organizational functions. Cross-departmental coordination enables sophisticated optimization that Structured properties cannot match.

Technical implementation reaches genuine sophistication. Advanced schema markup includes proximity details, special offers, and custom properties. Server-side rendering or prerendering eliminates JavaScript dependencies. Advanced optimization delivers page speeds under 1 second.

Content structure demonstrates expertise. Extensive FAQ content covering 60 or more questions addresses edge cases and niche traveler scenarios that competitors overlook. The content extends beyond standard operational answers into situational specifics: questions families with young children ask, questions guests with accessibility requirements need answered before booking, questions business travelers ask about meeting space configurations.

At this level, content architecture is not only correct. It is advanced. FAQ schema extends beyond the dedicated FAQ page into contextual question-answer pairs embedded on room pages, amenity pages, and event pages, each with its own FAQPage markup. Answer-first formatting incorporates specific details that competitors leave vague: not "the pool is heated" but "the pool maintains 82 degrees year-round with a separate 92-degree spa accessible from 6 AM to 10 PM without additional charge." Differentiated positioning establishes unique value. Content depth signals authority on specific topics. Detailed policy documentation addresses concerns proactively.

The content does more than answer retrieval queries. It gives AI platforms enough differentiated, structured material to construct a recommendation rather than a mention. The AI does not recommend your property because it found your name on enough platforms. It recommends your property because your content answered the traveler's specific question with more precision than any competitor's content could.

Citation presence builds measurable authority. A strong presence emerges through 8 to 12 editorial placements annually in authoritative publications. Strategic positioning in citations reinforces brand narrative. Co-occurrence patterns link the property to desirable attributes in AI training data.

Measurement capability matures at this level. Weekly testing occurs during optimization initiatives. Monthly standard testing continues. Competitive benchmarking reveals strategic insights.

Attribution modeling connects visibility to business outcomes through proxy metrics.

Organizational integration completes. A dedicated AI visibility coordinator role exists. Weekly cross-functional coordination meetings connect marketing, operations, and IT. Executive sponsors review strategic performance. Budget allocation gets formalized through annual planning.

Properties at this level appear consistently across platforms with favorable, differentiated descriptions. The specific citation rate varies based on how all five Visibility Score components contribute to the overall composite. Some Integrated properties achieve high citation rates. Others reach this level through exceptional positioning quality and information accuracy that compensate for moderate citation frequency. The composite score determines placement, not any single component.

Business impact becomes visible through directional evidence. Multiple proxy metrics tend to move in a consistent positive direction. Branded search volume may increase as AI recommendations drive curiosity. Direct booking percentages may rise as travelers who discover you through AI validate and convert on your website. OTA dependency may decline as organic discovery channels strengthen. These patterns represent observed correlations at this maturity level, not guaranteed outcomes. The strength of the signal depends on your market, your competitive set, and how effectively your content converts the visibility into bookings.

Level 4: Optimized (80 to 100 Points)

Properties that reach this level establish advantages that competitors find extremely difficult to overcome.

Technical implementation achieves excellence. Advanced schema implementation uses custom extensions. Advanced rendering optimization occurs. Exceptional performance delivers sub-0.5-second page loads. Continuous technical monitoring catches issues before they impact visibility.

Content structure at this level achieves full coverage across every page type and every traveler research scenario. Room pages, amenity pages, event pages, policy documentation, and the FAQ library all carry appropriate schema, answer-first formatting, and specific quantified details. Content extends into territory competitors have not addressed: neighborhood guides with walking times to specific venues, seasonal activity recommendations with dates and pricing, and operational details for edge-case traveler needs. The content architecture is not only correct and consistent. It is differentiated enough that AI platforms select this property's content as the authoritative answer over competitors who provide generic descriptions of similar features.

Citation presence establishes unquestionable authority. Tier 1 success is achieved through 1 to 3 placements in national publications or major industry recognition. Citation diversity creates resilience across platform algorithm changes. Co-occurrence patterns are strongly established in AI training data.

Measurement capability becomes industry leading. Real-time monitoring systems track performance. Sophisticated attribution modeling connects AI visibility to business outcomes. Competitive intelligence anticipates competitor moves. Platform evolution tracking detects changes before competitors notice.

Organizational integration becomes cultural. AI visibility is embedded in how the organization thinks about marketing. Quality standards are maintained through review processes and accountability systems. Succession planning ensures continuity beyond any individual team member.

The Sixt case study demonstrates this level's business impact. Sixt partnered with Yext, managing data consistency across 1,312 locations on more than 100 digital platforms. Within six months, Sixt measured a 29% increase in Google customer actions compared with the previous year. While Sixt applied this at enterprise scale, the mechanic is identical for a single property. Excellence in data consistency yields the same relative lift whether you manage one location or one thousand.

The Optimized property has addressed the hardest problem in AI visibility: the Primary Bias introduced in Chapter 1. Large language models carry a statistical preference for brands that dominated twenty years of internet content. That preference is not a ranking signal a property can adjust. It is embedded in the model's training data. An independent property that was not prominent enough to appear frequently in that training corpus starts every query at a structural disadvantage.

An Optimized independent property has built enough bridge entities to counteract that disadvantage. These are citations from Tier 1 and Tier 2 sources that the AI already trusts. The AI recommends these properties not because their schema is perfect, though it is. The AI recommends them because the sources it respects have vouched for them. Authority transfers through association. The property did not change the training data. It built enough external authority that the retrieval process overrides what the training data alone would produce.

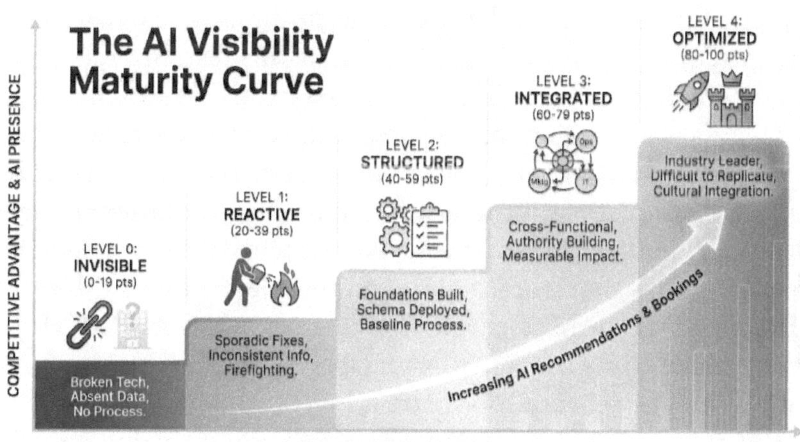

Assessing Where You Actually Stand

Most hotels misjudge their maturity level by one or two stages. Some overestimate, discovering that strong general impressions mask specific gaps. Others underestimate, learning through testing that their existing work already cleared early-stage requirements. Both miscalibrations create planning problems. Accurate assessment prevents wasted effort in either direction.

Test yourself against four dimensions.

Technical foundation: Does complete schema markup exist across all key pages, beyond your homepage? Does your website pass reader mode testing consistently across all content pages? Can AI platforms access and parse your content without JavaScript execution requirements?

Content structure: Can AI platforms find, parse, and extract the information on your website? This question applies to every content type, not only your FAQ page. Room descriptions, amenity details, policy documentation, location information, and editorial content all feed AI retrieval. Test three conditions across your key pages. First, is the content accessible? Load your FAQ page, a room page, and an amenity page in browser Reader Mode. If content disappears on any page, those entries are invisible to AI crawlers. Content inside JavaScript accordions, click-to-expand elements, or dynamically loaded tabs fails this test. Second, is the content marked up with appropriate schema? Hotel schema on your homepage, Product schema on room pages, FAQPage schema on your FAQ content, and Location Features schema on amenity pages each give AI platforms a structured signal for different types of traveler queries. Third, does your content lead with specific, quantified answers rather than marketing descriptions? "Heated rooftop pool open May through October, 6 AM to 10 PM, no additional fee" gives the AI an extractable fact. "Enjoy our stunning rooftop pool experience" does not.

FAQ content provides concentrated retrieval value because a single well-structured FAQ page lets the AI satisfy multiple sub-queries from one page load. Target 30 or more question-answer pairs in answer-first format covering the operational topics travelers ask most frequently. That said, FAQ content alone does not constitute content structure. Room pages without Product schema, amenity pages without operational details, and policy pages written in legal language rather than plain answers all represent content structure gaps that limit AI visibility regardless of how strong your FAQ page performs.

Measurement discipline: Do you test AI visibility monthly across multiple platforms using standardized methods? Can you quantify your visibility relative to competitors? Do you track trends showing improvement or decline over time?

Organizational integration: Does someone own AI visibility as a primary responsibility with explicit accountability? Do multiple departments coordinate AI visibility efforts through regular communication? Does leadership review AI visibility metrics and allocate resources based on performance?

The gap between perception and reality often surprises people when they apply this framework. A property might believe it operates at a solid Structured level based on general impressions. When the team evaluates against the specific criteria, they discover they are late Reactive. They have awareness and sporadic execution without processes.

What This Means for Your Planning

Your current maturity level determines which implementation roadmap you should follow from Chapter 9. High-risk properties at Invisible or early Reactive levels need the foundation sprint. Medium-risk properties at Reactive or Structured levels should follow the six-month comprehensive build. Properties at Structured or Integrated pursuing market leadership can attempt the 12-month advanced path.

Maturity level also determines realistic expectations. Properties that discover they already operate at Structured or Integrated levels gain a different advantage. Their implementation timelines compress because the foundational work is behind them. Their focus shifts to the capabilities that differentiate rather than the infrastructure that qualifies. Properties at early Structured should not expect to achieve Optimized status within one year. The progression requires time for capabilities to compound.

Understanding maturity curves prevents two common mistakes. The first: starting advanced optimization before establishing foundations. This wastes resources on tactics that cannot work without underlying infrastructure. The second: maintaining an emergency mindset after you build foundations. This burns out teams and prevents sustainable operations from developing.

Seasonal patterns persist despite platform transformation. AI tools and traditional search both show identical mid-year dips and late-summer rebounds. Underlying human behavior patterns transcend platform changes. Properties planning optimization launches should account for these cycles rather than assuming AI platforms eliminate seasonality.

Your choice determines whether you build sustainable competitive positioning or temporary tactical advantages that competitors quickly overcome.

The maturity framework tells you where you stand. Now you need the technical knowledge to build visibility. Two categories of work determine your results. On-site optimization addresses what you control directly: your website, your content, and your technical infrastructure. Off-site influence addresses what you shape indirectly: citations, reviews, media coverage, and the broader web presence that AI platforms reference when making recommendations.

Both matter. Neither alone proves sufficient. The next chapter starts with the half you control: your own website.

6
TECHNICAL FOUNDATIONS AND ON-SITE OPTIMIZATION

YOUR WEBSITE SERVES two audiences now. Human visitors judge visual appeal and user experience. AI systems parse structured data and extract factual information.

Most hotels optimize beautifully for humans while remaining completely invisible to AI platforms.

The Problem Living in Your Content

A traveler asks ChatGPT for hotel recommendations. ChatGPT mentions your property and provides links to Booking.com for comparison. The traveler books through the OTA. A reservation appears in your property management system labeled as a Booking. com booking. You pay the commission. Nothing in that transaction tells you how the guest found your Booking.com listing. The OTA does not share upstream referral data with properties. The AI conversation that created initial awareness and directed the traveler toward your property never appears anywhere in your data. You did not misattribute the booking. You never had the attribution signal to begin with.

A major Gulf airline conducted an audit that revealed this pattern at scale. Despite ranking on page one of Google for premium flight queries, the airline was completely omitted from AI responses to "best business-class airlines," while Qatar Airways and Singapore Airlines consistently appeared. The audit revealed the cause: incomplete schema markup, inconsistent information across their website and Wikipedia, and conflicting data on travel sites. Strong performance in traditional search provided no protection against AI invisibility.

Hotels face identical problems. Your property details appear inconsistently across different pages. The homepage lists check-in at 3:00 PM. The FAQ says 4:00 PM. The policies page mentions early check-in without specifics. Amenity lists vary between sections. The pet policy page says dogs must be under 50 pounds. The booking page says 40 pounds. Google Business Profile lists 60 pounds.

This fragmentation undermines AI visibility because automated systems cannot determine which version represents accurate information. They encounter conflicts and either skip mentioning you or provide incorrect details that cost you bookings.

The industry calls this semantic dilution. When slightly different versions of the same fact appear across your pages and platforms, the AI embeds each version separately. You do not get one strong representation of your property. You get several weak ones competing with each other. Google reconciles these conflicts over time. AI retrieval systems do not. They average the conflicting signals, produce lower-confidence embeddings, and move on to a competitor whose information is clean.

How AI Systems Actually Process Your Information

Most hotels do not understand how their information ends up in AI responses. It is not a single lookup. It is an automated research process.

Google's VP of Product Robby Stein revealed how this works in an October 2025 interview. When their AI constructs a response, it performs what they call "query fan-out." The AI does not answer from stored knowledge alone. It automatically generates dozens of background searches, using Google Search to fetch real-time data and evaluate quality signals.

A traveler asks: "Pet-friendly hotels in downtown Austin with parking."

The AI does not pull a pre-written answer. It automatically generates and executes searches for: Austin downtown hotels, pet-friendly accommodations Austin, hotel parking downtown Austin, pet policies Austin hotels, downtown Austin lodging with amenities.

AI Query Fan-Out Process

The AI becomes the searcher, issuing queries and evaluating your content using the same quality signals that have always mattered.

Nectiv's research analyzing 8,500 ChatGPT prompts across commercial search categories revealed specific patterns. ChatGPT triggered search in 31% of instances, averaging over two queries per prompt. The behavior intensifies for local businesses. Prompts with local intent triggered background searches 59% of the time, nearly double the overall average. Hotels live in this category. When travelers ask location-based questions about where to stay, ChatGPT does not rely on training data. It actively searches, conducting real-time research to ground its recommendations.

Those queries skew longer than standard search behavior. Three-quarters of all queries contained five or more words. The research also identified recurring terms ChatGPT adds during background research. "Reviews" appeared in 702 of 2,648 searches analyzed. The current year appeared often. "Features" and "comparison" appeared across categories, signaling the platform's tendency to evaluate options against each other rather than in isolation.

Properties optimized only for short-tail keywords miss the longer phrases ChatGPT searches for. Content lacking comparison frameworks, feature specifications, and review integration fails to connect with the queries ChatGPT automatically generates.

Stein confirmed this: "At the end of the day, actually something's searching. It's not a person, but there are searches happening. And each search is paired with content. So, if for a given search, your webpage is designed to be extremely helpful... a lot of the core signals, is this a good piece of information for the question, they're still valid."

This technical reality should provide confidence. The work you have done for traditional SEO does not become obsolete. It becomes the foundation that AI systems use during their background research process.

Why Token Economics Shape Everything That Follows

Before walking through each technical layer, you need to understand the economics that govern how AI platforms process your content. This understanding explains why the specific recommendations in this chapter take the form they do.

Large language models do not read web pages the way humans do. They process text as tokens, units of meaning roughly equivalent to three-quarters of a word. Every token an AI system processes costs the platform operator money. Input tokens (the text the system reads from your website) carry a direct cost. Output tokens (the answer the system generates) cost three to five times more. A single traveler query that triggers Query Fan-Out and retrieves content from a dozen websites might process tens of thousands of tokens across retrieval, evaluation, and response generation.

These costs accumulate at scale. ChatGPT handles hundreds of millions of queries daily. Gemini processes billions of searches across Google's infrastructure. Every token consumed during retrieval represents a computational expense the platform must justify through the quality of the answer it produces. This economic pressure creates a selection mechanism that directly affects your property's visibility.

AI platforms optimize aggressively for token efficiency. They prefer content that delivers maximum useful information per token consumed. A page filled with marketing language, welcome messages, and vague descriptions forces the system to process hundreds of tokens before reaching an extractable fact. A page that opens with specific, quantified details about your property delivers useful information immediately. The system spends fewer tokens to get better data. Your content becomes computationally cheaper to use.

This preference operates at every stage of retrieval. During Query Fan-Out, the AI decides which pages to retrieve based on title tags and meta descriptions. Pages signaling high information density earn retrieval. Pages signaling promotional content get skipped. During content parsing, the AI breaks retrieved pages into chunks and evaluates each chunk for relevance. Sections packed with specific facts generate useful chunks. Sections filled with adjectives and brand voice generate noise the system must process and discard.

Token economics explain why the FAQ page architecture described later in this chapter carries such strategic weight. A single FAQ page with 40 clearly headed questions and fact-dense answers lets the AI retrieve one URL and extract answers to multiple sub-queries. The alternative (40 separate pages each requiring individual retrieval) consumes 40 times the processing budget for the same information. At scale, AI platforms favor the architecture that delivers more answers per retrieval cycle. They have financial incentive to do so.

You do not need to understand the technical details of tokenization. You need to understand the principle it creates. AI platforms reward content that delivers specific, extractable facts with minimal processing overhead. They deprioritize content that forces them to spend tokens parsing through promotional language, vague descriptions, and structural noise. Every recommendation in this chapter serves this underlying economic logic. Dense, specific, well-structured content is computationally cheaper for AI systems to use. Cheaper content gets used more often. More frequent use means more frequent recommendations.

Entity-Intent Mapping and Bridge Entities

In traditional search, a traveler typing "family friendly hotel" triggered a keyword match. Google looked for those specific words on your page. AI search works differently. The engine converts that query into a numerical coordinate within a high-dimensional mathematical space. Engineers call this vector space.

Think of it as a map with hundreds of dimensions instead of three. On this map, concepts like luxury, beach, and relaxation cluster in one region. Concepts like budget, airport, and convenience cluster in another. Every word, every phrase, every entity occupies a specific position based on its semantic meaning and its relationships to other concepts.

When a traveler asks "Where should I stay for a stress-free weekend?" the AI does not scan pages for the phrase "stress-free." It maps the intent behind that question (relaxation, ease, minimal friction) to the entities that occupy the same region of vector space. Your hotel's spa. Your streamlined check-in process. Your location on a quiet residential street. If those attributes exist in your content with enough descriptive specificity, the AI plots your property in the same neighborhood as the traveler's intent.

Your goal is to surround your brand with enough descriptive signals that the AI positions your property in the right region of that map. Vague marketing language places you nowhere specific. Quantified, detailed descriptions of what you offer and why it matters give the AI the coordinates it needs.

The AI does not stop at the intent the traveler stated. It infers the intent the traveler did not. A business trip query triggers assumed needs for proximity to transportation, quiet rooms, reliable Wi-Fi, workspace, and early breakfast availability. A family vacation query triggers assumed needs for connecting rooms, kid-friendly dining, pool access, and proximity to activities. The traveler asked for "a good hotel for our family trip to San Diego." The AI generated sub-queries about childproofing, highchair availability, and distance to the zoo.

This is latent intent extraction. The AI builds a profile of unstated requirements based on the context embedded in the original prompt and searches for properties that satisfy the full profile, not the literal question.

The strategic implication is direct. Your content must answer questions travelers have not yet thought to ask. A property optimized for the explicit query "business hotel in Scarsdale" captures one search. A property whose content also addresses commute time to Manhattan, availability of early check-in before morning meetings, printing services in the business center, and quiet room guarantees captures the five or six latent intent sub-queries the AI generates around that single prompt.

This is where quantified specificity earns its value. "Close to the train station" does not satisfy a latent intent query about transportation proximity. "0.4 miles from the Metro-North Scarsdale station, 35-minute express service to Grand Central Terminal, complimentary station shuttle departing every 15 minutes from 6:00 AM to 10:00 PM" does. The AI needs extractable facts to match against latent intent. Vague descriptions provide nothing to extract.

Bridge entities extend this concept. When an AI performs Query Fan-Out, it breaks a single question into a network of sub-tasks. Bridge entities are the logical anchors that connect your property to the broader context of a traveler's trip. In hospitality, a bridge entity is often a landmark, a seasonal event, or a specific traveler need. The Javits Center. South by Southwest. Pet-friendly accommodations with on-site dog walking.

Bridge entities matter because AI platforms reason through connections. A traveler asks "I am attending a conference at the Javits Center and want a hotel with a serious gym." The AI has to connect two nodes: the Javits Center location and high-end fitness facilities. If your hotel content explicitly links your property to both of those entities, you become the logical answer when the AI resolves that connection.

This is how you build co-occurrence patterns deliberately. Chapter 5's maturity levels describe co-occurrence as the outcome. Bridge entity strategy is the method for getting there. Each explicit connection between your property and a high-authority concept generates repeated associations that AI platforms absorb from training data and real-time retrieval. When your website, your media coverage, your OTA listings, and your review responses all connect your brand to the same bridge entities, the co-occurrence pattern compounds across sources. The AI stops treating the association as incidental. It starts treating it as definitional.

The strategy is direct. Identify the bridge entities that define your competitive position. Convention centers within walking distance. Annual events that drive bookings. Specific traveler needs your property serves better than competitors. Then build content that explicitly connects your brand name to those entities with specific, quantified details.

The Three Technical Layers

Think of AI-accessible websites as three layers working together. Each layer serves a specific function. All three must work properly, or the system fails.

Layer 1 is rendering accessibility. The server must provide the text before the browser paints the screen. If AI systems cannot read your text in the code source, nothing else matters.

Layer 2 is structured data. Machine-readable information through schema markup using JSON-LD format. Without structured data, AI platforms must parse natural language, which introduces interpretation errors.

Layer 3 is content architecture. Information organized logically with clear hierarchies, consistent formatting, and semantic HTML, enabling accurate extraction and comprehension.

Properties that implement all three layers provide complete AI accessibility. Partial implementation delivers partial results. Strongly structured data cannot compensate for poor rendering accessibility. Excellent content architecture proves less effective without proper schema markup.

Optimizing for the Agentic Click

Before an AI model reads your schema or processes your content, it makes a retrieval decision. That decision happens at the snippet level.

When AI platforms run background searches through Query Fan-Out, they evaluate results the same way a search engine displays them: title, URL, and description. If those three elements do not signal that your page contains the relevant answer, the AI moves on. Your content never gets read. Your schema never gets parsed. The retrieval fails before it begins.

This inverts a core principle of traditional SEO. For years, marketers wrote meta descriptions that teased the answer, creating curiosity gaps designed to earn human clicks. AI systems have no curiosity. They need confirmation that your page holds the data they are looking for.

Title tags must include the specific entity or question the traveler is asking. A title reading "Our Amenities" tells the AI nothing. A title reading "Pet Policy, Parking Rates, and Pool Hours at The Meridian Hotel Downtown" tells the AI exactly what facts the page contains.

Meta descriptions must deliver the answer, not promise it. A description stating "Learn about our wonderful pet-friendly accommodations" gives the AI no reason to retrieve the page. A description stating "Dogs and cats welcome, 50-pound limit, $35 nightly fee, ground-floor rooms, advance booking required" confirms the page holds extractable facts. The AI retrieves it.

LinkedIn's AI search optimization guide validates this approach across industries: write meta descriptions as short, direct answers to the primary query the page addresses. Use full, natural-language URL slugs that read like conversational phrases rather than abbreviated internal shorthand. Include connector words such as "how," "what," and "why" to signal intent. Keep meta descriptions between 140 and 160 characters for clarity and complete display. The principle works the same whether the page describes B2B marketing tactics or hotel pet policies. AI systems evaluate the snippet before deciding whether to retrieve the page. The snippet must confirm the answer exists.

Think of this as optimization step zero. Every technical foundation in this chapter depends on the AI choosing to read your page in the first place.

Google's January 2026 announcement of Chrome Auto Browse extends this principle beyond AI search platforms. Chrome itself now functions as an agentic browser, autonomously navigating websites on behalf of users. Your title tags, meta descriptions, and content structure must pass the retrieval test whether the visitor is human, an AI search crawler, or an agentic browser acting on a traveler's behalf. Microsoft's February 2026 rewrite of the Bing Webmaster Guidelines introduced a directive-by-directive breakdown that Google has not yet published. Understanding these controls matters because Bing powers ChatGPT's retrieval infrastructure. What you allow or restrict on Bing surfaces across the entire Microsoft and OpenAI ecosystem.

Four directives now govern how your content appears in Copilot and AI-generated answers. NOARCHIVE prevents your content from being used in Copilot responses or grounding results entirely. NOCACHE limits Copilot to citing only your URL, title, and snippet, stripping all richer context from citations. DATA-NOSNIPPET and NOSNIPPET reduce citation quality by restricting what text the AI can extract. Bing explicitly recommends against NOCACHE on any page you want cited with depth.

The update also introduced a data-snippet attribute that gives you section-level control. You can designate specific text blocks as citable while restricting others. For hotel properties, this means you can mark your pet policy, parking rates, and amenity details as eligible for AI citation while keeping promotional copy or legal boilerplate outside the extractable zone.

Audit your existing meta directives before assuming AI platforms can access your content. A single misconfigured tag can exclude an entire page from Copilot grounding results, regardless of how well the rest of your optimization performs.

Making Your Content Actually Visible

AI platforms access content through automated crawlers that behave differently from human browsers. The reader mode test provides simple validation. Open any page on your website in reader mode (Chrome, Safari, or Firefox). Does the content completely display? Do images appear with descriptions? Does the page structure remain logical? If reader mode fails to display content properly, AI crawlers will likely experience similar problems.

Microsoft's guidance emphasizes: "AI assistants don't read a page top to bottom as a person would. They break content into smaller, usable pieces, a process called parsing. These modular pieces are what get ranked and assembled into answers."

Common accessibility failures include JavaScript-dependent content frequently missed by crawlers optimizing for speed. While some bots can execute JavaScript, they prioritize static HTML for efficiency during real-time Query Fan-Out. Content loaded asynchronously through AJAX requests may not appear to automated systems. Images without proper alt text attributes remain invisible to text-based crawling. Navigation elements relying on JavaScript for functionality prevent crawlers from discovering linked pages.

Server response latency creates a failure mode most properties overlook. AI agents operate with shorter timeout thresholds than traditional search crawlers. If your Time to First Byte is slow, the agent abandons the retrieval before the page loads. A CDN combined with server-side caching ensures immediate server response. Properties with TTFB exceeding two seconds risk systematic exclusion from AI retrieval during Query Fan-Out, where speed determines which pages get processed and which get skipped.

Server-side rendering solves most accessibility problems by generating complete HTML before sending pages to browsers or crawlers. For properties that find full server-side rendering impractical, prerendering services offer affordable alternatives. The most effective delivery point is the edge layer, the globally distributed network sitting between the requester and your server. AI crawlers hit the edge first. If the pre-rendered page is waiting there, the crawler receives complete HTML instantly. No JavaScript execution. No rendering delay. Human visitors still get the full dynamic experience.

Turning Your Website Into a Database

Schema markup transforms your website into a machine-readable database of property information. This structured data enables algorithms to reliably extract precise facts rather than parsing natural language descriptions, which introduce interpretation errors.

The foundational Hotel schema establishes basic entity recognition. This entity recognition feeds into what Google calls its Knowledge Graph, a structured database of entities and their verified attributes. When your schema, citations, and business listings all confirm the same facts about your property, the Knowledge Graph builds a confident record that AI systems draw on when generating responses. When those sources conflict, the record degrades.

Zero-click search behavior validates structured data's strategic importance. When over one-quarter of U.S. desktop searches resolve inside platforms without generating click-throughs, schema markup becomes your primary visibility mechanism. AI systems extract your structured data to construct answers. Properties without thorough schema lose representation in these direct-answer formats.

A basic Hotel schema implementation should include name, address, telephone number, star rating, amenities, check-in and check-out times, payment methods, and cancellation policy. Extended implementation adds room types, pricing, availability, operational hours, and services.

Here is what this looks like in practice:

```json
{
  "@context": "https://schema.org",
  "@type": ["Hotel", "LocalBusiness"],
  "@id": "https://www.yourhotel.com/#hotel",
  "name": "The Grand Hotel",
  "url": "https://www.yourhotel.com",
  "telephone": "+1-512-555-0100",

  "address": {
    "@type": "PostalAddress",
    "streetAddress": "200 Congress Avenue",
    "addressLocality": "Austin",
    "addressRegion": "TX",
    "postalCode": "78701",
    "addressCountry": "US"
  },

  "starRating": {
    "@type": "Rating",
    "ratingValue": "4"
  },

  "checkinTime": "15:00",
  "checkoutTime": "11:00",

  "amenityFeature": [
    { "@type": "LocationFeatureSpecification", "name": "Heated Outdoor Pool", "value": true },
    { "@type": "LocationFeatureSpecification", "name": "Fitness Center", "value": true },
    { "@type": "LocationFeatureSpecification", "name": "On-Site Restaurant", "value": true },
    { "@type": "LocationFeatureSpecification", "name": "Business Center", "value": true },
    { "@type": "LocationFeatureSpecification", "name": "Free Wi-Fi", "value": true },
    { "@type": "LocationFeatureSpecification", "name": "Valet Parking", "value": true },
    { "@type": "LocationFeatureSpecification", "name": "Pet Friendly", "value": true },
    { "@type": "LocationFeatureSpecification", "name": "Concierge Service", "value": true },
    { "@type": "LocationFeatureSpecification", "name": "Accessible Rooms", "value": true }
  ],

  "paymentAccepted": "Visa, Mastercard, American Express, Discover, Cash",
```

That is simplified for readability. The complete implementation includes more fields. The pattern is clear: structured information AI platforms can reliably parse.

Schema validation is critical. Errors in schema markup render it invisible to the algorithm. Use Google Rich Results Test to validate implementations before deployment. Achieve zero errors before considering implementation complete. A single syntax error may break the entire schema block.

A newer proposal complements traditional schema markup. The llms.txt file is a lightweight Markdown document placed in your website root that identifies which pages contain your most substantive content. Jeremy Howard, co-founder of Answer.AI, proposed the specification to address how AI systems waste context window capacity processing navigation menus, scripts, and boilerplate text when they retrieve web pages. By pointing to substantive pages in a clean, structured format, the file aims to improve signal-to-noise ratio during retrieval. The file works alongside schema markup and FAQ content rather than replacing them.

Adoption requires honest context. The specification was designed primarily for developer documentation sites, and early adopters are overwhelmingly technology companies like Stripe, Cloudflare, and Anthropic, which uses llms.txt for its own Claude documentation. No major AI platform, including OpenAI or Google, has confirmed that its models read llms.txt files during inference. Server log analysis by companies that have implemented the file shows that major AI crawlers do not currently request it. The specification may gain traction as AI retrieval matures. It may not. Properties with comprehensive technical foundations (schema markup, FAQ content, rendering accessibility) can consider llms.txt as low-cost experimentation. The implementation requires a few hours to create the initial file and quarterly maintenance thereafter. Properties still building basic infrastructure should prioritize those foundations first. Do not treat llms.txt as a substitute for the structural work described in this chapter.

Organizing Information for AI Comprehension

Proper HTML structure helps AI platforms understand the organization of content and the relative importance of information elements.

Heading hierarchy establishes document structure through proper H1-H6 usage. Use only one H1 per page as the primary page title. Nest subsequent headings logically, with H2 for major sections, H3 for subsections. Never skip heading levels. Generic headings like "Learn More" provide no useful information. Specific headings like "Pet Policy Details" or "Airport Shuttle Service" help AI systems understand what content follows and match it to relevant queries.

LinkedIn's content optimization research reinforces this principle with a specific test. Replace a vague heading like "Overview" with "What B2B Marketers Need Before Launching a Lead Gen Campaign." Replace "Best Practices" with "Channels That Drive Qualified B2B Leads." The pattern applies identically to hospitality. Replace "Guest Services" with "Valet Parking, Concierge Hours, and Airport Shuttle Schedule at The Meridian Hotel." Every heading should communicate a complete idea so that both readers and AI systems understand the focus of the section before reading a single word of body copy.

List structures organize related items for easy extraction. Use ordered lists for sequential items such as check-in procedures. Use unordered lists for non-sequential items such as amenities. Hotels often create fake lists through line breaks or dashes. This looks fine to humans but confuses AI models. HTML list elements provide semantic meaning that text formatting cannot convey.

Table structures organize data with clear relationships. Use tables for information that naturally fits rows and columns: room types with prices, amenities with hours, and packages with inclusions.

Image alt text provides textual descriptions for visual content. "Pool area at The Grand Hotel showing heated outdoor pool with mountain views" proves more useful than "hotel pool." Alt text serves accessibility, search indexing, and AI comprehension simultaneously.

Visual elements extend beyond static images. LinkedIn's research confirms that AI systems rely on captions, filenames, and surrounding text to interpret the purpose of any visual asset on a page. Use descriptive filenames like "heated-rooftop-pool-meridian-hotel.png" rather than "IMG_4582.png." For properties embedding video content, optimize titles, tags, and descriptions so metadata clearly reflects what the video covers. Add transcripts and structured data like VideoObject schema to give AI systems a text-based understanding of video content. Properties hosting virtual tours, room walkthrough videos, or event footage on YouTube should embed those videos on the relevant website pages. The embed creates an association between your domain and a trusted video platform, strengthening retrieval signals in both traditional search and AI systems.

Footer content deserves more attention than most properties give it. LLMs parse footer content for brand and service signals that reinforce entity understanding. Your footer appears on every page of your site. That repetition creates strong signal density. Include your property name, location, star classification or property type, and primary service categories in readable text within the footer. Not hidden in code. Visible, crawlable text that AI systems encounter on every page they visit.

Internal linking architecture helps AI systems understand relationships between content sections on your site. Use descriptive anchor text that communicates the destination page's topic. "See our complete pet policy with fees and weight limits" tells the AI what the linked page contains. "Click here" tells it nothing. Structure your site so that primary content pages link to supporting detail pages and those detail pages link back. LinkedIn recommends three to five meaningful internal links per 1,000 words of content. More than that dilutes value and overwhelms readers. Keep your most important pages within two clicks of the homepage so crawlers reach them efficiently. A FAQ page buried four navigation layers deep will be crawled less frequently than one accessible from the main menu.

Every H2 and H3 section on your page must function as an independent, extractable answer unit. If the AI pulls that single section into a synthesized response, does it deliver a complete answer? Does it mention your property by name? Does it include quantified details that distinguish you from competitors?

The property name requirement matters more than most hotels realize. When the AI extracts a single sentence, pronouns disconnect the answer from the entity. "We offer complimentary parking" could belong to any hotel. "The Meridian Hotel provides complimentary valet parking" forces attribution. Never use pronouns when referring to your property in any content block that might be extracted independently.

Writing Content AI Systems Actually Use

Beyond technical structure, the content itself requires optimization for AI discovery. AI systems favor direct answers over marketing narratives.

Answer-first structure places the specific answer at the beginning of content blocks. Traditional marketing copy builds context before revealing information. AI-optimized content inverts this pattern.

Traditional structure: "We understand that traveling with pets can be challenging. After extensive guest feedback, we developed solutions meeting diverse needs. Pet-friendly rooms are available for guests traveling with dogs or cats."

Answer-first structure: "Pet Policy: Dogs and cats welcome. Maximum weight 50 pounds. Pet fee $35 per night. Available in designated ground-floor rooms. Advance request required during booking."

The first version forces the AI to guess. The second version feeds the AI the exact facts it needs to recommend you. Do not make the machine work to understand your business.

LinkedIn applies the same principle to their own content pages, calling it answer-block formatting. Their recommendation: start major sections with a 30-to-80-word block that directly addresses the main topic in the section heading. Follow that block with deeper context, examples, and sources. The approach mirrors the traditional SEO pillar-and-waterfall content model. Lead with the definitive answer. Let the rest of the page break it down. Properties that front-load their answers earn retrieval. Properties that build toward their answers lose to competitors who do not make the AI wait.

The data behind this is striking. An analysis of 1.2 million verified ChatGPT citations found that 44.2% of all citations come from the first 30% of a page, what researchers call the "ski ramp" pattern. The middle third of content accounts for 31.1% of citations. The final third drops to 24.7%. Content buried past the halfway point is 2.5 times less likely to be cited than content placed at the top. For hoteliers, this means pet policies, parking rates, and signature amenity details belong in the first paragraphs of each content section, not at the end of a description that builds toward the answer.

Microsoft's research explains: "Write for intent, not just keywords. Use phrasing that directly answers the questions users ask. Avoid vague language. Terms like 'innovative' or 'eco' mean little without specifics. Instead, anchor claims in measurable facts."

Policy precision eliminates ambiguity. "Early check-in subject to availability" becomes "Early check-in available starting at 12:00 PM, subject to room availability. Guaranteed early check-in at 12:00 PM available for $25 surcharge paid at check-in."

Quantification strengthens answers. "Close to downtown" becomes "0.3 miles from Convention Center, 0.5 miles from Theater District, 1.2 miles from Waterfront Park."

This specificity matters at a measurable level. Research analyzing citation patterns across 1.2 million ChatGPT responses found that heavily cited content carries an entity density of 20.6%. Standard English text runs at 5 to 8%. The gap is not marginal. Entity density measures the frequency of specific proper nouns, named locations, brands, and measurable facts within a piece of content. A sentence referencing "The Meridian Hotel, 0.3 miles from Austin Convention Center, adjacent to the Sixth Street entertainment district" carries far more citation weight than a sentence describing "our convenient downtown location." Name the landmarks. Name the distances. Name the neighborhood. Every specific, named element raises the probability that the AI pulls your content into its answer.

Context matters. Instead of "Our rooms feature soundproof windows," write "Our rooms feature double-pane soundproof windows, reducing street noise by 35 decibels, ideal for light sleepers in our downtown location." The additional context helps algorithms understand not what you offer alone, but why it matters and how it compares.

AI engines extract concise, "snippable" pieces of content and weave them into answers. Content eligible for snippet extraction shares four characteristics. Concise answers provide one- to two-sentence responses addressing specific questions. Structured formatting uses lists, tables, and question-answer blocks that AI platforms can extract. Strong headings signal where complete ideas start and end. Self-contained phrasing creates sentences that make sense when pulled out of surrounding context.

Write every policy statement, amenity description, and operational detail as if algorithms will independently extract it. "Our fitness center includes 8 cardio machines, free weights up to 50 pounds, and operates 24 hours daily" works as a standalone snippet. "We have a great fitness center with everything you need" does not.

The FAQ Page Architecture AI Prefers

Traditional SEO discouraged standalone FAQ pages. The conventional wisdom buried questions at the bottom of service pages, distributing them across the site to support individual page rankings. AI retrieval works differently.

When an AI platform runs Query Fan-Out, it retrieves a limited number of URLs per background search. Each retrieval costs processing time. A standalone FAQ page containing 30 or 40 clearly headed questions lets the AI satisfy multiple sub-queries from a single URL retrieval. One page load answers questions about pet policies, parking rates, check-in procedures, cancellation terms, and accessibility features simultaneously. The AI gets dense, structured information without burning retrieval cycles across six different pages.

Build a dedicated FAQ library as a standalone page on your website. Not a collapsed accordion buried in the footer. A prominent, crawlable page with each question as a proper heading and each answer in answer-first format with specific, quantified details.

Use H2 headings for category groupings: Reservations, Policies, Amenities, Location, Accessibility. Use H3 headings for individual questions. Write each answer as a self-contained statement that makes sense when extracted independently. Deploy FAQPage schema across the entire page so every question-answer pair becomes machine-readable.

Start with 20 to 30 questions covering the operational information travelers ask most frequently. Expand toward 60 or more as you identify patterns from actual AI queries and guest inquiries. Thirty excellent question-answer pairs on a single well-structured page outperform sixty mediocre answers scattered across the site.

The FAQ strategy connects to latent intent extraction described earlier in this chapter. Forty well-structured questions covering operational details, policies, and situational specifics do not only answer questions travelers type into AI platforms. They answer the latent intent sub-queries the AI generates on the traveler's behalf. Your front desk knows what business travelers ask about when they call. Your concierge knows what families need before they arrive. That institutional knowledge, translated into structured content, feeds the latent intent extraction process that determines whether the AI recommends you or skips you.

Comprehensive content also serves a defensive purpose. When AI platforms lack verified information about your property, they do not leave gaps. They fill them with plausible guesses. A platform that cannot find your pet policy may invent one based on properties it considers similar. A platform missing your parking rates may fabricate a number that frustrates guests on arrival. Structured FAQ content and validated schema data reduce this risk by giving AI platforms verified facts to work with rather than generating approximations. You are not writing content for marketing purposes alone. You are writing it to prevent AI platforms from making things up about your property.

This content work connects directly to the Answer Spiral described in Chapter 3. Travelers do not ask one question and book. They refine their queries across multiple platforms, narrowing from broad discovery through specific comparison to final validation. Each stage of the spiral triggers different sub-queries during retrieval. Content optimized for a single query captures one moment in the spiral. Content covering operational details, policies, edge cases, and situational specifics captures the full arc of a traveler's iterative research process.

What Google Actually Rewards

October 2025 brought explicit confirmation from Google's VP of Search, Liz Reid, about what content performs in AI Overviews. The click data reveals a clear pattern.

"What we see is people want content from that human perspective," Reid explained. "They want that sense of like, what's the unique thing you bring to it. And actually, what we see on what people click on, on AI Overviews, is content that is richer and deeper."

Surface-level content fails. Users click through, realize they learned nothing new, and bounce back to search. Google tracks these "bounce clicks" and adjusts what appears. The system learns what satisfies users and surfaces more of it.

Reid revealed something critical: Google expanded the definition of spam. The company now treats repetitive content the same as traditional spam for ranking purposes. Content that "doesn't add very much, kind of tells you what everybody else knows" gets downranked.

Your content might be well-written, accurate, and properly formatted. If it echoes what competitors already published, it falls into Google's expanded spam category. Origin does not matter. A human repeating widely known information gets downranked the same as AI-generated spam.

Reid explained what gets upweighted: content "from someone who really went in and brought their perspective or brought their expertise, put real time and craft into the work."

That final word matters. Craft means mastery, not efficiency. Google's algorithms now identify and reward original perspectives based on actual experience, demonstrable expertise from specialized knowledge, and substantial effort visible in the depth.

This connects to the writing guidance earlier in this chapter. Write from experience, not research. Explain why your fitness center includes specific equipment based on three years of guest feedback. Describe how your pet policy evolved through operational challenges. Share insights competitors cannot replicate because they did not live through the same decisions.

Reid clarified that AI-generated content does not automatically equal spam. Google evaluates by merit, not origin. AI content demonstrating expertise and a unique perspective meets the quality bar. AI content repeating widely known information gets downranked.

Microsoft moved to the same position in its February 2026 Bing Webmaster Guidelines rewrite. The previous Bing policy classified machine-generated content as malicious and promised automatic penalties. The rewritten language targets content produced without editorial oversight, quality control, or originality. Aligning Bing's standard with Google's. Both platforms now evaluate content by the human judgment applied during creation, not by origin. Properties using AI tools with genuine editorial oversight and institutional specificity operate within both platforms' published standards. Properties generating volume without substance face the same outcome on Bing that Google described: exclusion from indexing and AI-generated answers alike.

The AI Content Flood and Why It Matters for Your Strategy

The quality standard Google describes exists in direct response to a measurable problem. Originality.ai tracked AI-generated content in Google's top 20 search results from February 2019 through September 2025, testing 500 informational keywords monthly across 10,000 websites per period.

In February 2019, 2.27% of top search results contained AI-generated content. By July 2025, that number hit 19.56%. Nearly one in five search results now comes from AI content farms rather than human authors.

Google's March 2024 algorithm update specifically targeted AI spam. The update dropped AI content levels from 8.48% in December 2023 to 7.43% by early March 2024. Properties that relied heavily on AI-generated content saw rankings collapse overnight. Every website that received a manual penalty from Google during the March 2024 update used AI-generated content. Half of those penalized sites had 90% to 100% of their posts generated by AI.

Google's 2025 Search Quality Rater Guidelines made their position explicit: "If all or almost all of a page's main content is AI-generated and little to no originality is added, raters should apply the lowest rating."

This creates a compound problem for hotel discovery. Travelers increasingly ask AI platforms for recommendations rather than searching on Google. The search results travelers still see contain more AI-generated content from competitors and content farms than ever before. Google actively penalizes low-quality AI content, creating volatility in search rankings.

The research documents another pattern. As AI content saturates the web, future AI models will be trained on datasets containing more machine-generated material. A May 2023 study found that models trained on AI-contaminated datasets generate increasingly generic and predictable results over successive iterations. This creates a feedback loop. More AI content trains worse

AI models, which generate more generic content, which trains even worse models. Hotels publishing quality human-created content provide value to travelers today and to AI training datasets tomorrow. Properties that rushed to AI content generation did not degrade the web alone. They corrupted the training data that future AI models will use to decide who gets recommended.

Why Static Content Creates Algorithmic Risk

Google is introducing AI-powered features in Search and Discover that prioritize trending topics and recent updates, using AI-generated previews to surface fresh content from multiple publishers. Properties relying on static websites face measurable risk. If your digital presence generates no fresh signals (new posts, updated pages, current commentary), you concede discoverability. AI engines now interpret content freshness as a proxy for relevance.

Do not confuse freshness with recency. AI models check dates to ensure validity. For non-news queries, they prioritize authority over newness. Research shows large language models frequently cite sources that are six to twelve months old when those sources carry strong citation networks from other trusted pages. Your goal is not to churn out new updates. Your goal is to update the last modified date on your core anchor content, signaling that existing authority remains valid. Freshness maintains relevance. Citation depth builds trust. You need both working together.

LinkedIn recommends four specific freshness practices that apply directly to hotel content. Display the "Last Updated" date on every key page, ideally near the title or footer. For evergreen guides, add a year-specific update note signaling that the page reflects current information. Review and update high-value content every six to twelve months with new examples, metrics, or operational changes. Update FAQ schema after every content revision so metadata matches the current page. These practices require minimal effort and signal ongoing relevance to AI retrieval systems that interpret stale content as unreliable content.

The speed at which fresh content enters AI retrieval varies by platform. Posts on high-authority social platforms can appear in AI search results within hours. LinkedIn articles from accounts with established followings have appeared in AI-generated answers the same day they were published. Reddit threads addressing specific traveler questions achieve similar velocity. YouTube content from creators with subscriber authority enters retrieval systems faster than new pages on low-authority domains.

This speed differential matters for tactical planning. When a property needs to address a reputation issue, announce a renovation completion, or respond to market changes, social platform content reaches AI retrieval systems faster than website updates on most hotel domains. Properties that maintain active presences on LinkedIn, Reddit, and YouTube create rapid-response channels for AI visibility that static website content cannot match.

Static content retains value for foundational information. Your check-in policy, amenity details, and property description serve important functions. Static architecture alone cannot maintain visibility. The strategy requires hybrid implementation: authoritative anchor content paired with regular updates signaling active relevance.

The Implementation Priority

Your homepage should communicate who you serve and what your property delivers in clear, parseable text early in the page body. LLMs process homepage content more reliably than they navigate menus or interpret visual layouts. A homepage that relies on imagery, dropdown navigation, or JavaScript-driven content carousels to explain the property's value proposition creates a comprehension gap for AI retrieval. State your property's identity, location, primary guest segments, and distinguishing characteristics in the body text. The schema markup then validates what the visible content already declares.

Technical foundation implementation should follow priority ordering.

Phase 1 focuses on rendering accessibility. Ensure content displays properly in reader mode. Fix JavaScript dependencies preventing content access. Implement server-side rendering or prerendering as needed. This foundation must be in place before other optimizations can succeed.

Phase 2 implements core schema markup. Start with the basic Hotel schema on the homepage. Add extended operational fields. Implement the room Product schema. Deploy the FAQ schema for policy questions. Validate all implementations thoroughly.

Phase 3 optimizes content architecture. Fix heading hierarchies across all pages. Implement proper list and table structures. Write descriptive alt text for images. Ensure semantic HTML throughout the site.

Phase 4 refines content for AI discovery. Develop detailed FAQ content. Restructure information in answer-first formats. Add specificity to policy statements. Quantify location descriptions. Create content that directly answers traveler questions.

Phase 5 maintains and improves the foundation. Validate schema quarterly. Monitor technical performance. Update content as property information changes. Test rendering accessibility regularly. The technical foundation requires ongoing maintenance, not one-time implementation.

Those traditional foundations include technical measurement capabilities that most properties ignore. You need to isolate AI referral traffic from general referral noise. The technical approach uses regex patterns in custom channel groupings. Match source strings containing platform identifiers: ChatGPT, Perplexity, Gemini, and Claude. Group them separately for analysis. This systematic filtering enables the measurement framework from Chapter 2. You cannot track AI performance without isolating AI sources.

Search marketing still delivers. Google Ads, Google Hotel Ads, and organic listings consistently contribute over 50% of hotel website bookings. This performance persists despite the traffic transformation documented throughout this book. You do not abandon channels that work. You prepare for when they deliver less while maximizing current performance. Build AI visibility capabilities now, while existing traditional channels still generate revenue.

Your technical foundation determines whether AI models can access, understand, and accurately represent your property. Get this wrong, and nothing else matters. Get it right, and you create the platform for everything that follows.

The citation networks in the next chapter amplify these foundations through authoritative external signals. Together, technical excellence and off-site authority create sustainable AI visibility.

7

CITATION NETWORKS AND OFF-SITE INFLUENCE

YOUR WEBSITE ALONE cannot deliver the visibility you need.

A hotel can invest fifty thousand dollars in a website redesign. The team can create beautiful property photography. Developers can implement perfect schema markup. Writers can develop comprehensive FAQ content answering every conceivable question. The technical foundations can score near-perfect.

Yet visibility in AI recommendations remains weak.

The property appears in perhaps a third of queries. Competitors with objectively worse websites appear more frequently in AI responses. The reason: AI platforms assess trust through citation networks spanning review platforms, media mentions, and authoritative sources across the entire web.

Think of it this way. Your website functions as your resume. Citations serve as your references. Nobody makes hiring decisions based solely on what candidates claim about themselves.

The Trust Hierarchy That Determines Visibility

AI platforms treat information sources differently by establishing trust hierarchies based on source authority. Research from Similarweb analyzing the top 1,000 websites receiving AI referrals in June 2025 revealed that twenty websites accounted for approximately 70% of all travel-related AI citations. Not a single hotel's own website ranked among the top ten most-cited sources.

McKinsey quantified the sourcing breakdown. Own-site content accounts for 5% to 10% of the sources AI platforms reference when generating hotel recommendations. External citations provide the other 90% to 95%. Review platforms, booking sites, publishers, user-generated content, and affiliate networks supply most of what AI engines use to answer traveler questions. The VertoDigital audit referenced in Chapter 3 found a higher on-site share (25%) when measuring answer content rather than source count. Both confirm the same directional reality: external sources dominate.

This inverts traditional SEO logic. Search engines primarily index your owned content. AI platforms primarily reference everything except your owned content.

The reverse also holds. Ahrefs found that 28% of ChatGPT's most-cited pages have zero organic visibility in Google. Content that traditional search ignores can earn prominent AI citations through citation authority and platform-specific relevance. The two discovery systems reward different signals, and properties that treat Google rankings as a proxy for AI visibility operate on a false assumption.

The shift also eliminates the traditional traffic-generation model that justified citation building for two decades. Users increasingly get answers directly from AI platforms rather than visiting websites. Your TripAdvisor listing no longer matters primarily because it sends referral traffic. It matters because ChatGPT reads that listing when researching your property, and the information accuracy there determines what the platform tells travelers. Citations establish whether you appear in AI answers at all, not whether people click through afterward.

Tier 1 sources establish unquestionable credibility. Major news publications like the New York Times and Wall Street Journal. National travel magazines like Travel + Leisure and Condé Nast Traveler. Authoritative reference sources like Wikipedia for entities meeting notability criteria. AI platforms treat Tier 1 sources as ground truth. Profound's analysis found Wikipedia appearing in nearly one of every six ChatGPT conversations containing citations, functioning as the default knowledge layer the model consults for baseline facts before turning to specialized sources. When major publications mention your property, AI platforms believe the information without question. According to Similarweb data from June 2025, news and media sites received 770% more AI referrals compared to June 2024, with Reuters receiving 1.8 million AI referral visits in a single month.

These placements prove difficult to obtain. You need genuinely newsworthy stories or extraordinary properties to secure consistent Tier 1 coverage. Most independent hotels will never achieve it. Platform evolution patterns validate pursuing these placements despite accessibility challenges. Wikipedia and government reference sources maintained strong positions across both traditional search and AI platforms through Q3 2025, demonstrating that the highest-authority sources persist through algorithmic changes. Each Tier 1 placement becomes a long-term asset rather than a temporary ranking factor.

Tier 2 sources provide strong authority. Regional media outlets. Trade publications like Hotel Business and Lodging Magazine. Authoritative travel blogs with substantial readership and editorial standards. Most hotels should concentrate resources here. Tier 2 sources deliver optimal return on investment through achievable authority gains. Relationship development and strategic storytelling secure placements. A regional newspaper feature provides meaningful authority without requiring national media connections.

Tier 3 sources establish foundational legitimacy. Review platforms like TripAdvisor and Google. Booking sites like Expedia and Booking.com. Business directories like Bing Places and Yellow Pages. Local listings through chambers of commerce and tourism boards. Every property requires a complete Tier 3 foundation. These citations are straightforward to obtain through claiming and optimization. You control most of the information. Tier 3 alone will not make you competitive. It is the minimum threshold required before advanced strategies can take effect.

Tier 4 sources contribute negligible trust signals. User-generated platforms without editorial standards. Low-quality directories. Link farms. Content aggregators. Avoid investing time here.

The AI Citation Trust Hierarchy

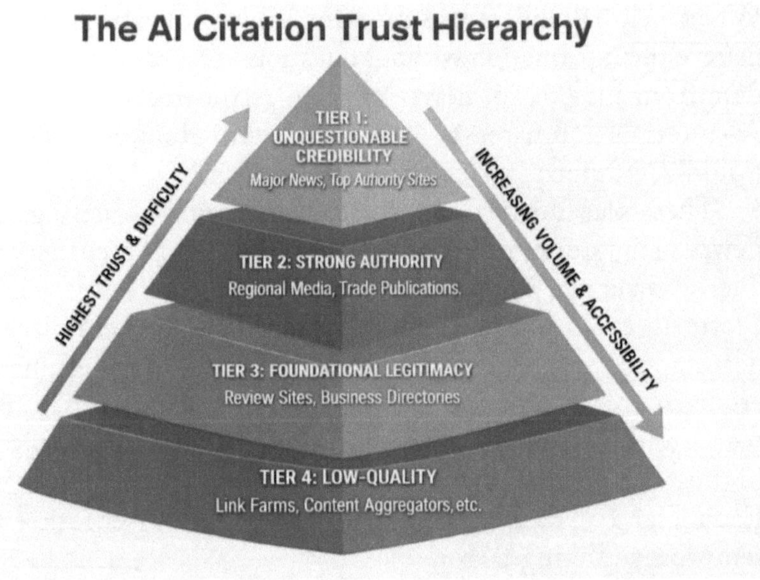

Why Consistency Matters More Than Volume

Inconsistent business information across platforms undermines citation value. AI engines cross-reference information from multiple sources. When they discover conflicting details, trust decreases.

Consistency requires identical formatting everywhere. "The Grand Hotel" differs from "Grand Hotel" or "Grand Hotel Seattle" in AI parsing. Choose one name format and implement it universally. Address formatting must match down to abbreviation choices. Choose "Suite" or "Ste" and maintain that choice. Phone formatting must follow one standard. URL references must use your primary domain everywhere. The specific format matters less than universal consistency.

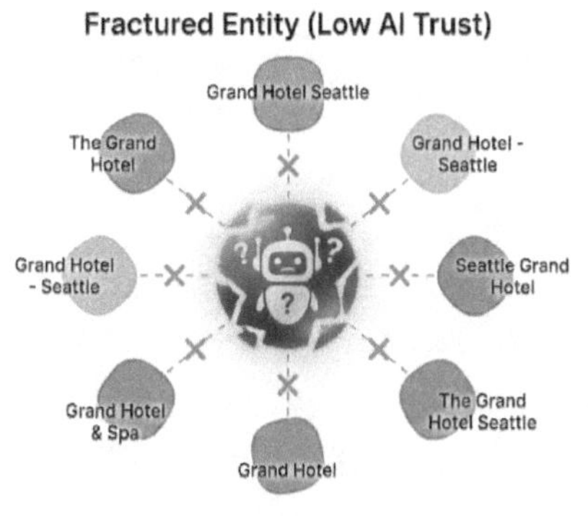

As detailed in Chapter 5, Sixt's data consistency initiative across 1,312 locations drove a 29% lift in Google customer actions. That result followed directly from how the Knowledge Graph rewards verified, uniform data across platforms.

The Three Market Categories That Change Everything

In Chapter 1, you identified your Market Tier. Your citation strategy must adapt to that reality.

If you are in a Major Metro, you cannot out-shout Marriott. Abandon broad terms. Your path is ultra-niche dominance. Become the undisputed authority on "Pet-Friendly Luxury in Brooklyn" rather than a generic option in NYC.

If you are in a Regional Hub, this is a fair fight. You can match brand visibility by locking down local media relations. The brands are too large to invest in the Austin Chronicle or the Nashville Scene. You must own those relationships.

If you are in an Emerging Market, speed is your weapon. The first property to build a serious Tier 3 foundation becomes the default answer for the entire destination.

Building Your Citation Foundation

Most properties should complete Tier 3 before pursuing Tier 2 opportunities. The foundation establishes baseline legitimacy, enabling advanced work. Citation building timelines reflect relationship development patterns from PR and media relations work. Track your actual timelines and adjust expectations accordingly.

Tier 3 represents the foundation of your citation network: the platforms where you can claim and manage your property information directly. These include your Google and Bing Business Profiles, major OTA listings, review platforms, and business directories. None of these sources carry the editorial authority of a newspaper feature or the cultural weight of a viral social media mention. Their value lies in consistency and completeness. When AI platforms cross-reference information about your property, Tier 3 sources provide the baseline data those systems use to confirm your identity, verify your attributes, and establish that your business exists as a legitimate entity. Without this foundation, higher-tier citations lose their anchoring context.

Google and Bing Business Profiles. Google Business Profile optimization requires completing every field. Claiming and adding basic information is not enough. Upload at least 20 photos from multiple angles. Verify business information accuracy. Respond to all reviews within 48 hours.

Business profile relationships with AI platforms vary significantly by system. Google's Gemini draws directly from Google Business Profile as a primary data source. BrightLocal's research confirms Gemini frequently cites GBP information when generating responses. ChatGPT operates differently, drawing from Bing and partner content rather than accessing GBP directly. For ChatGPT visibility, Bing Business Profile matters because Bing provides ChatGPT's search infrastructure. Microsoft enables direct synchronization from Google Business Profile to Bing Places. Maintain complete, identical profiles across both platforms.

Google's AI Overviews incorporate GBP information directly, often presenting profile data in summaries without requiring click-throughs. LocalFalcon's research documents how these summaries shift discovery patterns, with GBP data replacing traditional search results for many queries. While broad travel queries rely on OTAs, BrightLocal's late 2024 research found that for specific local lookup queries, ChatGPT cited the business website 58% of the time. Your website is the authority for facts (phone number, address). OTAs are the authority for rankings. For Gemini, GBP functions as a primary source rather than an amplifier.

Major OTA listings require consistent information management. Booking.com, Expedia, and Hotels.com all need identical property details. Check-in times must match exactly. Pet policies must be stated identically. Amenity lists must use consistent terminology. Cloudbeds found that 55% of AI citations came from OTA sites. Inconsistency here destroys entity recognition.

Review platforms demand attention. TripAdvisor, Yelp, and Google Reviews all contribute citations that AI models reference. Active review response signals engagement. Recent reviews indicate operational currency. High review volume suggests popularity.

Review responses also appear on pages that AI platforms already crawl and process, making them a likely source of attribute information. A response that reads "Thank you for your review" adds nothing to the citation network. A response that reads "We are glad you enjoyed the rooftop pool and the complimentary breakfast. Our chef changes the menu seasonally, and the spring offerings you experienced reflect our focus on locally sourced ingredients" introduces specific, keyword-rich information into a high-authority source that AI platforms already trust. Every review response is a citation opportunity. Properties that treat review management as customer service alone miss the dual function: maintaining reputation while simultaneously feeding structured attribute information into the sources AI platforms reference most frequently.

Business directories require methodical claiming and completion. Bing Places, Yellow Pages, Apple Maps, and industry-specific directories all contribute to overall presence. The individual impact of each directory remains small. The cumulative effect of consistent directory citations establishes foundational legitimacy.

The Tier 2 Building Strategy

Industry trade publications regularly feature properties implementing innovative practices. Hotel Business, Lodging Magazine, and Hotel Management all need content. The key is identifying story angles that serve publication audiences rather than promoting your property. Renovation projects solving design challenges interest readers. Sustainability initiatives reducing operational costs provide value. Technology implementations improving guest experience offer lessons.

Regional media outlets cover local business developments. Newspapers and magazines in your market need hospitality stories. Properties expanding operations, hiring locally, implementing community programs, or adapting to market changes provide newsworthy content. Develop relationships with journalists covering hospitality beats. Follow their work. Share relevant information when stories warrant coverage. Avoid generic promotional pitches. Offer specific story angles with documented outcomes. Relationships develop through consistent professional engagement over months, not through aggressive one-time pitching.

Authoritative travel blogs with editorial standards provide valuable citations. Identify blogs serving your target traveler segments. Family travel blogs for family-focused properties. Business travel blogs for corporate hotels. Luxury travel blogs for high-end properties. Evaluate blog quality through traffic data, engagement metrics, and editorial voice. Avoid blogs featuring obvious paid content without disclosure.

One nuance worth addressing directly. Current LLMs do not reliably distinguish between paid editorial placements and organic coverage. A well-crafted advertorial on a reputable travel publication can generate the same citation authority as earned media, provided the publication itself carries editorial credibility. Properties that place sponsored content on high-authority sites can accelerate their citation presence, particularly when organic editorial relationships take months to develop. Any paid placement should comply with FTC disclosure requirements and the publication's own editorial guidelines.

The opportunity has limits. Low-quality publications add negligible citation value regardless of payment. Advertorials reading as promotional copy perform poorly because surrounding site quality matters more than any single article. This dynamic may not persist. As AI platforms develop the ability to identify paid content, the citation value of advertorials could diminish. Treat paid editorial as a supplement to earned media strategy, not a replacement.

Paid syndication follows similar logic. Distributing content through syndication networks extends reach across multiple publications. Citation value scales with the reputation of the sites carrying the syndicated content. Syndication through Reuters, the Associated Press, or established industry wire services carries meaningful authority. Syndication through low-traffic content farms does not. Ten placements on authoritative hospitality publications generate more citation value than two hundred listings on generic sites.

Reddit and YouTube

Treat these platforms as search engines. You are not posting for likes. You are posting to create a permanent, indexable answer to a specific question.

Reddit represents an emerging Tier 2 citation opportunity that most hotels ignore. The platform's visibility in AI search grew substantially through 2025, with desktop visits nearly matching Facebook in European markets and overtaking it in the U.S. by Q3. AI platforms increasingly reference Reddit discussions when researching hotels because users provide unfiltered operational details and comparative assessments that traditional sources lack.

The scale of Reddit's citation advantage is striking. Profound's analysis of approximately 238,000 social platform citations from ChatGPT responses between October and December 2025 found that Reddit captured 3 to 4 percent of all citations, more than ten times the volume of any other social platform. Ninety-nine percent of those citations pointed to individual discussion threads rather than subreddit homepages or user profiles. ChatGPT does not cite Reddit because the platform carries brand authority. It cites Reddit because specific threads contain self-contained, structured answers to specific questions. The implication for hotels is precise: a single well-written response to a traveler's question in r/travel generates more citation value than an optimized subreddit presence or a polished Reddit profile.

Warning: Do not sell on Reddit. If you post a link to your booking engine, you will be banned. You are there to answer questions, not to advertise.

The strategic approach requires patience and authenticity. Identify subreddits serving your target markets (r/travel, city-specific tourism forums, special interest communities aligned with your property focus). Contribute genuinely helpful information, answering traveler questions rather than promoting your property. Share operational insights that demonstrate expertise. Over quarters, this participation establishes authority that AI platforms recognize when researching hotels in your market, generating citations that competitors cannot easily replicate.

YouTube citations offer similar strategic value through a different content format. The platform maintains 70% to 75% desktop reach according to Datos Q3 2025 data, yet hotels rarely pursue video content citations. AI platforms reference YouTube content when researching properties because video provides operational details and visual confirmation that text alone cannot deliver.

The same Profound analysis revealed a counterintuitive pattern in how ChatGPT cites YouTube. Sixty-five percent of YouTube citations pointed to channel pages rather than individual videos. Individual videos accounted for only 2.3 percent of citations. Channel subpages (the /videos, /shorts, and /community tabs) added another 14 percent. Combined, channel-level citations represented nearly 80 percent of YouTube's total share within ChatGPT. The data confirms that ChatGPT treats YouTube as a creator authority platform, not a video content platform. A hotel that produces a single property tour video on a low-authority channel generates far less citation value than a mention within an established travel creator's channel that ChatGPT already recognizes as authoritative. One caveat applies. Profound's data covers ChatGPT only. Gemini, with its native YouTube integration, may cite individual videos more heavily. The channel-first pattern should inform ChatGPT strategy specifically, not serve as a universal rule across all AI platforms.

Partner with travel content creators rather than producing all content internally. Identify YouTubers covering your market with established audiences and editorial credibility. Offer property access and operational insights that serve their content needs rather than requesting promotional coverage. The resulting videos generate citations that AI platforms reference when answering questions about your market.

Both Reddit and YouTube strategies share a fundamental principle. Community-driven citations develop through contribution rather than promotion. You provide value to platform audiences through expertise sharing. This generates organic mentions that AI platforms treat as more authoritative than paid placements.

LinkedIn follows a similar authority pattern. Profound's citation data showed that 47 percent of LinkedIn citations in ChatGPT pointed to personal profiles, more than double the 21 percent directed at company pages. LinkedIn articles on the Pulse platform captured 14 percent. The pattern reinforces what the Reddit and YouTube data demonstrates from different angles. AI platforms favor individual expertise over institutional presence. A hotel general manager who contributes thoughtful commentary on LinkedIn builds citation authority that the property's company page cannot replicate. The same principle applies to industry professionals whose LinkedIn profiles establish them as sources on hospitality topics in specific markets.

Publishing on respected, niche industry sites can produce remarkably fast inclusion in LLM responses. Properties that secure placements on authoritative hospitality publications have seen their content referenced in AI answers within hours of publication. The publication's domain authority accelerates the retrieval timeline. A mention on a site that AI platforms already trust enters the citation network faster than identical content published on a lower-authority domain.

What Actually Works in Practice

Three principles determine the effectiveness of citation building across all activities.

Consistency establishes identity. Accurate names, addresses, and phone numbers across 50 platforms establish the prerequisite for entity identity. They ensure the AI knows you exist as a verified entity. Two hundred platform listings with inconsistent information destroy that confidence. Fifty platforms with identical formatting build it.

Consistency alone does not establish authority. Authority comes from the sentiment of the citation. Is your brand mentioned as a solution to a traveler's problem, or does it appear as one data point among many in a directory listing? The distinction determines whether AI platforms recognize you or recommend you. Top-ranking listicles, active Reddit threads, and authoritative editorial content carry more weight in recommendation logic than clean NAP data across 200 directories. Directory consistency prevents confusion. Strategic placement on high-value pages earns citations.

This progression clarifies why citation building requires sustained investment rather than campaign-based bursts. Each tier takes time to develop. Directory consistency requires weeks of corrections across dozens of platforms. Editorial relationships require months of professional engagement before yielding coverage. Authoritative features require a track record of newsworthiness that cannot be manufactured on demand. The progression takes quarters, not weeks. Properties that start building now accumulate compound advantages that late movers cannot shortcut.

Profound's broader analysis of ChatGPT web sourcing behavior explains why this volume matters. Among conversations that included citations, ChatGPT averaged approximately six unique citations per conversation and four unique citations per individual turn. Sixty-six percent of cited turns contained one to four distinct sources. The model triangulates. It does not select a single winner and defer to that authority. It pulls from multiple sources and constructs a composite answer. Getting cited once does not guarantee prominence. You compete for share of voice within a set of sources, not for sole ownership of an answer. Building substantial citation volume addresses this reality. Properties with thin citation networks may appear in one of those six sources. Properties with deep networks appear in three or four, establishing the repetition that shifts the AI from mentioning your property to recommending it.

Context determines citation value. Not all mentions carry equal weight. AI platforms disproportionately favor listicles and comparative reviews. Pages titled "Top 10 Hotels in Austin" or "Best Luxury Resorts for Families" function as pre-validated recommendation lists that AI systems can extract and summarize with minimal processing. A single mention on one of these pages delivers more citation value than dozens of directory listings.

This changes where you invest citation-building resources. Instead of pursuing presence on low-traffic directories, identify the pages that already rank in AI citations for your target queries. Run the prompts travelers use. Document which URLs the AI platforms cite in their responses. Those are the pages that matter. Your goal is to appear on those specific pages through editorial outreach, updated information submissions, or earned media relationships.

Properties can also create their own high-citation-value content. The "How to Choose the Best Hotel in [Destination]" format targets the same traveler intent as listicles while positioning your property as the authoritative voice. These guides perform well in AI retrieval because the AI processes them as recommendation content addressing evaluative queries.

To scale this approach, map your property against different traveler segments and use cases. Business travelers attending conventions. Families visiting during school breaks. Couples celebrating anniversaries. Pet owners needing ground-floor access. Each combination generates a specific guide targeting a specific query pattern that AI platforms encounter during Query Fan-Out. Ten well-crafted guides covering ten distinct traveler scenarios create ten opportunities for AI citation from your own domain.

One critical execution detail: mention your property by name in the opening paragraph. A guide titled "How to Choose the Best Downtown Austin Hotel for a Conference" that recommends your property in the first two sentences gives the AI an extractable, attributed recommendation. A guide that waits until paragraph six to mention your name risks the AI never reaching it during snippet extraction.

Quality outweighs quantity. A single Tier 1 citation from a major publication delivers more authority than dozens of Tier 4 directory listings. Focus resources on higher-authority sources rather than accumulating low-value mentions. Maintenance proves as important as initial building. Citations degrade over time through platform changes, business information updates, and competitive activities. Quarterly audits and corrections maintain citation value

From Mentions to Recommendations

The Visibility Score framework measures whether AI platforms mention your property. Citation Rate tracks frequency. Positioning Quality tracks where you appear and how favorably. These components tell you whether you are visible.

They do not tell you whether you are being sold.

There is a critical distinction the hospitality industry has not yet internalized. A mention and a recommendation are fundamentally different outcomes. They require different strategies. They produce different business results. Most properties conflate them, treating any appearance in an AI response as a win.

A mention is the AI naming your property. "Hotels in downtown Austin include The Meridian, Hotel Lux, The Grand, and Austin Place." You appear. The AI acknowledges your existence. You occupy a position in a list. For measurement purposes, this registers as a citation. Your Citation Rate improves.

A recommendation is the AI endorsing your property as the answer to a specific traveler need. "For conference attendees who need a quiet room within walking distance of the convention center, The Meridian is the strongest option. Its double-pane soundproofing reduces street noise by 35 decibels, and the 0.3-mile walk to the convention center takes under seven minutes." The AI has not named you. It has advocated for you. It has connected your specific attributes to the traveler's specific problem and concluded that you are the solution.

The difference between these two outcomes determines whether AI visibility generates bookings or generates vanity metrics.

Why the Distinction Matters

AI platforms construct recommendations through a synthesis process. During Query Fan-Out, the model retrieves information from multiple sources, evaluates the evidence, and assembles a response. When that response includes your property name alongside generic descriptions that could apply to any hotel, you received a mention. The AI found you in its retrieval results and included you for completeness.

When the response connects your property to specific traveler needs with attributed reasoning, you received a recommendation. The AI found enough structured, specific, differentiated information about your property to conclude that you solve the traveler's stated problem better than alternatives.

Mentions come from presence. Your name appears on enough platforms with enough consistency that the AI recognizes you as a valid entity. The consistency and citation network work from this chapter builds mention capability.

Recommendations come from positioned authority. The AI has access to specific, quantified, differentiated information about your property that it can match against specific traveler intent. The content architecture from Chapter 6, the bridge entity connections, and the co-occurrence patterns described in Chapters 5 and 6 all contribute to the AI selecting you as the answer rather than listing you as an option.

The Mention Trap

Properties that invest heavily in mention building without progressing to recommendation building end up in a frustrating position. Their Citation Rate scores climb. They appear in 40%, 50%, 60% of tested queries. Leadership sees the numbers improving and assumes the strategy works.

The Positioning Quality score tells a different story. The property appears frequently, in the middle of lists, with generic descriptions, as one option among five or six. The AI mentions the property because it cannot ignore a well-cited entity. It does not recommend the property because it lacks the specific, structured information needed to advocate for it.

This is the difference between the Visibility Score's Citation Rate component and its Positioning Quality component. Properties with high Citation Rate scores and low Positioning Quality scores are stuck in the mention trap. Visible, but not compelling. Present, but not preferred.

What Recommendation Building Requires

Moving from mentions to recommendations requires a shift in how you think about your content, citations, and competitive positioning.

Your content must explicitly state why your property solves specific problems. Not what you offer. Why it matters for a specific traveler in a specific situation. "450-square-foot rooms with king beds" is a mention-level description. "450-square-foot rooms with king beds and double-pane soundproofing that reduces street noise by 35 decibels, located on the quiet east side of the building away from the entertainment district" is a recommendation-level description. The second version gives the AI enough information to advocate for you when a traveler asks about quiet hotels downtown.

Your citations must position your property as a solution, not a listing. A directory entry with your name, address, and star rating generates mentions. A listicle that names your property as the top recommendation for business travelers attending conventions, with specific reasons cited, generates recommendations.

Your bridge entity connections must be explicit and specific. A generic "near the convention center" association generates mentions when travelers ask about convention hotels. An explicit connection stating "0.3-mile walk to the Javits Center, complimentary shuttle running every 20 minutes during convention weeks, dedicated business center with printing and video conferencing" generates recommendations. The AI needs specific, attributable facts to build its case.

Measuring the Progression

Track Citation Rate and Positioning Quality independently. A property with a 60% Citation Rate and a Positioning Quality score of 35 has strong mention capability with weak recommendation building. The priority shifts from citation volume to content specificity and bridge entity development. A property with a 25% Citation Rate and a Positioning Quality score of 75 gets strong recommendations when mentioned but lacks the citation foundation for consistent visibility. The priority remains citation network expansion.

The strategic goal is clear. Build mentions first through citation network consistency, technical foundations, and platform presence. Then convert those mentions into recommendations through specific content, explicit bridge entity connections, and positioned authority on the pages AI platforms trust most.

Mentions get you into the conversation. Recommendations get you the booking.

Your website creates the foundation. Citations establish trust. Both prove necessary. Neither alone proves sufficient.

You now understand what to optimize and where authority comes from. The question becomes: how do you know if your optimization works? Traditional analytics cannot answer this question. You need measurement frameworks designed for AI visibility.

8

THE VISIBILITY SCORE FRAMEWORK

CHAPTER 2 EXPLAINED why AI visibility requires different measurement standards. This chapter shows you how to measure it.

You need a way to determine whether your optimization efforts produce results. AI discovery does not provide perfect attribution. Neither does SEO, paid media, or brand measurement. The absence of perfect attribution does not eliminate the necessity of disciplined measurement. Directional evidence, consistent patterns across multiple data points, is enough to govern progress.

This chapter presents a structured framework for assessing AI visibility. The component weights (30%, 25%, 20%, 15%, and 10%) represent informed initial estimates designed to enable testing, comparison, and refinement over time. Track these components separately and analyze which ones correlate with your business metrics. Expect to adjust the weights based on what you observe at your property.

This Visibility Score framework adapts emerging AI measurement practices for hospitality application. The five components reflect metrics that leading AI visibility platforms track independently. The specific weighting reflects the operational priorities of properties managing perishable inventory, where citation absence and information inaccuracy carry immediate revenue consequences that other industries may not experience with the same urgency.

The Visibility Score combines five measurements into a 0 to 100 point scale.

The Five Components

Citation Rate (30% weight): How often AI platforms mention you when travelers ask relevant questions. This forms the foundation. If you remain invisible, nothing else matters. Citation Rate receives the highest weight because visibility is the most fundamental requirement.

Platform Spread (25% weight): How many platforms show you consistently. Appearing on all four major platforms (ChatGPT, Gemini, Perplexity, Claude) signals broad accessibility. Missing from one entirely reveals platform-specific problems. Platform Spread receives substantial weight because diversification provides resilience against any single platform's algorithm changes.

Positioning Quality (20% weight): Where you appear when mentioned and how platforms describe you. AI platforms generate answers probabilistically. Position varies across identical queries. Research conducted by SparkToro and Gumshoe.ai across 2,961 prompt runs in late 2025 found fewer than 1-in-1,000 responses containing the same brand list in the same order. Treat position scores as directional indicators, not fixed standings. A consistent pattern of first and second position mentions across multiple months signals stronger AI consideration than a pattern of fourth and fifth. Detailed positive descriptions outperform minimal factual mentions regardless of position. The distinction between mentions and recommendations described in Chapter 7 becomes measurable through this component.

Information Accuracy (15% weight): Whether AI platforms provide correct details about your property. Wrong pet policies cost bookings. Incorrect parking costs create guest frustration. Accuracy matters even when visibility succeeds.

Competitive Context (10% weight): How your visibility compares to direct competitors. Relative positioning reveals whether you gain ground, lose ground, or maintain position over time. This component receives the lowest weight because it is inherently relative and depends on your specific market. The score matters more than its weight suggests. The Primary Bias described in Chapter 1 means the AI enters every query with an inherited preference for globally dominant brands. Competitive Context scoring measures whether your optimization efforts override that inherited bias or fall further behind it. A rising score means your citation networks, structured data, and content authority build enough signal to compete against the training data advantage global brands carry by default. A declining score means the bias is winning.

The final score maps to maturity levels from Chapter 5:

- 0 to 19 = Invisible
- 20 to 39 = Reactive
- 40 to 59 = Structured
- 60 to 79 = Integrated
- 80 to 100 = Optimized

Why Manual Testing

Tools like BrightLocal, Semrush, and a growing category of dedicated AI visibility platforms track some of these signals. These newer platforms monitor brand mentions across AI engines, track citation sources, measure competitive share of voice, and analyze how AI bots crawl your site. The category is maturing rapidly, with new entrants and feature expansions appearing monthly. The reader familiar with SEO tooling will wonder whether manual testing is necessary. Three reasons it remains essential at this stage.

First, existing tools measure different things. Traditional SEO platforms track rankings, backlinks, and GBP performance. The dedicated AI visibility platforms described above are expanding rapidly, but remain inconsistent in methodology and expensive for most independent properties. None yet capture all five components measured here. Bing Webmaster Tools now reports AI citation data for the Microsoft and Copilot ecosystem (Chapter 2), providing one platform-specific signal. That signal supplements manual testing. It does not replace the cross-platform, qualitative assessment this framework provides.

Second, manual testing provides qualitative insight that automated tools cannot. Description quality, the difference between a mention and a recommendation described in Chapter 7, requires human judgment. An automated tool can tell you that ChatGPT named your property. It cannot tell you whether the description was favorable, accurate, or detailed enough to drive a booking decision.

Third, the act of reading AI responses about your property teaches you things no dashboard can convey. You see how platforms describe your competitors. You notice which attributes get highlighted and which get ignored. You discover information errors you did not know existed. That qualitative understanding informs strategy in ways that metrics alone cannot.

As automated tools mature, they will absorb portions of this testing workload. Evaluate emerging platforms against the five Visibility Score components in this chapter. If a tool reliably measures Citation Rate and Platform Spread with data you can verify against your own manual results, it earns a place in your measurement stack. If it reports numbers you cannot validate, treat it as directional input rather than ground truth. For now, manual testing remains the most reliable and comprehensive approach because you control the methodology and can verify every data point.

The 20-Question Testing Library

You test 20 core questions monthly across four platforms. That creates 80 total tests: a manageable workload that provides meaningful trend data without burning out your team.

The questions are organized in four categories that mirror the Answer Spiral described in Chapter 3. Travelers move from broad discovery through location and amenity specifics to competitive comparison. Testing across all four categories reveals where in that research journey your property appears and where it disappears.

Broad Discovery (4 questions):

1. Best hotels in [your city]
2. Luxury hotels [your city]
3. Boutique hotels [your city]
4. Family-friendly hotels [your city]

Location-Based (5 questions):

1. Hotels near [major landmark]
2. Hotels in [neighborhood name]
3. Hotels close to [venue]
4. Hotels with a view of [landmark]
5. Hotels within walking distance to [district]

Amenity-Focused (5 questions):

1. Hotels with pool in [city]
2. Pet-friendly hotels [city]
3. Hotels with free parking [area]
4. Hotels with best breakfast in [city]
5. Hotels with rooftop bar in [city]

Use Case (6 questions):

1. Best hotels for business travel in [city]
2. Where should I stay with kids in [city]?
3. Where should I stay for a weekend trip in [city]?
4. Best value hotels in [city]
5. Wedding venue hotels [city]
6. I need a hotel near [venue] for a conference next month

A note on prompt wording. Small changes in phrasing produce different results. "Best hotels in Austin" and "What are the best hotels in Austin?" and "Recommend a hotel in Austin" can return different properties. Resist the urge to keep refining prompts between testing cycles. The value of this framework comes from consistency over time, not comprehensiveness in any single month. Twenty fixed prompts tested identically each month produce trend data you can act on. Twenty different prompts each month produce noise you cannot interpret.

How to Run the Tests

Timing matters. Complete all 80 tests within three days maximum. Speed prevents algorithm shifts from skewing results.

Environment consistency prevents contamination. Use a fresh context window for every query. If the platform allows, use Incognito mode. For platforms requiring login (like ChatGPT Plus or Gemini Advanced), you must manually click "New Chat" before every single question. Never ask two test questions in the same thread, as the AI will use the first answer to bias the second.

Documentation enables analysis. Screenshot every response. Save as YYYYMMDD_platform_category_number.png (example: 20261015_chatgpt_amenity_21.png).

Record results in a spreadsheet with these columns: Date, Platform, Prompt number, Prompt text, Mentioned (Yes/No), Position (1st/2nd/3rd/4th/5th+), Description quality (Detailed positive

/ Moderate positive / Neutral / Minimal / Negative), Accuracy ratings for Location / Contact / Hours / Amenities / Policies / Pricing (each rated Perfect / Partial / Wrong / Not mentioned), Competitors mentioned, Screenshot filename, Notes.

Time investment for core testing: Two hours running tests across 80 queries. One hour verifying results. Two hours scoring and analyzing. One hour reporting. Total: 6 hours monthly for Visibility Score measurement.

Full AI visibility maintenance requires additional time beyond testing. Schema validation adds 2 to 3 hours quarterly. Citation monitoring adds 2 to 3 hours monthly. Content updates vary by property needs. Properties at Structured maturity or above should budget 12 to 15 hours monthly for comprehensive maintenance, including testing. The 6-hour testing protocol represents the measurement floor, not the operational ceiling.

Component Score Calculations

Citation Rate. Count how many of your 80 tests mentioned your property. Divide by 80. Multiply by 100.

Formula: (Total mentions / 80 tests) x 100 = Citation Rate Score

Example: Your property appeared in 19 of 80 tests. (19 / 80) x 100 = 23.75, rounded to 24.

Platform Spread. Count how many platforms mentioned you at least once. Score: 4 platforms = 100 points. 3 platforms = 75. 2 platforms = 50. 1 platform = 25. 0 platforms = 0.

Example: ChatGPT mentioned you 18 times, Gemini 14 times, Perplexity 6 times, Claude 0 times. Three platforms = 75 points.

Positioning Quality. For each mention, score position and description quality.

Position scoring: First mention = 25 points. Second = 20. Third = 15. Fourth = 10. Fifth or beyond = 5. No clear position = 12.

Quality scoring: Detailed positive description = 25 points. Moderate positive = 20. Neutral detailed = 15. Minimal description = 10. Negative description = 0.

Add position + quality for each mention. Average all mention scores. Multiply by 2. Cap at 100.

Example: 38 mentions across all tests. 8 were first position with detailed descriptions (50 points each) = 400. 12 were second position with moderate descriptions (40 each) = 480. 18 were third position with minimal descriptions (25 each) = 450. Total: 1,330. Divided by 38 = 35 average. Multiplied by 2 = 70 points.

Information Accuracy. For each mention containing specific property details, score accuracy across six categories (0 to 5 points each): Location, Contact, Hours, Amenities, Policies, Pricing. Accurate = 5, Partial = 3, Wrong = 0, Not mentioned = skip.

Calculate each mention's accuracy: (Total points earned / Maximum possible) x 100. Average across all mentions containing information.

Example: 38 mentions, 22 contained specific details. 15 were completely accurate (100% each). 5 had one error (83% each). 2 had multiple errors (60% each). Average: (15 x 100 + 5 x 83 + 2 x 60) / 22 = 93 points.

Equal weighting across six categories assumes equal importance. Your property might find certain accuracy categories matter more. Track which errors cost bookings.

Competitive Context. Run the same 20-question test for 3 to 5 direct competitors quarterly (not monthly). Calculate their Citation Rates. Average them. Divide your Citation Rate by that average. Multiply by 100. Cap at 150.

Example: Your Citation Rate is 24%. Competitors average 54%. Calculation: (24 / 54) x 100 = 44 points.

Overall Score Calculation. Multiply each component by its weight. Add them up.

- Citation Rate: 24 × 0.30 = 7.2
- Platform Spread: 75 × 0.25 = 18.75
- Positioning Quality: 70 × 0.20 = 14.0
- Information Accuracy: 93 × 0.15 = 13.95

- Competitive Context: 44 × 0.10 = 4.4
- Overall Visibility Score: 58.3, rounded to 58 points.

Using Your Scores for Decisions

The overall score provides directional measurement for tracking improvement over time. Do not over-interpret score differences of 3 to 5 points. Measurement variation and platform fluctuation create noise at that level. This applies with particular force to Positioning Quality scores, where response-to-response variation in mention order is a structural feature of how AI systems generate answers. Three or more months of position data reveal patterns. A single month reveals a snapshot. Focus on trends over 3 or more months showing sustained improvement or decline, component-specific insights revealing which dimensions need attention, competitive gaps requiring strategic response, and correlation with business metrics showing which components matter for your property.

What the Numbers Reveal

Example 1: Invisible Maturity (19 Points). A 120-room independent property finishes its first month of testing. Citation Rate: 4 points (3 mentions across 80 tests, competitors average 52%). Platform Spread: 25 points (only ChatGPT shows the property). Positioning Quality: 25 points (fifth position with minimal descriptions when mentioned). Information Accuracy: 38 points (wrong address, outdated phone number, missing pet policy). Competitive Context: 7 points (7% of competitive average).

Overall: 4 x 0.30 + 25 x 0.25 + 25 x 0.20 + 38 x 0.15 + 7 x 0.10 = 19 points. Invisible.

Everything needs attention. Citation Rate and Platform Spread require immediate focus.

Example 2: Reactive Maturity (38 Points). A different property has sporadic presence. Citation Rate: 18 points (appears in 18% of queries). Platform Spread: 50 points (2 of 4 platforms).

Positioning Quality: 38 points (third or fourth position with minimal descriptions). Information Accuracy: 62 points (pet policy and parking costs are incorrect). Competitive Context: 33 points (33% of competitor average).

Overall: 38 points. The diagnostic is clear: fix the pet policy and parking information (Accuracy) and establish presence on the missing platform (Spread).

Example 3: Structured Maturity (58 Points). After six months of focused work, a property implements processes. Citation Rate: 34 points (27 mentions across 80 tests, competitors average 58%). Platform Spread: 75 points (ChatGPT, Gemini, and Perplexity; Claude shows zero). Positioning Quality: 52 points (second or third position with moderate descriptions). Information Accuracy: 86 points (accurate across most categories with minor amenity inconsistencies). Competitive Context: 59 points (59% of competitive average).

Overall: 10.2 + 18.75 + 10.4 + 12.9 + 5.9 = 58 points. Structured.

The property appears in relevant queries with reasonable frequency. Information accuracy runs high. Platform coverage spans three of four platforms. The competitive gap narrows. Priority shifts to closing the Claude gap and improving Positioning Quality through content differentiation.

How to Spot Trends

Single-month scores give snapshots. Multiple months reveal patterns.

Three-month trends compare the current month to three months back. A property moving from 38 to 58 gained 20 points over 90 days, averaging 6.7 points per month.

Six-month trends reveal whether early momentum sustains. A property moving from 19 to 58 gained 39 points, averaging 6.5 points per month. Consistent improvement rate suggests execution is working.

Component-specific trends matter most. Track each component separately. Platform Spread may have jumped from 25 to 75 between months 2 and 3 after implementing Gemini and

Perplexity optimization. Citation Rate may have improved steadily each month. Positioning Quality may have remained flat until content differentiation work produced results in month 5. Component trends reveal which initiatives produced results and which dimensions remain resistant.

When Your Score Does Not Move

Properties doing serious work sometimes see three months of effort produce no overall score improvement. This happens. Two patterns explain most plateaus.

The first is lag time. Schema improvements, citation building, and content restructuring take 60 to 90 days to register in AI platform behavior. AI models do not re-crawl your website daily. Training data updates on longer cycles. Citation authority accumulates gradually. A property that completed major technical work in month two should not expect score movement until month four or five.

The second is component masking. One dimension improves while another declines, producing a flat overall score. A property might gain 8 points in Positioning Quality through content differentiation while losing 7 points in Competitive Context because a competitor launched their own optimization initiative. The overall score barely moves. The component breakdown reveals that your work produced results and that a new competitive threat requires response. During plateaus, the component-level analysis matters more than the headline number.

Common Testing Problems

Platform returns inconsistent results for identical queries. Run the same query twice, get different answers. This happens, especially on Perplexity. Solution: Test once per prompt per platform per month. Accept variation. Trend tracking over multiple months smooths single-instance differences.

Multiple properties mentioned without clear ordering. ChatGPT sometimes lists "Several great options include…" without explicit ranking. Solution: Assign 12 points for position. Note "unclear ordering" in your spreadsheet.

Competitor mentions confuse scoring. Some responses mix properties into combined descriptions. Solution: Count as mentioned for both properties. Score positioning and quality based on how each property gets described within the combined response.

Testing takes longer than expected. The first month always runs long. Solution: Your second month goes faster. By month three, testing time drops 30% to 40%. Build extra buffer for the first month.

The Monthly Testing Cycle

Concentrate testing into one focused week rather than spreading it across the month.

Monday: ChatGPT testing (45 to 60 minutes in months one and two, 30 minutes by month three). Execute all 20 questions. Screenshot results. Document in spreadsheet.

Tuesday: Gemini testing (30 minutes). Same protocol.

Wednesday: Perplexity testing (30 minutes). Same protocol.

Thursday morning: Claude testing (30 minutes). Same protocol.

Thursday afternoon: Verification pass (2 hours). Review all screenshots. Verify scoring accuracy. Resolve ambiguous cases. Check competitor mentions for consistency.

Friday: Analysis and reporting (3 hours). Calculate component scores. Compare to previous month. Identify trends. Create executive summary. Plan next month's optimization priorities

This cycle becomes routine by month three. The discipline matters more than perfection.

What Measurement Enables

The Visibility Score cannot prove that optimization caused an increase in bookings. Discovery happens privately across platforms through pathways too complex to track. Measurement enables five capabilities that change AI visibility from speculative experiment into a manageable business function.

Priority identification: Component scores reveal which dimensions need attention. Low Citation Rate requires content and citation work. Low Platform Spread requires platform-specific optimization. Low Positioning Quality requires differentiation emphasis. Low Information Accuracy requires a correction focus.

Competitive intelligence: Comparative analysis reveals whether you gain ground, lose ground, or maintain position.

Optimization validation: Score improvements following optimization initiatives suggest effectiveness. Citation Rate jumping from 34% to 42% after FAQ expansion validates content investment.

Early warning: Score declines signal problems before business metrics reveal damage. Detecting competitive threats through measurement rather than occupancy decline enables proactive response.

Strategic confidence: Evidence-based decision-making replaces assumption-based strategy. You optimize based on what testing reveals rather than what you hope might work.

You measure the current state. You identify the problems. You implement the corrections. You verify the improvement. Measurement without execution produces nothing. The next chapter provides implementation roadmaps matching your specific situation: your maturity level, your competitive urgency, and your available resources.

9
IMPLEMENTATION ROADMAPS

THESE IMPLEMENTATION ROADMAPS reflect how hotels actually execute complex, cross-functional initiatives under real operational constraints. They are based on two decades of leading digital transformation in hospitality, watching properties succeed and fail across mobile optimization, direct booking acceleration, and social integration. The patterns are consistent. Execution fails when timelines ignore staffing reality. Execution succeeds when work is sequenced correctly, expectations are realistic, and leadership commits to sustained focus.

Use them as structured starting points, not rigid formulas.

The First 48 Hours

Before choosing a roadmap, do reconnaissance. These four actions require no budget, no technical help, and less than three hours total. Complete them this weekend.

Run the 20-question test from Chapter 8 on ChatGPT alone. One platform, 20 prompts, one hour. You will learn more about your AI visibility in that hour than in any strategy meeting. Screenshot every response.

Check your website in reader mode. Open Chrome, navigate to your homepage, click the reader mode icon. Do the same for your rooms page, your FAQ page, and your amenities page. If content disappears, AI platforms cannot see it either. Ten minutes reveals whether your site has a rendering problem.

Verify your Google Business Profile. Is it claimed? Is every field completed? Are the photos current? Does the address match your website exactly? Thirty minutes of verification often reveals errors that have persisted for years.

Search for your hotel by name on ChatGPT, Gemini, Perplexity, and Claude. Not category queries. Your actual hotel name. Read what each platform says about you. Screenshot the responses. Thirty minutes of reading will show you exactly how AI platforms represent your property to travelers right now.

These actions do not optimize anything. They establish your starting position. The screenshots become your before picture. Every improvement you make over the coming months measures against what you captured this weekend.

Your ChatGPT-only test does not produce a formal Visibility Score. That requires the full 80-test protocol described in Chapter 8. Use your initial results as a rough indicator to determine your starting maturity level. If your property appeared in fewer than 4 of 20 prompts, start with Invisible. If it appeared in 4 to 8 prompts, start with Reactive. If 9 to 12, start with Structured. If 13 or more, start with Integrated. These thresholds approximate what the full scoring protocol would reveal. Run the complete assessment when you have time. Start optimizing now.

Your First Optimization Move

Your baseline results from the First 48 Hours reveal your maturity level. Your first optimization action depends on where you land.

If you scored Invisible (0 to 19 points), your immediate priority is rendering and schema. Check whether AI platforms can read your website at all. Fix JavaScript rendering issues blocking access. Deploy basic Hotel schema on your homepage. Nothing else matters until the AI can see your property.

If you scored Reactive (20 to 39 points), your immediate priority is content. Expand your FAQ library to cover the operational questions your front desk answers daily. Write answer-first content with specific, quantified details. The AI can find you. It does not find enough useful information to recommend you.

If you scored Structured (40 to 59 points), your immediate priority is platform-specific optimization. You have foundations in place. Start the Gemini optimization work described in the six-month roadmap. Close gaps on the platform where you perform weakest.

If you scored Integrated or higher (60+ points), your immediate priority is the mention-to-recommendation progression from Chapter 7. You appear consistently. You need to appear with differentiated, advocacy-level positioning that converts visibility into bookings.

Choosing Your Path

Three factors determine which roadmap fits your property: your current maturity level from Chapter 5, your competitive urgency from the Market Tier assessment in Chapter 1, and your available resources.

If your resources do not match your ambition, extend your timeline. Never compress quality work into insufficient hours. An eighteen-month transformation executed well always outperforms a six-month initiative executed poorly.

Pick the **90-Day Foundation Sprint** if your Visibility Score sits between 0 and 39 points, your risk level shows high urgency, and you can commit substantial weekly hours across your team with budget for external specialists.

Pick the **Six-Month Comprehensive Build** if your Visibility Score runs 20 to 59 points, your risk level indicates medium urgency, and you can sustain moderate weekly commitment across your team for two quarters.

Pick the **12-Month Leadership Path** if your Visibility Score runs 40 to 79 points, you want market leadership, and you can dedicate someone's primary focus to this work for a full year. If your Visibility Score already exceeds 80, you have achieved leadership positioning. Shift focus to maintenance, competitive defense, and the emerging platform strategies described in Chapter 10

AI Implementation Roadmap Decision Matrix

Decision Factors	90-Day Foundation Sprint	Six-Month Comprehensive Build	Twelve-Month Leadership Path
Visibility Score (0-100)	0 - 39 (Invisible/Reactive)	20 - 59 (Reactive/Structured)	40 - 79 (Structured/Integrated)
Risk Level	High Urgency	Medium Urgency	Strategic Opportunity
Resource Commitment	Substantial Weekly Hours	Moderate Weekly Hours	Primary Focus (Dedicated)
Budget Availability	External Specialists	Sustained (2 Quarters)	Full Year Optimization
Primary Goal	Basic Functionality	Solid Competitive Positioning	Market Leadership / Dominance

The 90-Day Foundation Sprint

This aggressive timeline compresses work that might naturally require four to five months into 90 days. The compression proves feasible based on sprint methodologies from agile project management, but it requires sustained focus and adequate resources.

This pace demands genuine urgency. You cannot ask your marketing manager to handle this alongside everything else. You need a project lead with decision-making authority, a technical resource with access to your CMS and DNS, and a content resource who can write 30 or more FAQs. You will likely need external help for schema implementation, FAQ development, and citation platform optimization.

Where this roadmap breaks: Week 5, when content development stalls because the person writing FAQs gets pulled to cover a staffing shortage or a seasonal demand spike. Protect that resource before you start. If you cannot guarantee their availability through Week 7, extend the timeline now rather than discovering the gap mid-sprint.

Weeks 1 through 2: Assessment and Planning. Start with a technical audit. Test multiple pages across browsers and validation tools. You need to know exactly what breaks, where rendering fails, and which schema is missing or wrong. Run baseline Visibility Score testing as described in Chapter 8. Test those 20 prompts across all platforms. Document everything.

Present baseline results to whoever controls budget and staffing. Make it concrete: "We appeared in 6 of 80 tests while our main competitor appeared in 35." Get written commitment. Actual budget approval, staffing authorization, and multi-quarter timeline acknowledgment. This work does not deliver results in one quarter.

Weeks 3 through 4: Technical Foundation. Deploy basic schema markup. Implement the Hotel schema for your homepage and key pages. You need Organization, LocalBusiness, and basic Hotel types covering name, address, phone, description, and amenities. Validate everything using Google Rich Results Test. Zero errors establish the standard. Fix rendering issues blocking AI access. Technical work comes first because nothing else matters if AI platforms cannot read your site.

Weeks 5 through 7: Content Development. Create thorough FAQ content. Develop 30 or more questions that travelers actually ask. Not marketing questions you want them to ask. Real questions: "What time do you allow check-in?" "Do you allow pets?" "How much does parking cost?" Each answer runs 80 to 120 words, starts with the direct answer, then provides context. Focus on operational questions, the ones your front desk answers daily. Those same questions drive what travelers ask AI platforms before they ever call you.

Structure matters as much as the content itself. Deploy the FAQ as a dedicated, crawlable page with static text. Do not use accordion elements or click-to-expand formatting. Each question must be a proper H3 heading. Each answer must render without JavaScript execution. Deploy FAQPage schema covering every question-answer pair and validate using Google Rich Results Test before considering the work complete. A property that writes 35 excellent answers and deploys them inside JavaScript accordions without schema markup has done the content work and missed the architecture work. Both must happen during this sprint.

The FAQ page is the highest-priority content deliverable during this sprint because of its concentrated retrieval value. It is not the only content that needs attention. Review your room descriptions and verify they contain specific, quantified details rather than marketing language. Check that amenity pages document hours, fees, and seasonal availability in plain text. Confirm that policy pages state terms with the same directness the FAQ answers use. These pages do not require the same volume of new writing the FAQ demands. They require an editing pass that converts existing marketing copy into the specific, extractable format AI platforms need.

Weeks 8 through 10: Citation Foundation. Optimize your Google Business Profile completely. Fill every available field. Upload at least 20 photos. Verify all business information. Respond to every review within 48 hours. Then audit your citations. Document exactly how your name, address, phone, and URL appear on every major platform. Look for variations. File correction requests immediately. Citation corrections typically take two to six weeks to propagate across platforms. Corrections filed during Weeks 8 through 10 will not register in your Week 12 retest. Expect those gains to appear in Month 4 or 5. The Week 12 retest measures technical and content improvements. Citation impact shows up in subsequent quarterly testing.

Weeks 11 through 12: Measurement and Analysis. Retest your Visibility Score. Same 20 prompts. Same four platforms. Same documentation standards. Calculate all component scores. Compare to the Week 1 baseline. Write up what you learned.

The Six-Month Comprehensive Build

This roadmap builds significantly more capability. You move from sporadic presence to consistent visibility, from basic content to comprehensive coverage, from ad hoc testing to systematic measurement. The six-month timeline gives you room to do quality work without burning out your team. Actual duration may vary by 25% to 30% depending on your specific constraints.

Most properties should start here.

You need an AI visibility manager, a technical specialist, a content lead, and digital PR support. You will need external specialists for advanced schema optimization, comprehensive content development, Tier 2 citation outreach, and media relations.

Where this roadmap breaks: Month 3, when the initial score improvement from technical fixes plateaus and leadership questions the investment. The plateau is normal. Citation authority and content indexing take 60 to 90 days to register in AI platform behavior. Prepare leadership for this timing gap before you start, not after the budget review meeting where someone asks why scores stopped improving.

Month 1: Assessment and Foundation. Execute full assessments. This runs deeper than the 90-day sprint. Test all pages in reader mode, audit complete schema implementation, and test page speed with Core Web Vitals documentation. Baseline Visibility Score measurement expands. Test 20 prompts across all platforms. Run competitive testing for 3 to 5 direct competitors using identical prompts.

Month 2: Technical Excellence. Implement complete Hotel schema across all pages. Go beyond basic schema to include detailed amenity specifications, review aggregation, and event schemas. Add Product schema for each room type. Deploy FAQPage schema. Implement server-side rendering or prerendering if your site is JavaScript-heavy. Optimize Core Web Vitals for both human visitors and AI crawlers.

Month 3: Content Expansion. Develop your strategic FAQ library. Target 60 or more questions. Add the edge cases competitors overlook: "What if my dog weighs 52 pounds and your policy says 50?" "What if I need to check in at 11:00 PM?" Write detailed amenity descriptions with actual specifics AI systems can extract: "Fitness center includes 8 cardio machines (4 treadmills, 2 ellipticals, 2 stationary bikes), free weights up to 50 pounds, and two multi-station weight machines. Open 24 hours. Towel service available." Create detailed policy documentation. Make every policy clear, specific, and complete. After expanding your FAQ library, update your FAQPage schema to include all new question-answer pairs. Revalidate using Google Rich Results Test. Schema deployed in Month 2 covered your initial question set. The expanded content requires updated markup to remain visible to AI platforms.

Month 4: Citation Network Building. Complete your Tier 3 foundation. Claim and optimize all major platforms: Google Business Profile, TripAdvisor, Yelp, Booking.com, every OTA, and every directory where you should appear. Audit citation inconsistencies using professional tools. File correction requests for every error. Use the second half of Month 4 to prepare for Tier 2 outreach. Identify target regional publications and trade outlets. Build contact lists. Draft initial pitch angles tied to your property's differentiators. This preparation allows Month 5 to focus entirely on platform-specific optimization without also carrying the Tier 2 launch.

Month 5: Platform-Specific Optimization. Start with Gemini. Not ChatGPT.

ChatGPT remains the name most people recognize. Through mid-2025, it accounted for more than 80% of AI referral traffic. That number shifted by Q4. ChatGPT usage stabilized in the 33% to 34% range of AI search activity. Gemini tripled its share during 2025, reaching approximately 11%.

For hospitality, Gemini's strategic importance exceeds its market share number. Gemini connects directly to the Google ecosystem: Maps, Flights, Hotels, and the AI Overviews that now appear in more than 25% of all Google searches. When a traveler asks Google anything about hotels, Gemini mediates that answer. It draws from your Google Business Profile, your structured data, your review history, and your Maps listing. ChatGPT operates as a standalone conversation. Gemini operates as the intelligence layer across every Google surface where travelers already research and book.

If you are invisible to Gemini, you are invisible to the Google traveler.

Gemini values factual precision. Replace vague language with specific measurements. Ensure your Google Business Profile contains complete, accurate, current information. Verify that your schema markup validates cleanly, because Gemini pulls structured data from your site to cross-reference against its Maps and Hotels databases. Inconsistencies between your website and your Google listings create data conflicts that Gemini resolves by choosing a competitor with cleaner information.

Then optimize for ChatGPT. ChatGPT needs thorough, in-depth answers. Where Gemini rewards precision, ChatGPT rewards thoroughness. A detailed FAQ page that answers fifteen related questions in one location performs well in ChatGPT's retrieval process. Then address Perplexity (which favors source diversity across multiple authoritative references) and Claude (which favors well-structured information with clear hierarchies).

Month 6: Measurement Systems and Transition. Establish operational measurement systems that survive beyond this project. Document your monthly Visibility Score testing process. Create step-by-step procedure manuals. Execute final testing across all platforms. Generate your final report showing where you started, where you stand, what worked, what did not, and what comes next.

The 12-Month Market Leadership Path

This path pursues market leadership. You build advanced capabilities, aiming to appear more often than competitors, with better positioning, across more platforms. Some aspects may develop faster as team expertise builds. Others may require longer. Tier 1 media relationships sometimes take 18 or more months to establish. Adjust milestones quarterly based on actual progress.

This requires someone's primary focus. Not "among their responsibilities." Primary focus. You need an AI strategy lead making this their main priority, supported by technical, content, digital presence, and measurement specialists. You need dedicated external support: strategic content development partnerships, media relations programs, competitive intelligence analysis, and analytics consultation.

Where this roadmap breaks: Quarter 2, when the strategy lead leaves or gets reassigned and nobody has documented the work. Twelve-month initiatives outlast individual tenure. Build documentation into every phase. If the person driving this initiative departed tomorrow, could someone else read their files and continue without losing a month?

Quarter 1: Strategic Foundation. Execute deep competitive analysis. Test multiple competitors across all platforms using your expanded prompt library. Audit your Tier 3 foundation before launching Tier 2 work. The entry criteria for this path assume a Visibility Score of 40 or above, but a property at 42 may still have Tier 3 gaps that a property at 74 resolved months ago. Close any remaining Tier 3 gaps before directing resources toward Tier 2 outreach. Deploy advanced schema enhancements: proximity details, special offers, and custom properties that basic implementations skip. Develop a differentiated content strategy answering what makes you different from competitors and how you articulate that difference in ways AI platforms recognize. Launch your Tier 2 citation campaign.

Quarter 2: Platform Optimization. Execute platform-specific deep optimization, starting with Gemini for the reasons detailed in the six-month roadmap. Gemini optimization and Google ecosystem optimization are the same work. Properties that treat them as separate initiatives duplicate effort. Verify that every Gemini-facing data point aligns: Google Business Profile, website schema, OTA listings, and review platform information. Deepen ChatGPT, Perplexity, and Claude optimization. Expand your citation network through sustained Tier 2 outreach.

Quarter 3: Consolidation and Excellence. Secure additional Tier 2 placements. Develop advanced content assets that go beyond FAQs into territory competitors have not touched. Begin Tier 1 pursuit if your property warrants national-level coverage. Refer to your Market Tier from Chapter 1. Properties in Major Metro markets with genuine differentiators may warrant Tier 1 pursuit. Regional Hub and Emerging Market properties should continue concentrating on Tier 2 depth, where return on investment remains strongest. Execute comprehensive Q3 assessment.

Quarter 4: Leadership and Transition. Address remaining gaps identified in Q3 assessment. Establish operational maintenance systems. Document everything. Make this capability survive personnel changes. Execute comprehensive year-end assessment: where you started, where you stand, what maintaining this position requires. Define your ongoing maintenance commitment. Leadership positions erode without sustained attention. At minimum, continue monthly Visibility Score testing, quarterly competitive analysis, and monthly review response optimization. Assign 8 to 12 hours per month to monitoring, content refreshes, and citation maintenance. The intensive build year is over. The operational discipline is permanent.

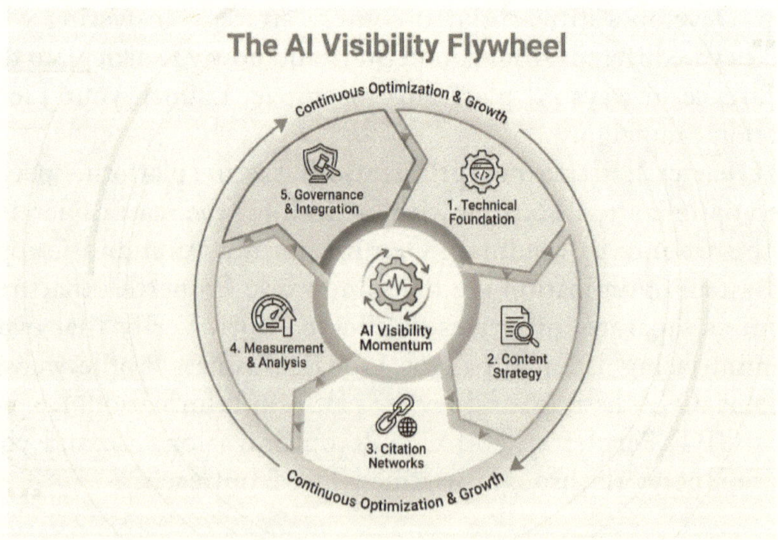

Switching Roadmaps

Sometimes the choice turns out to be wrong. A property that picked the 6-Month Build discovers it cannot sustain the pace. A property on the 90-Day Sprint realizes its technical debt runs far deeper than the initial audit revealed. A property on the 12-Month Path finds it is progressing faster than expected and can compress timelines.

Switching roadmaps is a sign of learning, not failure. The maturity framework from Chapter 5 and the Visibility Score from Chapter 8 provide objective signals for when a switch makes sense. If your Month 3 scores show you are still Invisible despite following the 6-Month Build, your technical foundation has gaps the roadmap cannot address at its current pace. Pause. Fix the foundation. Restart the clock. If your 90-Day Sprint scores show you already reached Structured maturity by Week 8, shift to the 6-Month Build's Month 4 activities rather than running out a timeline you have already surpassed.

Moving from Project to Operations

Finishing your roadmap does not mean you are done. It means you shift from building capability to maintaining it.

Monthly Visibility Score testing follows the same 20-prompt protocol from Appendix C, run across each platform where your property appeared during the build phase. Quarterly full-scope testing expands to all four major platforms regardless of previous results, capturing any shifts in platform behavior or competitive positioning. Content maintenance means reviewing and updating FAQ schema, property descriptions, and homepage narrative language whenever operational details change: seasonal rates, new amenities, revised policies, updated hours. Schema maintenance requires revalidating structured data after every website update through the Google Rich Results Test (see Appendix C for the validation walkthrough). Citation monitoring tracks your Tier 1 through Tier 4 mentions monthly, flagging any that have gone stale, been removed, or contain outdated information.

Resource requirements drop substantially in operational mode. Properties that maintained Structured maturity during testing typically need 8 to 12 hours per month of dedicated attention. Integrated maturity requires more, closer to 15 to 20 hours. Optimized demands sustained commitment, often a partial FTE or dedicated external partner.

Properties that reach operational stability have established AI visibility as a permanent business function. Not a temporary initiative. Not a marketing campaign. A permanent capability woven into how the property operates.

Adapting When Resources Fall Short

What happens when you cannot commit the resources your target roadmap requires?

Extend your timeline proportionally. If your roadmap assumes 15 weekly hours but you can sustain 10, multiply the timeline by 1.5. A six-month roadmap becomes nine months. A twelve-month path stretches to eighteen. Maintain the task sequence throughout. Technical foundations before content development. Content before citation building. The order matters more than the speed.

Focus external spending strategically. Hire specialists for complex schema implementation. Bring in media relations expertise for your initial Tier 2 outreach. Use consultants for technical audits where diagnostic precision saves weeks of trial and error. Execute the remaining work internally, accepting that generalists take longer.

The value does not come from timeline precision. It comes from having structured approaches to execution that prevent the paralysis that stalls too many digital initiatives in hospitality.

Evaluating External Help

Every roadmap references external specialists. The vendor market for AI visibility remains immature. Traditional SEO agencies may lack AI-specific expertise. Agencies claiming AI visibility capabilities may have rebranded existing services without developing new methodologies.

Three questions separate qualified partners from repackaged SEO vendors.

First, ask them to explain query fan-out and how it changes content strategy. If they cannot describe how AI platforms generate background searches and evaluate your content during retrieval, they are optimizing for a system they do not understand.

Second, ask them to demonstrate schema validation for a hotel website. Schema implementation is foundational to AI visibility. A vendor who cannot walk you through the Google Rich Results Test and explain what each error means lacks the technical capability this work requires. (Appendix C covers the validation process if you want to follow along during the conversation.)

Third, ask them to show you measured AI visibility improvement from a previous engagement. Not traffic increases. Not ranking improvements. Measured changes in how AI platforms mention, describe, or recommend a property. If they cannot produce this evidence, they have not done this work before.

The field will mature. Qualified vendors will become easier to identify as measurement standards solidify. For now, evaluate partners on demonstrated understanding of AI retrieval mechanics rather than marketing claims about AI expertise.

The Next Step

You have read the frameworks. You understand maturity levels, technical requirements, citation strategies, and measurement methodology.

Now you need to pick your path and walk it.

Choose your roadmap today. Not next week. Not next quarter. Today.

Start your baseline testing this week. Block the time on your calendar. Get the screenshots. Calculate your scores.

Present results to whoever controls budget and staffing within two weeks. Show them the competitive context from your testing.

Make the revenue implications concrete with the calculation framework from Chapter 8.

Get written commitment for resources before month-end. The work does not happen without explicit organizational support.

Then execute for months, not weeks. Follow your selected roadmap. Maintain discipline when results feel slow. Protect the work when competing priorities press against your timeline.

The hotels that will dominate AI visibility two years from now are starting execution this month. The window for building competitive advantage narrows every quarter as more properties begin structured optimization. The earlier you start, the harder your position becomes for competitors to displace.

10

ORGANIZATIONAL INTEGRATION AND GOVERNANCE

THE FRAMEWORKS IN the previous chapters explain how to build AI visibility. This chapter explains how to keep it alive.

Most hospitality initiatives fail for the same reason. Not because the strategy was wrong. Not because the tools were inadequate. They fail because the work never became part of how the organization operates.

AI visibility is especially vulnerable to this pattern. It touches marketing, technology, operations, and revenue without fully belonging to any of them. Without deliberate organizational design, it survives only as long as the person championing it remains in place.

If AI visibility remains a project, it will eventually disappear. If AI visibility becomes a business function, it will compound.

The difference is organizational integration.

The Pattern That Kills Initiatives

Properties spend three months building foundations. Schema gets implemented. FAQ content gets created. Citation building starts. Visibility Scores improve from the low twenties to the low forties. Real progress.

Then the marketing director takes a different position. The new director arrives with different priorities. Within four months, schema breaks during a website update. Content goes stale. Citation monitoring stops. Scores drop back to where they started.

The property treated AI visibility as a marketing campaign instead of a business capability. This chapter prevents that outcome.

The Ownership Problem

AI visibility touches everything without belonging to anyone. Marketing owns the content strategy. IT controls website infrastructure. Operations maintains information accuracy. Revenue management sets pricing that appears in AI responses.

Everyone has partial ownership. Nobody has complete accountability.

Schema breaks during website updates because IT does not know how to validate it. Content goes stale because marketing lacks refresh schedules. Citations drift toward inconsistency because nobody monitors them. Monthly testing gets skipped because nobody feels genuinely responsible for the outcome.

Ask hotel teams who owns AI visibility at their property. The answer usually involves a pause followed by some version of "we all kind of do." That answer guarantees failure.

Someone needs to wake up thinking about your AI visibility. Someone needs to check whether schema still validates after IT pushes a website update. Someone needs to notice when your Information Accuracy score drops three points. Someone needs to catch that a competitor displaced you from Gemini's top recommendation for business travelers in your market. Without that person, optimization dies through benign neglect rather than conscious decision.

Role Structures by Property Size

The right structure scales with your reality.

Small properties (under 100 rooms) combine roles. That works if you make it explicit. Assign AI visibility coordination to a specific person, whether the general manager or the marketing manager, with defined deliverables and protected weekly hours. Do not assume it will happen organically. Keep governance simple: monthly check-ins comparing Visibility Scores against the prior month and flagging any schema validation failures or citation losses. Quarterly reviews evaluating progress against your selected roadmap timeline. Annual planning sessions setting targets for the coming year. Keep documentation lean: one-page checklists and shared document folders. Bring in external specialists for peak demands like schema implementation, content strategy, and Tier 2 media outreach.

Medium properties (100 to 300 rooms) can justify dedicated coordination. The AI visibility coordinator role becomes a primary responsibility for someone rather than an addition to an already full workload. Build a small team with technical, content, and PR support executing coordinated work. Implement standard governance: monthly operational reviews that compare current Visibility Scores to prior periods and identify specific actions for the coming month. Quarterly strategic reviews that evaluate roadmap progress and adjust resource allocation. Annual planning sessions that set visibility targets, budget requirements, and staffing needs. Develop process documentation that people actually use rather than theoretical manuals nobody opens.

Large properties or groups (300 plus rooms or multiple properties) need dedicated AI Visibility Manager roles. The title itself matters less than the mandate. Your organization can adapt the name to fit existing structures. Full-time for single large properties. Portfolio responsibility for groups. This person coordinates specialized team members, manages vendor relationships, and maintains documentation enabling consistency across properties. Implement full governance: monthly operational reviews covering score trends, competitive shifts, and immediate action items. Quarterly strategic reviews assessing roadmap progress, vendor performance, and emerging platform changes. Annual planning encompassing budget allocation, staffing plans, technology investments, and competitive positioning targets. Build cultural integration through progress presentations, milestone recognition, and transparent performance dashboards.

The principle across all sizes: make ownership explicit, protect the time, and build governance that survives personnel changes.

The Documentation Discipline

Chapter 8 specifies the testing format, spreadsheet structure, and screenshot naming conventions. This section addresses why documentation discipline matters organizationally, not how to format the spreadsheet.

Your measurement work only matters if you can compare results over time and connect performance changes to specific actions you took. That requires three documentation habits.

First, maintain identical testing formats month to month. When you change formats, you collect data without learning from it. Consistency matters more than any specific format choice.

Second, archive actual AI responses. Six months from now, you will want to compare what ChatGPT said about your property in January versus June. Screenshots make that possible. Memory does not.

Third, log optimization activities with dates and details. When your Platform Spread score jumps eight points three weeks after you implement Gemini-specific optimizations, you want to know that connection. Activity logs make attribution possible even when perfect measurement does not exist.

Process documentation protects against turnover. When your marketing manager leaves, the replacement should execute monthly testing correctly within two weeks by reading your protocol. When your technical lead moves to another property, the new person should validate schema without reinventing the approach.

Essential documentation includes the monthly Visibility Score protocol with complete prompt library and scoring criteria, schema maintenance workflows and content update standards, and citation monitoring procedures with review response protocols. Store centrally with version control. Test documentation by having unfamiliar team members execute it. If they cannot follow it without asking questions, revise it.

The Governance Framework

Governance keeps work moving when initial enthusiasm fades and competing priorities emerge. Without it, AI visibility becomes the initiative everyone agrees matters but nobody actually does.

Monthly operational reviews cover the current Visibility Score and component breakdown, initiative progress, blockers, and next month's priorities. Keep these tactical and problem-focused. Sixty minutes with the AI visibility coordinator, marketing, IT, and operations representatives. Every monthly review should produce a one-page summary stored in a shared location. These summaries become the institutional record that enables continuity when personnel change.

Quarterly strategic reviews examine the full quarter's Visibility Score trends, competitive positioning, platform evolution, and resource allocation for the next quarter. Keep these strategic and forward-looking. Ninety minutes with department directors and the general manager.

Annual planning sessions analyze the competitive landscape, assess maturity level progression, develop the strategic plan, and create budget proposals for the next fiscal year. Half day with the leadership team.

When monthly reviews surface blockers that exceed the coordinator's authority, escalation should follow existing operational channels with one addition: frame the impact in Visibility Score terms. IT deprioritizing a schema fix is not a technical delay. It is a measurable visibility decline that compounds every week the validation errors persist. A Tier 2 media opportunity requiring unbudgeted spending is not a marketing expense. It is a citation gap that competitors will fill first. Visibility Score language gives leadership a concrete basis for prioritization rather than forcing them to weigh abstract digital initiatives against tangible operational demands.

The cadence matters more than the format. Properties that hold these meetings consistently maintain momentum. Properties that skip them when things get busy discover three months later that nobody has tested, schema broke, and scores declined.

AI Governance Meeting Rhythm: Sustaining Organizational Commitment

Warning Signs of Organizational Decay

Integration does not collapse overnight. It erodes. These signals indicate that your organizational capability is degrading before the Visibility Score confirms it.

Schema has not been validated in 90 or more days. Every website update risks breaking structured data. Properties that stop validating discover the damage months later when scores decline and they cannot identify the cause.

Monthly testing got skipped twice. The first skip feels like a scheduling conflict. The second skip establishes a pattern. By the third month, testing has become optional rather than operational.

Nobody can name the AI visibility owner when asked. If the answer requires checking an org chart or produces a pause, ownership has become theoretical rather than functional.

Leadership has not reviewed Visibility Scores in two or more quarters. When leadership stops reviewing, budget protection disappears in the next cycle. Governance without leadership attention is paperwork without power.

Citation monitoring has lapsed. Information accuracy degrades silently. Phone numbers change. Policies update. OTA listings drift. Without monitoring, the property discovers the problem when a guest complains that the AI told them parking was free.

Competitive tracking has dropped from quarterly reviews. A property can maintain every internal process and still lose ground because it stopped watching what competitors are doing. When a rival launches a structured optimization program and begins gaining share in AI recommendations, the property without competitive tracking will not notice until the gap becomes difficult to close. Competitive context is one of the five Visibility Score components for a reason. Ignoring it does not make the competition stop.

Property-controlled content has gone stale. Citation monitoring catches accuracy drift on OTAs and directories. It does not catch the property's own website. FAQ schema still reflecting last season's policies. Homepage narrative language describing a restaurant concept that changed six months ago. A property description referencing a renovated lobby as "coming soon" eight months after it opened. AI platforms weight a property's own site heavily during retrieval. Stale owned content undermines visibility in ways that no amount of external citation building can offset.

Catching these signals early costs hours. Catching them late costs months of rebuilding.

Building Organizational Literacy

Governance structures fail without broader understanding across your team. Your entire staff needs basic literacy about why AI visibility matters, even if they do not need to understand technical details.

Front desk staff do not need to understand Platform Spread optimization. They should understand that when they give guests wrong information about policies, that wrong information may end up in AI systems. Operations staff do not need to know about schema markup. They should understand that when they change fitness center hours without telling marketing, AI platforms start providing outdated information that creates guest frustration. Revenue managers do not need to grasp citation tier architecture. They should understand that when they adjust rates or modify packages without updating the website, AI platforms serve pricing information that no longer reflects reality. Sales and catering teams do not need to track Visibility Scores. They should understand that a new wedding package or group offering that exists only in a PDF brochure or email attachment is invisible to every AI system.

Build this literacy through regular communication. At monthly staff meetings, spend five minutes on AI visibility updates. Show the current Visibility Score trend in simple terms. Celebrate specific improvements and connect them to team contributions. "Information Accuracy jumped six points this month because operations helped us fix the 12 policy inconsistencies we discovered during testing."

Create simple explainer materials for new hires. A one-page overview should cover three things: what AI visibility means in plain language, why it affects the property's revenue, and how the new hire's specific role connects to it. Tailor the connection statement by department. A front desk version emphasizes information accuracy. A revenue management version emphasizes rate and package updates. An operations version emphasizes facility and policy changes. Update these one-pagers annually during your governance planning session, or sooner if your organizational structure changes. Make them part of standard onboarding so that every new team member arrives with baseline understanding.

For properties that want a ready-made foundation for this literacy work, The AI Literacy Playbook for Hoteliers provides frameworks designed for hospitality teams. The principles in this chapter apply whether you build your own materials or adapt existing resources.

Recognition reinforces literacy. When Information Accuracy improves, recognize the operations team. When Citation Rate increases following FAQ expansion, recognize the content writer. When a revenue manager's consistent rate updates keep pricing accurate across platforms, recognize that contribution. People care more about work when they see how it matters.

When literacy fails, the consequences are specific and measurable. A front desk manager posts a temporary policy change on the property's Facebook page or LinkedIn profile that contradicts the website. As Chapter 4 explains, not all social platforms are equally walled. Facebook posts and LinkedIn updates live on the open web where AI crawlers can access them, unlike Instagram and TikTok content that remains locked inside their ecosystems. AI platforms pick up the open-web social post as the more current source because it carries a more recent timestamp. Guests arrive expecting the temporary policy. The property spends weeks correcting information across platforms while its Information Accuracy score drops. The damage started with a single post from someone who did not understand that AI platforms monitor every public-facing channel on the open web, not only the website.

One connection deserves emphasis. AI visibility and guest experience are reinforcing systems, not separate initiatives. Guest experience generates the reviews, social media mentions, and word-of-mouth signals that AI platforms use to build citation authority. A property with strong AI visibility but declining service quality creates a fragile system. The reviews will eventually undermine the citation network. The AI will reflect the contradiction. Operations staff maintaining service excellence contribute to AI visibility whether they know it or not. Making that connection visible to your team strengthens both systems simultaneously.

Dealing With Leadership Resistance

You will face resistance. Budget gets questioned. Priorities get challenged. Resources get threatened. What follows reflects patterns that work when leadership pushes back.

When leadership questions ROI. Do not promise attribution you cannot deliver. Be direct about measurement limitations. Then pivot to directional evidence.

"I cannot draw a straight line from Visibility Score improvements to specific bookings. The attribution gap is narrowing but remains wide. Here is what I can show you: our score improved from 28 to 55 points over six months. During that same period, branded search increased by 18%, direct traffic grew by 12%, and the OTA booking percentage declined from 34% to 29%. Multiple signals moving in a consistent positive direction."

Show competitive context. "Our three main competitors average 67 points. We are at 55. That gap means they appear in recommendations where we do not."

Frame the risk. "Travelers are asking AI platforms for recommendations right now. Either we appear in those recommendations, or we do not. The longer we wait, the harder it gets to catch up."

When the budget gets threatened. Defend measurement capability above everything else. You can reduce optimization intensity temporarily. You cannot stop measuring without going blind.

"I can pause citation building for a quarter. I can defer platform-specific optimization. If we stop monthly testing, we lose our ability to track whether anything we are doing works. That is the one capability I need to protect."

Explain the maintenance cost trap. "We are spending $3,000 monthly on maintenance. If we skip maintenance for three months to save money, we will probably spend $8,000 fixing what breaks. Deferred maintenance costs more than sustained maintenance."

Frame the competitive cost of going dark. Every month without active optimization is a month competitors advance unopposed. Properties do not hold position by standing still. They hold position by matching the pace of competitors who are building citation networks, expanding schema coverage, and testing across platforms. A budget pause is not a freeze. It is a controlled retreat that concedes ground you will need to retake later at higher cost.

Offer scaling options. "We can reduce from Integrated-level optimization to Structured-level maintenance. Budget drops from

$25,000 annually to $15,000. We maintain what we have built. We stop advancing for now. When budget returns, we resume from a stable position rather than rebuilding from failure."

When priorities shift. Acknowledge competing demands without pretending they do not exist. Other things do matter. Show you understand that reality.

"I understand the renovation is consuming substantial resources. Here is what cannot be deferred without damage: monthly testing (6 hours), schema validation (3 hours), citation corrections (4 hours). That is 13 hours monthly, keeping what we have built from degrading. Everything else can pause until bandwidth returns."

Minimal maintenance at 13 hours monthly can sustain Structured maturity for roughly two to three quarters before degradation becomes measurable. Beyond that window, citation networks thin as listings go stale, schema errors accumulate undetected after website changes, and competitive positioning erodes as rivals continue advancing. If a reduced-resource period will extend beyond six months, revisit the Warning Signs checklist from earlier in this chapter quarterly to catch degradation before it compounds.

Connect to their priorities in their language. If they focus on direct bookings, frame AI visibility in direct booking terms. "Properties with improving visibility scores also see branded search increases, direct traffic growth, and declining OTA booking share. The more often you appear in AI trip planning tools, the more likely guests bypass the OTAs entirely."

The Sustainability Principle

Lasting AI visibility comes from organizational design, not projects.

Properties that sustain visibility build three forms of durability. Structural durability comes from explicit ownership, protected budgets, and governance rhythms that survive personnel changes. Process durability comes from documentation that enables consistent execution and decision frameworks that guide work under uncertainty. Cultural durability comes from shared literacy, visible accountability, and recognition that reinforces why this work matters.

Most properties will not build all three simultaneously. That expectation is neither realistic nor necessary. Structural durability typically comes first because it requires decisions rather than development. Assign ownership. Protect the budget. Establish the meeting cadence. Process durability follows as the team documents what works and discards what does not through the first two quarters of execution. Cultural durability takes the longest because it requires repeated demonstration that the work produces results people can see and connect to their own contributions. Building sequentially is expected. Building all three within the first year is the goal.

When these three operate together, AI visibility becomes part of how the hotel functions rather than something a single champion protects.

The technical frameworks in Chapters 6 through 9 show you what to do. This chapter shows you how to make that work last. What determines your outcome is not what you know. It is what you institutionalize.

CONCLUSION

The data in this book points one direction. Discovery shifted. Traffic patterns changed. AI platforms now mediate a growing share of how travelers find hotels. The specific percentages vary by study, methodology, and market. The direction never varies.

What remains uncertain is not whether the transformation happened. It is which properties will respond in time to benefit from responding.

What the Evidence Demands

Two disciplines determine whether you succeed. On-site technical excellence means the AI can read your property, parse your data, and extract accurate facts. Off-site citation authority means the AI trusts what it finds. On-site data tells the AI what you claim. Off-site citations tell the AI whether to believe it. Neither alone proves sufficient. Both together create the compounding advantage that AI systems reward.

The distinction between mentions and recommendations separates properties that appear from properties that convert. A mention puts your name in a list. A recommendation advocates for your property as the answer to a specific traveler need. The progression from one to the other requires structured content built from institutional knowledge your competitors cannot replicate, citation networks that accumulate authority over quarters, and bridge entity connections linking your property to the landmarks and events defining your market. These assets compound over time. A competitor can implement schema in a week. A competitor cannot replicate two years of citation network development.

The Answer Spiral from Chapter 3 explains why these assets matter more than they did under the funnel model. Travelers no longer move through predictable stages on measurable platforms. They spiral through iterative AI conversations where each answer generates the next question, cycling across platforms until they reach sufficient confidence to book. Your content must answer questions at every point in that spiral because you cannot predict where a traveler will enter or what platform will retrieve your information. The walled garden reality from Chapter 4 compounds the challenge. Each platform operates independently. Strength on one transfers nothing to another. The only work that serves every platform simultaneously is the technical foundation and citation infrastructure this book teaches you to build.

The Choice

You face three risks. Not two. Three.

The risk of early action means investing in infrastructure with directional measurement rather than perfect attribution. You act on pattern recognition rather than conclusive validation.

The risk of delayed action means waiting for comprehensive evidence while competitors build citation networks, establish algorithmic momentum, and claim positioning that grows more expensive to challenge with each passing quarter.

The risk of inaction means focusing on channels with perfect measurement while travelers research hotels through platforms your analytics cannot detect.

All three paths carry uncertainty. The question is which uncertainty you can accept.

A reasonable objection follows: what happens when every property optimizes? Technical foundations will become baseline requirements rather than competitive advantages. Schema markup and citation consistency will be expected, not differentiating. The advantage shifts permanently to content depth, citation authority, and the mention-to-recommendation progression. Those assets resist replication because they require time, institutional knowledge, and sustained organizational commitment. Properties that start building now create advantages that late movers cannot shortcut.

Most properties have not started. The window remains open. It will not remain open indefinitely.

Beyond Hospitality

This book used hotels as the case study. The transformation it documents does not stop at hotel lobbies.

Every framework in these pages has a direct equivalent outside hospitality. The translation requires changing terminology, not methodology.

The Visibility Score (Chapter 8) works for any business willing to run 20 prompts monthly across the platforms their customers use. A law firm tests "best estate planning attorney in [city]" instead of "best hotel in [city]." A retailer tests "best running shoes for wet pavement" instead of "best hotel near the convention center." A SaaS company tests "best project management tool for remote teams under 50 employees" instead of "best boutique hotel for business travelers." The five components measure the same dimensions regardless of industry. Citation Rate tracks how often AI mentions you. Platform Spread measures whether you appear across ChatGPT, Gemini, Perplexity, and Claude. Positioning Quality evaluates whether the AI recommends you or lists you. Information Accuracy catches errors the AI repeats about your business. Competitive Context benchmarks you against alternatives.

The citation tier framework (Chapter 7) translates with equal precision. For a law firm, Tier 1 sources include legal publications and major news outlets covering notable cases. Tier 2 includes bar association journals, regional legal media, and respected practice-area blogs. Tier 3 includes Avvo, Martindale-Hubbell, Google Business Profile, and legal directories. For a retailer, Tier 1 includes national publications and major consumer review outlets. Tier 2 includes category-specific publications, influential product reviewers, and trade media. Tier 3 includes Google Merchant Center, Amazon product listings, and shopping comparison platforms. For a SaaS company, Tier 1 includes major technology publications and analyst firms. Tier 2 includes G2, Capterra, industry analyst reports, and vertical trade publications. Tier 3 includes product directories, integration marketplaces, and business listing platforms.

Bridge entities (Chapter 6) apply wherever your business connects to a context larger than itself. A restaurant's bridge entities are the theater district, the sports arena, the annual food festival. A law firm's bridge entities are the courthouse, the financial district, the university whose faculty refer clients. A retailer's bridge entities are the seasonal events, the athletic competitions, the lifestyle categories that connect products to purchase intent. When someone asks an AI for dinner near a specific venue or a lawyer near a specific courthouse, the same retrieval logic determines which businesses surface.

The mention-to-recommendation progression (Chapter 7) applies wherever AI synthesizes answers from multiple sources. A restaurant that appears in AI responses as one option among twelve with no distinguishing detail is stuck in the same mention trap described for hotels. A financial advisor whose AI description reads "experienced wealth manager" competes against every other advisor with the same generic positioning. The content differentiation principles in Chapter 6 apply identically. Specific, quantified, structured information earns recommendations. Vague descriptions earn mentions at best.

Hospitality provided the right lens because hotels sit at the intersection of local search, review platforms, booking systems, and complex multi-factor intent. That complexity revealed the full scope of the challenge. The principles revealed through that lens apply to every business where customers research before they decide.

If your customers ask AI before they choose, this book is about you.

What Comes Next

The Visibility Score gives you measurement capability where none existed. The maturity levels tell you where you stand. The technical foundations transcend any individual platform. The implementation roadmaps reflect how hotels actually execute change under real constraints. The organizational integration framework makes the work survive beyond any single champion.

Measurement will remain imperfect. The attribution gap described in Chapter 2 is narrowing, not closing. That limitation is acceptable because the alternative is not better measurement. The alternative is measuring nothing while competitors build visibility you cannot see and capture bookings you cannot track.

These are tools. They produce nothing without execution.

Choose your roadmap. Start your baseline testing. Present the competitive context to whoever controls resources. Get written commitment. Then execute for months, not weeks, protecting the work when competing priorities press against it.

The businesses leading AI visibility two years from now will not be the ones with the largest budgets or the most sophisticated technology. They will be the ones that recognized the pattern, committed to the work, and built organizational systems that made the work irreversible.

The transformation is not coming. It arrived. Your response determines what happens next.

EPILOGUE
WHAT COMES NEXT

This book documents how AI platforms are reshaping discovery. The frameworks address the current transformation. This epilogue addresses where that transformation leads.

The preceding chapters provided implementable frameworks supported by current data. What follows shifts to emerging developments that remain early-stage and speculative. Consider this section strategic context for your planning horizon, not operational guidance you should act on today.

From Recommendation to Transaction

McKinsey identified the evolution beyond what this book addresses. Their research points to AI models becoming autonomous booking agents that make purchase decisions on behalf of users. OpenAI launched advertising inside ChatGPT in early 2026, and other platforms are building similar revenue models. The next phase converts AI from a recommendation engine to a transaction executor.

Google's Q4 2025 earnings confirmed the trajectory. Gemini 3 Pro became their fastest-adopted model in company history, processing three times the daily volume of its predecessor. Google announced a Universal Commerce Protocol built alongside retail industry leaders, creating an open standard for agentic commerce. The Chrome Auto Browse capability described in Chapter 6 represents one piece of this infrastructure. The path from recommendation to transaction is no longer theoretical. Google is building the commercial rails.

The pace accelerated further in February 2026 when Google released an early preview of WebMCP, a protocol for how AI agents interact with websites. WebMCP allows websites to publish structured "tool contracts" that tell AI agents what actions are available and how to execute them. Instead of an agent guessing how to navigate a booking form, the website declares its capabilities through a standard browser API. Google identified travel as a primary use case, describing agents that search, filter, and handle bookings through structured data. WebMCP and UCP address different sides of the same shift. UCP standardizes how agents discover products and complete purchases. WebMCP standardizes how agents interact with the website itself. The attribution consequence deserves equal attention. When research, comparison, and booking complete inside a single agent interface, the page visit data that currently enables retargeting, behavioral analysis, and journey mapping disappears. Marketers receive booking confirmation details. The path that produced the booking remains invisible. Properties that have built the technical foundations described in Chapter 6, structured data, rendering accessibility, machine-readable content, are already closer to WebMCP readiness than properties still relying on JavaScript-heavy interfaces designed for human navigation.

This changes what is at stake. Right now, you compete for visibility in conversational recommendations. Travelers still make final booking decisions. When AI engines evolve to autonomous booking, the AI makes the decision itself. Today, the AI suggests. The trajectory points toward a future where the AI buys. If you are not in the suggestion set, you will not be in the transaction set when that shift arrives.

The Agent That Does Not Wait

Everything in this book assumes the traveler initiates discovery. A person asks a question. An AI retrieves information. Your property either appears or it does not.

That assumption may not hold.

A new category of AI tooling is emerging. Open-source platforms like OpenClaw allow users to run self-hosted AI agents on their own hardware, connected to the chat applications they already use. OpenClaw accumulated over 100,000 GitHub stars within weeks of its launch, signaling substantial developer demand for autonomous agents operating outside corporate AI platforms. These agents monitor, compare, and act on behalf of the user continuously, without waiting for a prompt. OpenAI acquired OpenClaw in early 2026, signaling that this capability will likely move from open-source experiment to mainstream product before the end of 2026. The technology is early. Adoption patterns beyond the developer community remain unclear.

What matters is what it signals. OpenAI launched apps inside ChatGPT built on the Model Context Protocol as an open standard, with Booking.com and Expedia among the initial travel integrations. Google announced its Universal Commerce Protocol alongside retail industry partners. The connectors are standardizing. The trajectory points toward a world where AI agents do not answer questions about hotels. They shop for hotels, autonomously, on schedules the traveler sets once and never revisits.

Three things change for hotels if that world arrives. Continuous automated rate comparison puts new pressure on fencing strategies and cancellation policies. The booking interface shifts from your website to the agent's messaging window, making structured data and API accessibility more important than visual design. Trust signals (accurate policies, consistent rates, clean data across platforms) replace advertising signals in the agent context. A human browsing ChatGPT sees sponsored placements alongside organic answers. An autonomous agent operating programmatically does not browse a visual interface. It evaluates information quality through API calls and structured data retrieval, bypassing the ad layer entirely.

None of this replaces the work described in this book. It amplifies the urgency behind it. An autonomous agent still needs to find your property, parse your data, and compare your offer against competitors. The technical foundations, citation networks, and structured data strategies throughout these pages provide the information architecture these emerging tools require. You are not preparing for one transformation. You are building resilience for continuous platform evolution.

What to Watch

Five developments will signal how quickly this transformation advances. Monitor them quarterly.

The first is AI platform booking integration. When ChatGPT, Gemini, or Perplexity allow users to complete reservations without leaving the conversation, the visibility infrastructure you have built becomes transactional infrastructure. Watch for expanded partnerships between AI platforms and booking engines. The Booking.com and Expedia integrations with ChatGPT were early signals. By January 2026, Accor became one of the first major hotel groups to launch a native app inside ChatGPT, allowing travelers to search properties, view loyalty-member rates, and access room details directly within the conversation before redirecting to the brand's own booking platform. That distinction matters. OTA integrations place intermediaries inside the AI layer. A hotel company building its own ChatGPT presence controls the brand experience and the loyalty relationship from the first interaction.

Not every hotel group can build a native AI platform app. A new category of technology has emerged to address that gap.

Several startups now offer MCP-based aggregation services that ingest a hotel's availability, rates, and inventory data and deliver it to AI platforms through a single structured connection. The model mirrors what connectivity providers did for online distribution a decade ago: aggregate supply so that individual properties do not need separate integrations with every new channel. Properties connected through these aggregators can surface direct booking links inside AI conversations without building custom apps or maintaining platform-specific partnerships. The category is new. No vendor has published verified performance data at scale. Evaluate these services the same way Chapter 9 recommends evaluating any AI visibility partner: ask for measured results, not marketing claims. The structural development worth watching is not any single provider. It is whether MCP-based distribution becomes a standard layer in hotel technology stacks, the way channel managers became standard a generation ago.

The second is Google AI Overview expansion into commercial verticals. Conductor's analysis found AI Overviews triggering on over 25% of Google searches, with informational queries appearing at significantly higher rates. When that percentage climbs substantially in travel-specific queries and those overviews include direct booking actions, the zero-click transformation accelerates. Properties without strong structured data and citation authority will lose the last remaining click-through pathways.

The third is autonomous agent adoption rates. The OpenClaw model represents one implementation. When major platforms ship always-on agent capabilities to mainstream users, the window between "recommendation" and "booking" collapses. Properties invisible to current AI recommendations will be excluded from autonomous purchasing entirely.

The fourth is AI platform paid placement. OpenAI launched ads inside ChatGPT in February 2026, serving sponsored content matched to conversation topics for users on Free and Go tiers. Google monetizes AI Overviews through its existing ad infrastructure. Perplexity launched sponsored follow-up questions and pulled back. The trajectory is clear even where the timeline is not. Chapter 2 describes a short paid test as a diagnostic tool, a way to confirm whether travelers in your market research hotels inside these platforms. That diagnostic value is real. Watch for what follows. As targeting matures and ad formats evolve beyond sponsored text, paid AI placement will grow from a measurement window into a channel requiring its own budget line and performance benchmarks. Properties will face allocation decisions between paid and organic AI visibility the same way they learned to balance Google Ads against SEO a decade ago. The properties that built organic authority first will spend less and convert more. The ones that skipped the foundation work will pay the difference.

The fifth is personalization depth. Chapter 4 documents the early stage of this shift. Google extends account-based personalization to AI responses. ChatGPT's memory features retain user preferences across sessions. Apple routes queries through on-device personal data before generating responses. Each platform implements personalization differently, using different data sources, different weighting, and different privacy boundaries. As personalization matures, two travelers asking the same question will receive increasingly different recommendations based on behavioral history the property cannot see or influence. The strategic response remains what Chapter 4 prescribes: build rich, segmented content addressing distinct traveler profiles so that personalization algorithms have specific material to match against. Properties maintaining generic, undifferentiated content will be systematically deprioritized as personalization deepens, regardless of their technical foundations or citation authority.

The Living Framework

This book is static. The transformation is not. Implementation outcomes, roadmap refinements, and platform evolution updates will be documented at www.vivanderadvisors.com/AI-Visibility. If you implement these frameworks, share your data. Your experience becomes the evidence base that informs the next evolution of these strategies. The industry learns from implementation, not theory.

One scope limitation deserves acknowledgment. The data, examples, and platform behaviors documented here reflect primarily English-language markets with a U.S. and European focus. The technical frameworks apply universally. Content strategies and citation networks operate differently in non-English markets where AI platform availability, source authority hierarchies, and traveler discovery patterns vary. Properties in multilingual environments should treat the strategic principles as transferable and the tactical details as requiring local adaptation. Practitioners implementing these frameworks in non-English markets have particularly valuable data to contribute.

The conclusion asked you to decide. This epilogue asks you to look further. The frameworks you build today serve the current discovery landscape. They also serve the transactional landscape forming behind it. The autonomous agents arriving next year will evaluate the same structured data, the same citation networks, and the same content specificity that determines your visibility today. Every month of accumulated authority makes your property harder to displace when the rules change again.

The window to establish early-mover advantages remains open. It will not remain open indefinitely.

APPENDIX

The following appendices are for execution. I have designed these resources to be adapted, copied, and pasted directly into your workflows.

- **Appendix A:** The exact scripts to use when your owner asks, 'Why are we spending money on this?'
- **Appendix B:** The raw Schema code your developers need.
- **Appendix C:** The Visibility Score Testing Protocol and Prompt Library for your monthly measurement.
- **Appendix D:** Frameworks to analyze your competitors.
- **Appendix E:** Checklists to keep the system running.
- **Appendix F:** The glossary of terms you need to know.
- **Appendix G:** A 15-minute diagnostic to find your starting line.

Treat these pages as working documents. Mark them up. Share them with your team. Make them yours.

APPENDIX A

ADDRESSING SKEPTICISM AND COMMON OBJECTIONS

This appendix consolidates responses to resistance you will encounter when presenting AI visibility initiatives. Chapter 1 documents the transformation. Chapter 2 explains why traditional analytics cannot detect AI-mediated discovery. Chapter 9 provides roadmap frameworks matching different urgency levels. This appendix gives you specific language for the conversations that follow when leadership questions investment.

Strategic Objections

"This feels like another SEO trend that will pass."

SEO trends come and go because they involve tactics within a stable system. This is not a tactic. The system itself changed. Travelers now receive answers without clicking any link. Your ranking became irrelevant the moment the AI started answering the question directly.

Two differences separate this transformation from previous SEO shifts. First, traveler behavior already changed. Pew Research Center found that 65% of U.S. adults regularly encounter AI-generated summaries in search results, and question-based queries trigger those summaries 60% of the time (Chapter 1). Hotel research queries follow exactly these question-based patterns. That behavior persists. It did not retreat after the novelty faded. Second, this transformation affects discovery itself, not a single marketing channel. When travelers change how they find hotels, properties must adapt or accept exclusion.

"This is all SEO with a new name. Our SEO team already handles this."

The core tactics do share DNA with traditional SEO. Structured data, clean content architecture, authoritative backlinks, answering questions clearly. Practitioners who have built strong SEO programs will recognize most of the building blocks. Google themselves said that good SEO produces good GEO results.

The recognition is accurate. The conclusion drawn from it is not. Chapter 5 explains why this framing fails. The core distinction: ranking selects pages from a list. Retrieval selects fragments of meaning from across the web, synthesizes them, and presents a single constructed answer. Your property can hold position one on Google while producing weak results when an AI system evaluates that same content for recommendation worthiness. A ranking metric will never reveal a retrieval failure.

The practical test: ask your SEO team whether they monitor your Visibility Score across ChatGPT, Gemini, Perplexity, and Claude. Ask whether they track the mention-to-recommendation progression. Ask whether they can tell you what ChatGPT says about your property when a traveler asks for recommendations in your market. If the answer to any of those questions is no, your SEO team is not covering this.

"We cannot afford to invest without proven ROI."

Reframe the question. Can you afford competitive vulnerability from non-investment? Competitors building citation networks now create advantages you cannot economically match later. The question shifts from "What ROI will this generate?" to "Can we accept invisibility while waiting for perfect evidence that arrives after competitors claim advantages?"

AI visibility operates as infrastructure, not as a campaign with attributable returns. Chapter 2 addresses this investment framework in detail. The Budget Objections section later in this appendix provides specific language for the executive ROI conversation, including competitive positioning frameworks and budget reallocation strategies.

"Our traditional channels still work fine."

Zero-click rates reached elevated levels and stayed there through Q4 2025. Position-one rankings lost 34.5% of clicks when AI Overviews appeared. Traditional channels degrade as AI adoption persists, whether you acknowledge it or not.

The strategic question: Do you wait for channel collapse before building alternatives, or do you diversify while traditional channels still deliver results?

"Our SEO team says our rankings are stable. Our dashboards show healthy traffic."

They may be right about the rankings. Chapter 1 explains why that misses the point. The Alligator Mouth Effect described in Chapter 1 reveals the pattern: open Google Search Console and compare impressions to clicks over the past 18 months. When those lines diverge, each impression generates less traffic than it did a year ago. AI Overviews answer the question your listing used to answer. The traveler reads the AI-generated summary and never clicks through. Your impression counted. Your click did not. A dashboard showing stable rankings masks structural erosion underneath.

"The data seems contradictory. Google still dominates, yet you claim AI is transforming discovery?"

Google maintained 95% desktop search share through Q3 2025. AI tools reached approximately 1.3% of desktop activity by Q4. Both statements are true because they measure different things. Traditional search remains the dominant interface. AI increasingly mediates what happens within that interface. Datos documented 27% of U.S. searches ending without clicks. Users search on Google, receive AI-generated answers, and never click through to your site. The search happened. The click did not. Your analytics show nothing.

This is the transformation: not platform replacement, but discovery pathway disruption within existing platforms. Semrush research confirms the pattern. Users who adopted ChatGPT increased their weekly Google sessions rather than decreasing them. AI expanded total research activity. The search behavior changed. The search volume did not collapse.

"AI platforms represent small traffic percentages. Why invest now?"

Citation networks take quarters to build through relationship development that compression cannot accelerate. Technical foundations require iterative refinement over months. Organizational capabilities develop through extended practice.

The Datos reports document the growth trajectory. AI tools' share of desktop events tripled from 0.24% to 0.72% by Q3 2025 and reached 1.3% by Q4, with the growth rate normalizing rather than continuing its vertical climb. E-commerce followed identical curves. In 1999, online booking represented a small percentage. The hotels that waited for it to become a large percentage now pay 25% commissions to Expedia. Small percentages during normalization phases precede structural entrenchment. Properties waiting for "significant" percentages miss the compounding advantage period when citation networks and algorithmic positioning establish themselves.

McKinsey found that only 16% of brands track AI search performance today. That measurement gap creates a first-mover advantage for properties that establish testing capability now.

"Small properties cannot compete against major brands."

Chapter 7 documents market tier realities. Tier 1 markets require niche focus for independents. Tier 2 markets enable competitive parity. Tier 3 markets offer leadership opportunities through first-mover advantages.

Focus the budget on the highest-impact foundations: technical excellence, citation consistency, and core content development. Extend timelines if needed. The 12-month roadmap becomes an 18- to 24-month execution. Prioritize ChatGPT and Gemini first, adding other platforms as budget allows.

"We are a branded or franchised property. Corporate controls our website and schema. What can we actually do?"

The technical foundations in Chapter 6 require corporate cooperation for branded properties. You cannot implement schema markup or modify server-side rendering independently. What you control: the content that feeds AI systems through local channels. Your Google Business Profile descriptions. Your responses to reviews. Your local media relationships and citation presence. Your property-specific FAQ content that corporate templates omit.

Focus resources on citation authority (Chapter 7) and content differentiation. Build the off-site presence that AI systems reference independently of your corporate website. Escalate schema and technical requirements to your brand's digital team with the competitive data from your Visibility Score testing. When you show corporate that competitor properties score 30 points higher, the conversation changes.

The leverage exists. Wyndham's 2026 Hotel Owner Trends Report found that 89% of hotel owners view brand partnership as beneficial for AI implementation, with 34% calling it essential. Owners expect their brands to lead on this. Use that expectation. Frame your request not as a complaint about corporate limitations, but as a specific ask aligned with what ownership groups already want from their brand partners.

"Will improving our OTA listings to boost AI citations conflict with our strategy to reduce OTA dependence?"

The tension is real and the answer requires holding two ideas simultaneously. OTA listings function as high-authority citation sources that AI platforms reference heavily. Cloudbeds found that 55% of AI citations came from OTA sites. Improving the accuracy and completeness of your Expedia and Booking.com profiles strengthens the information AI platforms use when deciding whether to recommend you. That optimization serves AI visibility regardless of where the eventual booking happens.

The strategic goal is not to abandon OTAs. It is to ensure that when AI platforms recommend your property, travelers have a path to book directly. Properties with improving Visibility Scores see branded search increases and direct traffic growth alongside their AI visibility gains. The AI recommendation drives awareness. Your direct booking infrastructure captures the conversion. OTA profile optimization feeds the citation network. Direct booking optimization captures the revenue. These are complementary investments, not competing ones.

"Why optimize for visibility at all if AI agents will handle the booking transaction directly?"

The reasoning behind this objection contains its own answer. AI agents that execute transactions are trained on the same data sources that power AI search recommendations. The knowledge graph, the citation networks, the structured data, the co-occurrence patterns documented throughout this book. An agent cannot book a property it does not recognize as a valid entity in its understanding of the market.

Visibility infrastructure is not a workaround for the current discovery model. It is the foundation for every model that follows. If the AI does not know your property exists today, the autonomous agent will not consider your property bookable tomorrow. The citation authority, bridge entity connections, and schema markup you build now become the admission criteria for transactional eligibility when agents begin executing purchases. Properties that wait for autonomous agents before building visibility will start from zero while competitors carry two years of accumulated algorithmic positioning.

"What happens when every property starts doing this? Will the advantage disappear?"

Technical foundations will become baseline requirements rather than competitive advantages. Schema markup and citation consistency will be expected, not differentiating. That is exactly what happened with mobile optimization and direct booking technology. Every property eventually adopted them. The properties that adopted early captured years of incremental revenue that late movers never recovered.

The advantage shifts permanently to content depth, citation authority, and the mention-to-recommendation progression. Those assets resist replication because they require time, institutional knowledge, and sustained organizational commitment. A competitor can implement schema in a week. A competitor cannot replicate two years of citation network development. A competitor cannot fabricate the institutional knowledge that produces the kind of specific, operationally rich content AI systems reward with recommendations rather than mentions.

The Conclusion addresses this competitive timing dynamic in detail. The core principle: most properties have not started, and the window will not remain open indefinitely

Measurement Objections

"How do we justify budget for a channel that lacks precise attribution and changes constantly?"

This question combines two fears. The first: that AI visibility measurement is too imprecise to govern spending. The second: that platform instability makes any measurement framework obsolete before it delivers value. Both fears are reasonable. Neither eliminates the need for disciplined measurement.

The Visibility Score framework (Chapter 8) acknowledges what we do not know while providing structure where none existed. Monthly testing follows documented protocols that anyone can replicate. Competitive benchmarking provides verifiable comparative data. Component-level analysis enables tactical decisions even without proven correlation to bookings. Imprecise measurement governed by consistent methodology outperforms no measurement governed by intuition.

Platforms will change algorithms. The measurement approach anticipates this through monthly trend tracking that captures shifts within weeks. The five-component framework measures fundamental dimensions that transcend specific platform implementations. Citation frequency matters regardless of how platforms determine mentions. Platform diversity matters regardless of which specific platforms dominate. Information accuracy matters regardless of how platforms source data. The specific component weights may require adjustment as the industry learns which components correlate with business outcomes. The methodology survives because it measures durable properties of visibility rather than platform-specific signals.

The parallel to traditional channel measurement is closer than most executives realize. SEO attribution has never been precise. Paid media attribution models disagree with each other by 15% to 30% depending on methodology. Brand marketing budgets operate on directional evidence. AI visibility measurement is younger and less validated. It is not categorically different from the attribution uncertainty that every other digital channel has always carried.

"No platform gives us data about AI visibility. We are measuring blindly."

That was accurate through January 2026. It is no longer fully true. Microsoft's Bing Webmaster Tools now includes an AI Performance dashboard reporting citation activity across Copilot, Bing AI summaries, and partner integrations. The dashboard shows total citations, cited pages, grounding queries, and citation trends over time.

This matters because Bing provides the search infrastructure powering ChatGPT. Citation data from Bing Webmaster Tools reflects activity across the Microsoft and OpenAI ecosystem, not Bing alone.

The dashboard does not solve every measurement problem. It covers one ecosystem. It reports aggregate citation counts, not individual traveler behavior. It cannot tell you whether a citation led to a booking. Those limitations remain real.

What it does provide: confirmation that your content participates in AI-generated answers, identification of which pages get cited most frequently, and visibility into the grounding queries that trigger retrieval of your content. Combined with the ChatGPT ad diagnostic described in Chapter 2 and the Visibility Score framework in Chapter 8, you now have multiple independent measurement signals where 12 months ago you had none. Third-party AI visibility platforms (Chapter 8) add another layer, though their methodologies measure simulated responses rather than actual platform activity.

The trajectory matters more than any single tool. Microsoft released AI citation data. Google will face pressure to extend Search Console reporting to AI Overviews and Gemini. The measurement gap this book describes continues to narrow. Properties that establish measurement discipline now will integrate these new data sources into existing frameworks. Properties that waited for platform data before acting lost the months between this announcement and whenever they decide to start.

"Our competitors invest heavily in traditional channels that still generate measurable bookings. Why divert resources to channels we cannot measure precisely?"

Traditional channels generating measurable results today deliver progressively fewer results tomorrow. This pattern appears consistent across every platform transformation. Diversification reduces risk even when individual channel ROI remains uncertain. Properties investing exclusively in traditional channels face concentrated vulnerability. Properties building a multi-channel presence create strategic resilience.

Platform Optimization Objections

"We perform well on Gemini yet poorly on ChatGPT. Should we invest in improving ChatGPT when Gemini already delivers results?"

Platform concentration creates strategic risk. Over-dependence on a single platform leaves you vulnerable to algorithm changes, competitive displacement, and shifts in market share.

ChatGPT retains the largest share of AI referral traffic. For hospitality specifically, Gemini carries outsized strategic weight because of its direct integration with Google Maps, Hotels, and AI Overviews. Properties performing well on Gemini benefit across every Google surface where travelers research. Optimizing for both platforms addresses the two largest sources of AI-mediated discovery. Similarweb data from June 2025 showed ChatGPT accounted for more than 80% of AI referrals to top websites. By Q4 2025, ChatGPT's overall usage share stabilized around 33%, but its referral dominance persisted.

Test whether Gemini-specific tactics transfer to ChatGPT. Sometimes optimizations that benefit one platform also improve others. Comprehensive FAQ content developed for Gemini may strengthen ChatGPT visibility by improving content depth and serving both platforms.

"Does strong performance on one AI platform transfer to the others?"

Each AI platform operates as an independent ecosystem with its own retrieval logic, its own data sources, and its own ranking signals. ChatGPT, Gemini, Perplexity, and Claude do not share citation indexes, do not synchronize quality assessments, and do not coordinate how they evaluate properties. Performance on one platform tells you nothing about performance on another.

The solution is not to optimize for each platform individually. The solution is to build an entity identity strong enough that all platforms recognize it independently. Accurate schema markup, consistent citation data across authoritative sources, and comprehensive structured content serve every platform simultaneously because they address the foundational requirements all AI systems share. Platform-specific tactics address the 20% of optimization that varies between systems. Entity identity addresses the 80% that remains constant across all of them.

"This feels overwhelming. How can independent hotels possibly optimize for four different platforms when we barely manage Google Business Profile?"

Start with one platform rather than attempting to optimize all four simultaneously. Build technical foundations first (Chapter 6). These simultaneously benefit all platforms. Server-side rendering helps all AI platforms. Schema markup serves multiple platforms. Information accuracy matters everywhere. Chapters 9 and 10 present resource-allocation frameworks scaled by property size.

"The platforms keep changing. How do we know optimization efforts today remain effective when platforms release new models or change algorithms?"

Eighty percent of optimization value comes from foundational work that survives algorithm changes. Accurate information, comprehensive content, strong citation networks, and technical excellence provide value regardless of platform evolution. Twenty percent comes from platform-specific tactics that may become obsolete. Accept that some tactical work will become outdated. That is the cost of participating in dynamic channels. Monthly measurement (Chapter 8) enables detection of platform changes before they erode your positioning.

"We already have good reviews on Google and TripAdvisor. Why worry about citations or media coverage?"

Review volume and quality matter significantly for AI visibility. They represent only one component of the authority signals AI systems evaluate. OTA sites account for 55% of AI citations (Cloudbeds), with twenty websites representing approximately 70% of all travel-related AI citations. Not a single hotel website ranked among the top ten most-cited sources.

AI models cross-reference information across multiple sources to establish trust. Your reviews tell AI platforms what guests think. Your citations tell AI platforms whether authoritative sources consider your property noteworthy. The combination creates the comprehensive authority picture that informs recommendation algorithms.

Testing Protocol Objections

"This testing protocol requires 80 individual tests monthly. How can small properties possibly dedicate resources to this measurement level?"

The core testing protocol takes 6 hours a month. Two hours running tests, one hour verifying, two hours scoring, one hour reporting. Adding schema maintenance and citation monitoring (Chapter 10), the total monthly commitment is approximately 13 hours. Anyone claiming it requires 25 or more hours is overcomplicating the process.

For properties lacking internal resources, reduce testing frequency to quarterly while maintaining baseline monthly attention to critical metrics. Quarterly testing provides sufficient trend data for strategic decisions while reducing the measurement commitment to approximately 6 hours per quarter. Concentrate testing into a single focused week rather than spreading it across the month. Monday through Thursday, execute platform testing. On Friday, verify, analyze, and report.

"Will this measurement become obsolete as AI platforms evolve algorithms?"

The methodology measures what you are to AI systems, not how any single platform's algorithm works. When an algorithm changes, your next monthly test captures the shift. You adjust tactics. You do not rebuild the measurement infrastructure.

Consider the parallel: Google has changed its ranking algorithm thousands of times since 2000. Properties that tracked rankings monthly caught every shift. The tracking methodology never became obsolete. The specific rankings changed. The discipline of measuring them did not. The same principle applies here. Adapt the specific prompt library as platforms evolve and traveler behavior shifts. The measurement principles remain constant while tactical applications adjust.

"How do we know when Visibility Score improvements actually drive booking revenue?"

You cannot attribute booking revenue to Visibility Score improvements with precision traditional analytics enabled. AI discovery operates through complex pathways that resist clean attribution.

Track directional indicators rather than seeking perfect attribution. Monitor branded search volume increases as a proxy for awareness growth. Measure direct traffic improvements. Track booking patterns alongside Visibility Score improvements, even without proving causation. Accept attribution limitations as an inherent characteristic of AI-mediated discovery. Infrastructure investments enable outcomes without directly causing them. Your Visibility Score improvements create conditions for discovery. The booking decisions follow complex pathways involving multiple touchpoints you cannot track.

"Does tracking AI visibility raise privacy compliance issues under GDPR or CCPA?"

AI visibility optimization and measurement do not involve tracking individual users. The Visibility Score framework measures how AI platforms represent your property in response to standardized test queries. You are testing the AI's knowledge of your brand, not monitoring traveler behavior. The testing protocol uses fresh browser sessions with no logged-in accounts, no cookies, and no personal data.

The optimization work throughout this book focuses on improving public information about your property. Schema markup structures facts you already publish. Citation networks ensure your business details appear accurately across public platforms. Content architecture organizes information you want travelers to find. None of this involves collecting, storing, or processing personal data.

The personalization layer discussed in Chapter 4, where AI platforms incorporate individual behavioral data into recommendations, happens on the platform side, governed by each platform's own privacy framework and user consent mechanisms. Your optimization strategy does not access, influence, or depend on any individual's personal data. You are making your public information more accessible to AI systems. The AI platform decides how to use that information in the context of each traveler's query and privacy settings. Those are separate responsibilities governed by separate compliance frameworks.

Budget Objections

"Our executive team demands measurable ROI for all marketing investments. How do we justify AI visibility spending without booking attribution?"

Reframe the conversation from ROI calculation to strategic necessity. AI discovery transformation happened whether hotels invest or not. Travelers use AI platforms for research regardless of property visibility.

Present the transformation as a participation requirement, not a channel experiment. Your executive team does not ask for precise ROI on the phone system or the property management software. Those are costs of operating. AI visibility is becoming a cost of being discoverable.

Document competitive positioning through baseline Visibility Score testing for your property and three to five direct competitors. Present competitive comparison showing relative positioning. Competitors scoring 15 to 25 points higher pose immediate threats. Competitors scoring 40 or more points higher dominate discovery channels.

"How do we prevent the AI visibility budget from becoming a permanent cost center consuming resources indefinitely?"

Structure the budget as an infrastructure investment transitioning to operational maintenance. Initial implementation requires project-level investment in building foundations, developing content, and establishing citation networks. As paid search effectiveness erodes through AI Overviews pushing organic results down, redirect spending from paid search to AI visibility. As OTA dependence declines through improved organic discovery, adjust the OTA budget allocation.

"Small independent properties with budgets under $15,000 annually cannot afford full AI visibility optimization."

Properties with limited budgets should extend timelines rather than attempting full optimization on insufficient resources.

The six-month roadmap becomes a 12-month execution. The 12-month leadership path extends to 24 to 36 months. Digital behavior entering normalization means competitive volatility decreases. Datos shows smaller swings, diversified attention, and emerging equilibrium across search, AI, and platform-based discovery. This post-transition landscape favors sustained execution over sudden breakthroughs. Brand advantages compound more slowly in stable markets than during explosive growth phases. Your extended timeline approach works because the market stabilized enough that consistency beats intermittent bursts of activity.

Use external resources strategically for specialized requirements. Hire a developer for the schema implementation sprint. Engage a content writer for FAQ development. Use a citation service for Tier 3 foundation building. External support reduces internal time demands while maintaining quality standards.

Implementation Objections

"These roadmaps seem impossibly ambitious. How can realistic properties execute these timelines without neglecting critical business activities?"

Most properties should start with the six-month comprehensive build. The six-month timeline reduces the intensity from an emergency sprint to a sustainable operational rhythm. The work distributes across quarters, enabling quality execution without team burnout.

Consider phased resource allocation. Month 1 requires intensive work, demanding a temporary resource surge. Bring in a consultant or agency for baseline testing, a technical audit, and competitive analysis. Subsequent months settle into a sustainable rhythm with predictable weekly commitments manageable alongside other responsibilities.

Accept that slower progression may allow competitors to establish advantages during your implementation period. Quality execution beats rushed implementation that fails validation and requires expensive rework.

"How do we adapt roadmaps when facing resource constraints?"

Extend timelines proportionally to available resources. If the roadmap requires 25 hours per week but you can sustain only 15 hours, extend the timeline by 67%. Maintain task sequence: technical foundations before content development, content before citation building.

"Our property faces high competitive urgency but lacks resources for a 90-day sprint. What do we do?"

High urgency without adequate resources creates a genuine strategic dilemma requiring difficult choices.

Option one: Secure additional budget through an emergency request demonstrating competitive threat. Present baseline competitive testing showing the positioning gap. Quantify the disadvantage. Make urgency concrete through data rather than assertion.

Option two: Extend the roadmap to four months while accepting quality compromises. Focus exclusively on the highest-impact activities. Implement basic schema. Create a 30-question FAQ instead of 60. Complete Tier 3 citations. Sacrifice comprehensiveness for speed while maintaining technical validation standards.

Option three: Accept that you cannot respond adequately to high urgency given resource constraints. Focus resources on traditional channels delivering measurable returns while monitoring AI visibility quarterly. Plan a response when budget permits.

None of these options feels satisfying. High urgency with inadequate resources creates genuine constraints requiring explicit trade-offs rather than assuming you can execute premium outcomes on minimal investment.

Organizational Objections

"Small independent properties with 10 to 15 employees cannot build organizational systems. How can realistic properties without corporate infrastructure implement these frameworks?"

Small properties carry a structural disadvantage in organizational capacity. They carry a structural advantage in the thing AI systems value most: specificity.

Large brands produce content at scale. That content is generic by necessity. A Marriott property page describes amenities the same way across hundreds of locations. AI systems trained on that data learn to associate the brand with broad category terms. They do not learn to associate it with the specific, high-detail attributes that answer precise traveler queries.

Your 12-room historic inn with ghost tours, a chef who forages ingredients from the surrounding hills, and a library of first-edition regional novels contains exactly the kind of high-entropy detail that AI systems cannot find anywhere else. That operational uniqueness translates directly into the content specificity that earns recommendations rather than generic mentions. In Tier 2 and Tier 3 markets, independents with strong niche positioning regularly outperform brands with vastly larger citation networks.

The organizational question is real. The answer is not to build corporate infrastructure. The answer is to make the responsibility explicit and the governance lean. The general manager owns AI visibility at 5 to 10 hours weekly for properties under 30 rooms. The marketing manager dedicates 10 to 15 hours per week for properties under 100 rooms. Add it to actual job descriptions with specific deliverables rather than hoping it happens alongside everything else.

Simplify governance to match your scale. Monthly 30-minute check-ins. Quarterly one-hour reviews. Annual half-day planning sessions. One-page checklists. A shared Google Docs folder. Simple templates from Appendix E. Elaborate operational reviews waste time that small teams do not have.

External resources fill capability gaps without permanent overhead. Technical contractors for schema implementation. Freelance content strategists for differentiation projects. PR consultants when pursuing Tier 2 placements. The investment profile for a small property is not less work. It is different work, focused on depth in your niche rather than breadth across categories.

"Our team changes constantly. How do we sustain AI visibility capability when people executing it keep leaving?"

Documentation quality determines turnover resilience. Comprehensive documentation enables effective execution without prior knowledge. When the marketing manager leaves, the new manager reviews the documented monthly testing protocol and executes testing correctly within two weeks.

Essential process documentation includes the monthly Visibility Score protocol (with complete prompt library, testing environment specs, scoring criteria, and troubleshooting guide), the schema maintenance workflow, content update standards, citation monitoring procedures, and review response protocols.

Cross-training creates redundancy, preventing single points of failure. External partnerships provide continuity during transitions. Build succession plans that explicitly identify internal candidates and document who knows what.

"These governance structures seem like unnecessary bureaucracy. Can we skip governance and focus on execution?"

Monthly operational reviews surface blockers early. Quarterly strategic reviews enable evidence-based strategy adjustments. Annual planning ensures continued leadership support and resource commitment. Governance prevents AI visibility from becoming invisible work that nobody prioritizes. The alternative creates a cycle of enthusiasm, followed by neglect, followed by crisis requiring expensive remediation. Consistent governance proves far less burdensome than repeated rescue efforts.

"We cannot dedicate someone's primary focus to this work. Everyone has multiple responsibilities. How do we make this realistic?"

Small properties combine roles. The marketing manager dedicates 10 to 15 hours weekly to AI visibility coordination alongside other responsibilities. Medium properties justify dedicated coordinator roles at 20 to 30 hours weekly. Only large properties or groups justify full-time AI Visibility Manager positions. Most properties implement AI visibility through combined responsibilities rather than dedicated positions. The key: making the responsibility explicit, allocating specific hours weekly, and establishing clear accountability for outcomes. Without explicit allocation, AI visibility becomes the thing that matters until something else demands attention.

Evidence and Validation Objections

"You admit to lacking comprehensive validation. Why should we invest based on frameworks you acknowledge require refinement?"

The Prologue addresses this directly. I cannot promise specific ROI from implementing these frameworks. I cannot prove these exact approaches will work for your property because we do not yet have enough completed implementations to make those claims.

Properties implementing these frameworks should use them to measure directionally, tracking whether optimization efforts lead to improvements in visibility. Track component correlations with business metrics to determine which dimensions matter. Share findings so the industry can refine frameworks based on actual implementations. Expect to adjust weights and methodology based on what correlates with outcomes at your property.

"You extrapolate timelines from mobile and social media transformations. AI might develop faster or slower. How reliable are these timeline projections?"

The timelines extrapolate from mobile optimization, social media adoption, and direct booking acceleration patterns. AI visibility may follow a similar progression or may differ as the industry learns more efficient approaches.

The underlying principle holds regardless of specific timing: transformation requires sustained effort. Citation networks need relationship development. Technical foundations require iterative refinement. Organizational capabilities develop through extended practice. Use these timelines as planning frameworks, adjusting expectations quarterly based on what you observe in your actual implementation.

"This entire book feels like speculation dressed as a framework. How can we trust recommendations built on pattern recognition rather than AI-specific validation?"

I am not offering proven certainty. I am offering structured frameworks for navigating uncertainty.

The Visibility Score gives you measurement capability where none existed. The maturity levels help you assess progress despite attribution gaps. The roadmaps provide timeline guidance based on how hotels execute complex initiatives.

You act on incomplete evidence because waiting for complete evidence means acting after competitive positioning has been lost. Early adopters take that calculated risk across every platform transformation. Some frameworks in this book will prove accurate. Some will require significant revision.

"Why should we become early implementers of unproven frameworks while you learn what actually works?"

Fair question deserving a direct answer. You should not implement these frameworks to help me validate them. You should implement them because the transformation already happened, and you need structured approaches for a response.

The transformation is real. The evidence is clear from documented traffic collapse, measured platform adoption, and observed shifts in user behavior. What remains uncertain: which specific optimization tactics deliver which specific outcomes under which conditions. That uncertainty does not eliminate the need for a response. It changes what response looks like.

Properties establishing competitive advantages through 2026 and 2027 will not have perfect evidence. They will act despite uncertainty, measure progress despite attribution gaps, and sustain commitment despite organizational challenges.

"What stops AI from hallucinating fake rates or offers for our hotel?"

Nothing stops it completely. AI platforms can and do generate inaccurate pricing, fabricated package details, and incorrect policy information. A revenue manager's worst scenario, ChatGPT quoting a $500 room at $50, is not hypothetical. It happens when the AI lacks structured, authoritative pricing data and fills the gap with inference.

This risk is the strongest argument for the technical foundations in Chapter 6, not an argument against them. AI hallucination about your property increases in direct proportion to the gap between what the AI needs to know and what you have made available in structured, machine-readable formats.

Schema markup with explicit pricing fields, validity dates, and room-type specifications gives the AI verifiable data to cite. When your Product schema states "King Suite, $289 to $349 per night, valid through Q2 2026," the AI has a structured fact to reference. When your schema contains nothing about pricing, the AI estimates based on whatever fragments it finds across OTA listings, outdated blog posts, and cached web pages that may reflect rates from two years ago. The estimate may be catastrophically wrong.

The Information Accuracy component of the Visibility Score measures this directly. Properties scoring below 70% on accuracy are actively exposed to hallucination risk. The AI is mentioning them with wrong details, which is worse than not being mentioned at all. A traveler who arrives expecting the rate ChatGPT quoted and discovers the actual price is 40% higher does not become a loyal guest. That traveler becomes a negative review.

Chapter 6 details the schema fields that prevent this. The monthly testing protocol catches inaccuracies before they compound. The maintenance cadence in Chapter 10 ensures pricing data stays current as rates change seasonally. The technical work in this book is not only about earning recommendations. It is about ensuring the recommendations the AI generates are accurate enough to convert into bookings rather than complaints.

"Can we use AI to write the content this book recommends?"

Yes, with constraints. Google's Search Quality Rater Guidelines state that if all or almost all of a page's main content is AI-generated and little to no originality is added, raters should apply the lowest rating. Google evaluates content by merit, not origin. AI content demonstrating expertise and a unique perspective meets the quality bar. AI content repeating widely available information gets downranked.

The practical boundary: AI tools can draft structured content efficiently. FAQ answers, schema descriptions, meta tags. The institutional knowledge that earns recommendations rather than mentions cannot be generated by a model that has never operated your property. A description of your pet policy that includes the operational reasoning behind your 50-pound limit, the ground-floor room requirement you implemented after carpet damage incidents, and the dog-washing station you added based on guest feedback contains details no AI can fabricate. That specificity is what separates properties AI platforms mention from properties they recommend.

Use AI for structure and drafting. Supply the institutional knowledge yourself. Review every output against the AI Context File described in Appendix E before publishing. Chapter 6 provides the quality framework for evaluating whether AI-assisted content meets the standard these platforms require.

APPENDIX B
SCHEMA IMPLEMENTATION GUIDE

This appendix provides the schema implementation specifications your development team needs to execute the technical foundations described in Chapter 6. Complete code templates are available for download at www.vivanderadvisors.com/AI-Visibility.

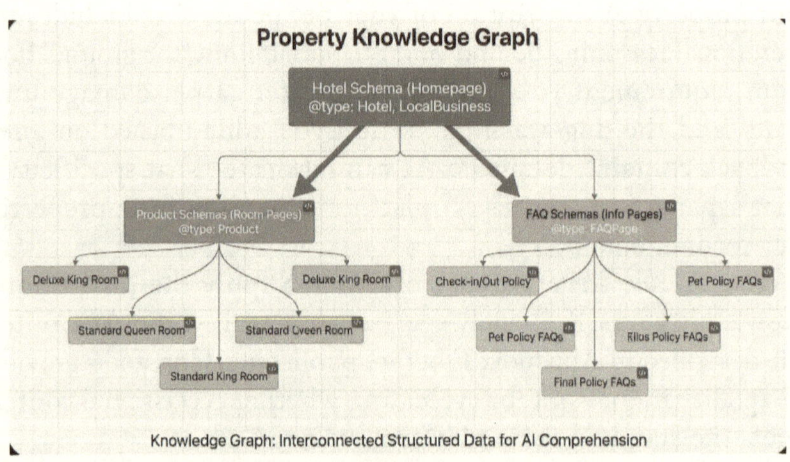

Knowledge Graph: Interconnected Structured Data for AI Comprehension

Implementation Format

All schema uses JSON-LD format placed in script tags within page HTML. Validate every implementation using Google Rich Results Test and Schema.org Validator before deploying to production. Zero errors required on both validators.

Maintain identical values for recurring fields across all implementations. If your hotel name appears in the core Hotel schema, the Room Product schema, and the FAQ schema, the name must match exactly in all three. Inconsistency confuses AI engines attempting entity recognition.

Six Required Schema Types

1. Core Hotel Schema (deploy on homepage)

Establishes your property's entity identity and essential operational information. This is the foundation every other schema references. Required fields include: property name and alternate names, physical address with geo-coordinates, contact information, check-in and check-out times, number of rooms, pet policy, smoking policy, star rating, aggregate review rating, payment methods, languages spoken, price range indicator, and primary amenity features with operating hours.

The @id property creates a unique identifier that connects all your schema objects into a single entity. Use the format https://yourhotel.com/#hotel for the hotel entity, https://yourhotel.com/#address for the address, and https://yourhotel.com/#room-deluxe-king (or similar) for individual room types. Reference these identifiers consistently across all schema objects on your site. The dual type declaration (Hotel and LocalBusiness) maximizes compatibility across AI systems. Without this schema, AI platforms treat every page on your site as disconnected information rather than details about one recognizable property.

2. Room Product Schema (deploy on individual room type pages)

Enables AI systems to understand your specific accommodations, capacities, and pricing. Deploy a separate Product schema for each distinct room type. Schema.org defines HotelRoom as the native type for individual rooms. The Product overlay adds the pricing fields (priceValidUntil, price, priceCurrency) that prevent the hallucination problem. Implement both types together by declaring the room as both HotelRoom and Product, or use Product alone if your development team prefers simplicity. Either approach validates correctly. Required fields include: room name and description, bed type, room size in square feet, maximum occupancy, view type, images, nightly rate with currency, rate validity date, and availability status.

This is the schema that prevents the hallucination problem described in Appendix A. When your Product schema states "Deluxe King Room, $279 per night, valid through Q2 2026," the AI has a structured fact to cite. When it contains nothing, the AI estimates from whatever fragments it finds across OTA listings and cached pages. Update the priceValidUntil field quarterly to prevent stale pricing data.

3. FAQ Schema (deploy on FAQ page or pages containing Q&A pairs)

Maps questions to answers in a format AI platforms extract directly. Chapter 6 emphasizes answer-first formatting: lead with the specific answer, then provide supporting detail. Each entry requires a Question type with a name property and an Answer type with a text property.

FAQ content requirements scale with your maturity level. At every level, the structural requirements matter as much as the count. Questions without FAQPage schema lose their structural signal. Answers without answer-first formatting reduce extraction accuracy. Content hidden inside JavaScript accordions or click-to-expand elements is invisible to AI crawlers regardless of how many questions it contains. Verify that your FAQ content passes all three conditions (accessible in Reader Mode, marked up with FAQPage schema, formatted answer-first) before focusing on expanding the number of questions.

Properties at Reactive maturity need 20 to 30 question-answer pairs covering essential operational information: check-in and check-out times, pet policies with fees, parking details, cancellation terms, and core amenity hours. These questions establish baseline retrieval value by giving AI platforms verified facts for the highest-frequency traveler queries. Properties at Structured maturity should maintain 30 to 60 questions expanding into broader traveler research categories: reservations, policies, amenities, location, and accessibility. At this level, the FAQ page becomes a retrieval asset that satisfies multiple sub-queries from a single page load during Query Fan-Out. Properties pursuing Integrated or Optimized status benefit from 60 or more questions covering edge cases and niche scenarios competitors overlook: accessibility configurations, family-specific needs, business traveler requirements, and seasonal considerations.

Start where you can execute quality content with correct structure. Expand as capabilities develop. Thirty properly structured questions outperform sixty unstructured ones.

Structure every answer with specific, quantified information. Not "Early check-in is available" but "Early check-in available starting 12:00 PM, subject to availability. Guaranteed early check-in at 12:00 PM available for $25 surcharge paid at check-in." The specificity is what earns AI recommendations over competitors providing vague answers.

4. Location Features Schema (extend core Hotel schema)

Detailed amenity specifications beyond the basic amenity list in the core schema. Document operating hours for every time-dependent amenity: fitness center, pool, restaurant, business center, spa. Include seasonal restrictions, capacity limits, age restrictions, and additional fees. This schema enables AI systems to answer the precise facility questions travelers ask during research.

5. Review Aggregate Schema (include in core Hotel schema or deploy on reviews page)

Provides AI systems with guest satisfaction data including average rating, total review count, and rating scale. Automate updates through your CMS or review management plugin to prevent staleness. Manual aggregation across platforms works for properties without automated solutions.

6. Event Schema (deploy on event or meetings pages)

Properties hosting events, conferences, weddings, or meetings should implement Event schema for each recurring or scheduled offering. Required fields include: event name, start and end dates, location reference linking to your core Hotel schema, description, ticket or pricing information, and organizer details. This schema enables AI systems to recommend your property when travelers search for event venues or conference hotels in your market. Properties without event or meeting space can skip this schema type.

Validation Checklist

After your developer implements the schema:

Test each page in Google Rich Results Test. Achieve zero errors before deployment. Address all warnings.

Test in Schema.org Validator. This tool catches edge cases the Google validator misses. Achieve zero errors.

Manually inspect page source to verify JSON-LD formatting. A single syntax error, whether a missing comma, an unclosed bracket, or an incorrect quote type, breaks the entire schema block. Test in multiple browsers on both mobile and desktop. Verify schema renders identically.

Document the implementation date. Schedule quarterly validation. Many properties implement schema correctly, then break it with subsequent website modifications. Regular validation maintains integrity.

Chapter 6 provides complete technical optimization guidance. Chapter 9 roadmaps specify the timing of schema implementation within your chosen timeline. Chapter 10 includes schema maintenance procedures to prevent decay.

Chapter 6 also covers the optional llms.txt file, a lightweight Markdown document placed in your website root that guides AI crawlers toward priority content. This appendix focuses on the six required schema types. Properties that have completed all six schema implementations can consider llms.txt as incremental experimentation with low implementation cost.

APPENDIX C
VISIBILITY SCORE TESTING PROTOCOL

This appendix provides the operational procedures for executing the Visibility Score framework detailed in Chapter 8. The scoring formulas, component weights, and calculation methodology appear in Chapter 8. This appendix covers what Chapter 8 does not: testing environment setup, an expanded prompt library for customization, diagnostic procedures for platform-specific gaps, and leading indicator monitoring through server logs. A downloadable testing spreadsheet template is available at www.vivanderadvisors.com/AI-Visibility.

Critical Testing Requirements

Before beginning any tests, establish proper testing conditions.

Use Incognito or Private Browsing Mode. Open a private browsing window to prevent personalization algorithms from skewing results.

Disable AI Memory and Personalization. Turn off memory features in ChatGPT, conversation history in Gemini, and any personalization settings in all platforms.

Set Specific Geographic Parameters. If testing in a large metropolitan area, specify the neighborhood, district, or region in your prompts. "Midtown" rather than "New York City." "Downtown Chicago" rather than "Chicago."

Confirm Rendering Accessibility. Before running monthly visibility tests, verify that your key content pages pass the reader mode test described in Chapter 6. Open each page in your browser's reader mode. If reader mode fails to display your property information, AI crawlers face the same limitation. A page that fails reader mode is invisible to retrieval regardless of how well it scores on content quality. Run this check monthly because site updates, CMS changes, and plugin additions can break rendering accessibility without warning.

Validate Schema Markup. Run your key pages through the Google Rich Results Test and Schema.org Validator monthly. Schema markup can break silently when developers push site updates, when CMS platforms auto-update, or when third-party plugins conflict with existing code. A property whose schema validated three months ago may have zero functioning structured data today. Monthly validation catches technical drift before it degrades your Visibility Score. Chapter 6 details the schema requirements. Appendix B provides the implementation guide.

These precautions ensure your measurements reflect genuine AI visibility rather than personalized results based on your search history or location data.

Proactive Retrieval Testing

The prompt library that follows measures how platforms currently represent your property. This is reactive measurement. You test, you observe, you document. A complementary practice tests your content before publishing to predict whether AI systems will retrieve it.

Retrieval simulation uses local LLM tools or services like LlamaIndex to process your web pages the way an AI retrieval system would. You submit a traveler query. The tool identifies which specific sections of your content a retrieval system would select as relevant chunks. If the tool selects the wrong section, or selects nothing, the AI platform will likely do the same.

This practice is optional for properties at Reactive and Structured maturity levels. It becomes increasingly valuable at Integrated and Optimized levels where content volume is high enough that retrieval precision determines which pages earn inclusion in AI responses and which get passed over.

Generate synthetic query variations to expand your testing beyond the standard prompt library. The Query Fan-Out process described in Chapter 6 means a single traveler prompt generates five to twelve background searches. If you target "family hotels in Austin," simulate the background queries the AI would generate: "hotels with kids clubs Austin," "Austin hotels with connecting rooms," "safe Austin neighborhoods for families with toddlers," "Austin hotels with cribs and highchairs." Test whether your content surfaces for those derivative queries, not only for the primary prompt. Properties whose content answers the primary query but misses the latent intent sub-queries lose recommendations to competitors whose content covers the full query fan-out surface.

The Expanded Prompt Library

Chapter 8 provides the core 20-prompt testing library across four categories. This appendix expands that library to 10 prompts per category and adds a fifth category for multi-criteria compound queries. Select prompts from across all five categories to build your monthly 20-prompt test set. A balanced approach uses 4 prompts each from Categories 1 through 4 and 4 from Category 5. Properties without complex multi-criteria demand can skip Category 5 and maintain the original 5-per-category structure from Chapter 8. Choose prompts most relevant to your property type, location, and target segments. Maintain the same 20 prompts month over month to enable trend comparison. One practical method for building a more informed prompt library uses data you already have. Filter your Google Search Console queries to 10 words or more by navigating to Performance, Search Queries, Add Filter, Query, Custom Regex, and entering the string: ^(?:\S+\s+){9,}\S+ Export those results and analyze them for patterns in how travelers phrase complex, multi-part questions about properties like yours. Queries this long read like prompts because many of them are. Search Console captures some AI Mode activity alongside standard search behavior, and the phrasing of these longer queries reflects how travelers structure conversational questions across both. The patterns you find inform which prompt categories and phrasings are worth adding to your monthly test set. Rotate prompts quarterly if you want to expand coverage while preserving core measurement consistency.

For all categories, replace location placeholders with your actual destination. Use the specific neighborhood or district if you are in a large metropolitan area (e.g., "SoHo" not "New York," "River North" not "Chicago"). Test exact phrases without modification each month.

Category 1: Sample of Broad Discovery Queries

These queries represent initial destination research where travelers explore options without specific requirements.

1. "Best hotels in [your city/region]"
2. "Where to stay in [your city/region]"
3. "Top-rated hotels [your city/region]"
4. "Recommended hotels [your city/region]"
5. "Popular hotels in [your city/region]"
6. "Luxury hotels [your city/region]"
7. "Boutique hotels [your city/region]"
8. "Best places to stay [your city/region]"

9. "Hotels in [your city/region] with good reviews"
10. "What are the nicest hotels in [your city/region]"

Category 2: Sample of Location-Based Queries

These queries emphasize geographic positioning and proximity to landmarks.

1. "Hotels near [major landmark]"
2. "Hotels in [your specific neighborhood]"
3. "Hotels walking distance to [attraction]"
4. "Downtown [your city] hotels"
5. "Hotels close to [convention center/airport/district]"
6. "Best hotels in [neighborhood] area"
7. "Where to stay near [specific venue]"
8. "Hotels with easy access to [transportation hub]"
9. "Hotels in the [geographic descriptor] of [city]"
10. "Centrally located hotels [your city]"

Customize landmarks and neighborhoods matching your actual location. Include the 3 to 5 most important proximity points for your property.

Category 3: Sample of Amenity-Focused Queries

These queries highlight specific facilities or features travelers seek.

1. "Hotels with pools in [your city]"
2. "Hotels with parking [your area]"
3. "Hotels with restaurants [your city]"
4. "Pet-friendly hotels [your city]"
5. "Hotels with fitness centers [your area]"

6. "Hotels with free breakfast [your city]"
7. "Hotels with airport shuttle [your city]"
8. "Hotels with meeting rooms [your area]"
9. "Hotels with rooftop bars [your city]"
10. "Hotels with spa services [your city]"

Select amenities matching your property features. Test the amenities you offer.

Category 4: Sample of Use Case Queries

These queries indicate specific trip purposes or traveler types.

1. "Business hotels in [your city]"
2. "Family-friendly hotels [your area]"
3. "Romantic hotels [your city]"
4. "Hotels for conventions [your city]"
5. "Weekend getaway hotels [your area]"
6. "Extended stay hotels [your city]"
7. "Group travel hotels [your area]"
8. "Wedding hotels [your city]"
9. "Accessible hotels [your city]"
10. "Budget hotels [your area]"

Select use cases matching your target segments.

Category 5: Sample of Multi-Criteria Compound Queries

These queries combine multiple criteria, creating more complex discovery challenges.

1. "Pet-friendly hotels near [landmark] with parking"
2. "Hotels in [neighborhood] with free breakfast and pool"

3. "Business hotels near [convention center] with meeting rooms"
4. "Family hotels in [area] with kitchenettes"
5. "Boutique hotels in [district] with restaurants"
6. "Hotels near [attraction] with accessible rooms"
7. "Extended stay hotels in [area] with full kitchens"
8. "Luxury hotels in [neighborhood] with spa and fitness center"
9. "Pet-friendly hotels in [area] with balconies"
10. "Hotels near [venue] with shuttle service and parking"

Create combinations that reflect common requirement patterns in your market.

Diagnosing Platform-Specific Gaps

The Platform Spread component tells you where you are missing. It does not tell you why. When your property appears consistently on three platforms but remains absent from the fourth, the cause typically falls into one of three categories.

First, technical exclusion. The platform's crawler cannot access your content. Check server logs for that platform's specific bot. If the bot is not visiting, the problem is rendering accessibility or robots.txt configuration, not content quality.

Second, citation network gaps. Each platform draws on different source hierarchies. Gemini draws heavily from Google Business Profile data. ChatGPT references Reddit discussions and review aggregators with notable frequency. Perplexity weights recent editorial content from news and media sources. If you are absent from the sources a specific platform favors, your content quality becomes irrelevant. Check whether your property has active presence on the high-citation domains that platform relies on. Reddit, LinkedIn, YouTube, and major OTA platforms appear consistently among the most-cited domains across AI platforms. Profound's analysis of 238,000 ChatGPT social citations found that citation patterns vary by platform type: Reddit citations point overwhelmingly to individual threads (99 percent), YouTube citations favor channel pages over individual videos (65 percent versus 2.3 percent), and LinkedIn citations prioritize personal profiles over company pages (47 percent versus 21 percent). These patterns may differ on Gemini, Perplexity, and Claude, reinforcing the importance of platform-specific testing rather than assuming uniform citation behavior. Chapter 7's citation tier framework identifies which sources carry the most authority.

Third, content specificity mismatch. Different platforms interpret query intent differently. A query that triggers your property on Gemini may fail on ChatGPT because ChatGPT's background search generates different sub-queries during Query Fan-Out. Test the same prompt on the underperforming platform, then ask follow-up questions probing why your property was excluded. The AI's explanation often reveals which content gaps to address.

Document platform-specific gaps in your monthly template's Notes column. Over two to three months, patterns emerge that point toward the structural cause rather than random variation.

A Note on Information Accuracy Weighting

The base scoring protocol in Chapter 8 weights all six accuracy categories equally. In practice, Policy and Pricing accuracy carry disproportionate business impact. An incorrect phone number creates a minor inconvenience. An incorrect pet policy or a fabricated room rate creates immediate guest frustration, negative reviews, and lost bookings. Properties at Integrated and Optimized maturity levels should consider applying a 1.5x multiplier to Policy and Pricing accuracy scores within the Information Accuracy component to reflect their higher transactional stakes. Properties at Reactive and Structured levels should use the standard equal weighting to keep the protocol simple during early implementation.

Leading Indicators: Passive Detection Through Server Logs

The Visibility Score protocol measures output: what AI platforms say about your property when asked. A complementary measurement tracks input: whether AI platforms are visiting your website at all.

Chapter 2 introduces server log monitoring for AI bot activity. This section provides the operational protocol for integrating passive detection into your monthly measurement cycle.

Filter your server logs monthly for the following user agent strings: ChatGPT-User (OpenAI crawling for real-time browsing or training), PerplexityBot (Perplexity indexing for live answers), Google-Extended (Gemini accessing your content), and OAI-SearchBot (OpenAI's dedicated search crawler). Record crawl frequency for each bot: daily visits, weekly visits, or no visits within the measurement period.

A drop in bot crawl frequency often precedes a drop in your Visibility Score by 30 to 60 days. The bots stop visiting before the AI stops mentioning you. This makes crawl frequency a leading indicator, the earliest warning that your technical infrastructure may be blocking the systems you are trying to reach. A property that scores well on active testing but sees declining bot activity should investigate rendering accessibility, server performance, and robots.txt configuration before the active scores follow the passive signal downward.

Add a "Bot Activity" row to your monthly documentation template. Record the crawl frequency for each platform's bot alongside your Visibility Score components. Over three to six months, correlations between bot activity trends and score trends become visible. These correlations tell you whether your technical foundation is strengthening or degrading independently of your content and citation strategy.

Bing Webmaster Tools now provides a third measurement layer for the Microsoft ecosystem. The AI Performance dashboard reports citation activity across Copilot, Bing AI summaries, and partner integrations. Add a 'Bing AI Citations' row to your monthly documentation template alongside bot activity and Visibility Score components. Chapter 2 describes the dashboard in detail. Over time, correlations between bot crawl frequency, platform-reported citations, and your manual Visibility Scores reveal whether all three signals move together or diverge, indicating either measurement consistency or gaps worth investigating

APPENDIX D
COMPETITIVE INTELLIGENCE TOOLKIT

Chapter 8 introduces competitive benchmarking as the fifth component of the Visibility Score. This appendix provides the operational framework: how to identify the right competitive set, execute quarterly competitor testing, extract actionable intelligence from the results, and translate findings into strategic response. Combine this competitive data with the Share of Search tracking methodology from Chapter 2 for a complete competitive picture.

Defining Your Competitive Set

Accurate competitive analysis requires three tiers of competitor identification. Traditional competitive sets miss properties AI platforms group with yours. AI-recommended competitors may differ in price, location, or property type while competing directly for the same traveler queries.

Primary Competitive Set (3 to 5 properties)

Properties competing for the same guests through traditional channels. Selection criteria: properties within 1 mile, similar room rates (within 20%), similar property type (boutique versus full-service versus extended stay), similar star rating, similar target segment focus.

Secondary Competitive Set (5 to 8 properties)

Alternative options travelers might consider despite differences in one or two characteristics. Selection criteria: properties within 2 to 3 miles, slightly different price positioning, different property types serving similar needs, different sizes offering similar amenities.

AI-Recommended Competitors (identified through testing)

This tier matters most for this book's purpose. Execute baseline Visibility Score testing and document every property AI platforms recommend in response to your test queries. These AI-recommended properties may not appear in traditional competitive sets. They represent actual competition in the AI discovery context.

Track mention frequency across your 80 tests, common queries triggering mentions, platform-specific recommendation patterns, and differentiators AI platforms emphasize. Some of these properties will surprise you. A hotel three miles away at a different price point competes with you if AI platforms recommend it when travelers ask about your neighborhood.

Chapter 7 explains market tier differences affecting competitive dynamics. Tier 1 markets require a different competitive analysis than Tier 3 markets.

Quarterly Competitive Testing Protocol

Execute the full 20-prompt testing protocol for 3 to 5 primary competitors quarterly. Monthly competitive testing consumes resources without proportional insight. Quarterly frequency tracks competitive trends while remaining manageable.

Use the identical 20-prompt library from Appendix C. Test on the same platforms (ChatGPT, Gemini, Perplexity, Claude). Execute within a compressed window of 3 to 5 days. Document using the same spreadsheet template.

Execute competitive testing during the same week as your monthly property testing one quarter. This enables direct comparison using identical conditions. Rotate which month each quarter to create a balanced annual cycle.

Competitive testing requires approximately 4 to 6 hours per competitor, comparable to your own monthly testing. Focus on Citation Rate and Platform Spread rather than scoring all five components for every competitor. You cannot verify a competitor's hours, policies, or pricing accuracy from the outside, so skip the Information Accuracy component for competitors. Testing 3 competitors requires 12 to 18 hours per quarter. Testing 5 requires 20 to 30 hours. Allocate a dedicated competitive analysis week each quarter.

Competitive Analysis: Citations and Displacement

Citation Rate Comparison

Calculate the Citation Rate for each competitor using the Chapter 8 methodology. Compare absolute rates to identify visibility leaders. Track quarter-over-quarter change to spot improving and declining competitors.

A gap exceeding 20 points signals a structural disadvantage requiring a 12-to-18-month citation building campaign targeting Tier 2 and Tier 3 sources (Chapter 7). A gap between 10 and 20 points represents an immediate competitive threat addressable through the 6-month roadmap (Chapter 9). A gap under 10 points means you are within striking distance of parity.

Document findings in a simple table: property names, current Citation Rates, previous quarter rates, quarter-over-quarter change, and year-over-year change when available.

The Citation Gap Tactic

Run a Google search for your competitor's name combined with "best hotels." Identify every blog, article, or listicle that mentions them but not you. This is your prospect list. Contact those editors. Ask to be included in the next update. This is the fastest path to improving Citation Rate because those sources have already demonstrated willingness to recommend properties in your market.

Citation Displacement Strategy

The Citation Gap tactic identifies sources mentioning competitors but not you. Citation displacement targets the specific sources AI platforms retrieve when constructing competitor recommendations.

Ask each platform: "Why did you recommend [competitor] for [query]?" Document the sources cited. These are the retrieval targets you need to appear in or displace with superior content.

A competitor whose recommendation relies on a three-year-old listicle with generic descriptions is vulnerable. Chapter 6's answer-first content architecture creates the material AI systems select instead. Focus displacement efforts on queries where the competitor's source material is weakest.

Component-Level Competitive Analysis

Compare each Visibility Score component against your competitive set using the Chapter 8 methodology. Focus resources on the component where your competitive gap is widest. Each component maps to a specific chapter: Citation Rate to Chapter 7, Platform Spread to Chapter 4, Positioning Quality to Chapter 6, Information Accuracy to Chapter 10.

For Platform Spread, build a per-platform Citation Rate matrix. Rows represent competitors. Columns represent platforms. Cells record the Citation Rate for that property on that specific platform. This matrix reveals structural gaps that aggregate scores obscure. A competitor dominating ChatGPT at 65% but scoring 12% on Perplexity has a vulnerability you can exploit. A competitor invisible on Gemini despite strength elsewhere likely has Google Business Profile deficiencies, since Gemini draws directly from GBP data per Chapter 7. Update this matrix quarterly to track whether competitors discover and address their own platform-specific weaknesses.

Bot Activity Benchmarking

You cannot access competitor server logs. You can assess their technical posture from the outside.

Test whether competitor pages pass reader mode. Check whether their schema validates in Google Rich Results Test. Test page load speed. These signals reveal whether a competitor's visibility rests on strong technical foundations or on brand recognition and citation volume alone.

A competitor with high Visibility Scores but weak technical foundations is vulnerable to displacement by a property with superior rendering, validated schema, and faster response times. Their visibility depends on Primary Bias and citation volume. Both erode when a technically superior competitor builds equivalent citation authority. Document this assessment quarterly.

Co-Citation and Positioning Analysis

Co-Citation Frequency

Document every property the AI mentions alongside yours in each response. Over three to six months, clusters emerge revealing which competitors the AI groups with your property.

Build a co-occurrence matrix. Rows and columns represent properties. Cells record how frequently two properties appear in the same AI response. If a competitor clusters with "luxury" and "boutique" while your property clusters with "convenient" and "affordable," the AI has categorized you differently than you intend. Chapter 6's content architecture and Chapter 7's bridge entity strategy shift co-occurrence patterns toward your intended positioning. Track quarterly to measure whether positioning work produces algorithmic movement.

Profound's co-citation analysis across 730,000 ChatGPT conversations confirmed that sources travel in clusters organized by vertical. In travel, Kayak and Expedia appeared together most frequently among cited domain pairs. In personal finance, NerdWallet and The Points Guy co-appeared in 14 percent of conversations citing either source. In technology, The Verge and TechRadar co-appeared in 10 percent. For hotels, this means the OTAs and review platforms appearing alongside your property in AI responses are not random. They reflect stable citation clusters that ChatGPT draws from repeatedly. Knowing your citation neighbors matters because your content competes within that cluster. If ChatGPT consistently pairs your property with Booking.com and TripAdvisor, your information accuracy on those platforms directly shapes the AI's composite answer about your hotel.

Competitive Bridge Entity Audit

For each bridge entity relevant to your market (convention centers, stadiums, cultural districts, annual events, transportation hubs), run a targeted query across all four platforms: "best hotel near [bridge entity]."

Create a matrix. Rows represent bridge entities. Columns represent competitors. Cells record mention frequency across multiple test runs, not position. AI platforms vary position significantly between identical queries. Whether a property appears at all is the reliable competitive signal. Unclaimed bridge entities represent the highest-value opportunities. Chapter 6's bridge entity strategy and

Chapter 7's citation guidance provide the methods for claiming them. Claimed entities require superior content specificity and stronger source citations to displace the incumbent. Document quarterly to track whether your bridge entity work shifts associations.

Differentiation Pattern Analysis

Document how AI platforms differentiate properties when recommending multiple options. Note which attributes platforms use to distinguish properties: location, amenities, price, style, service level. Create a differentiation map listing common attributes and noting which properties get associated with which characteristics. This reveals positioning opportunities and competitive overlaps. Chapter 6 emphasizes quantification and specificity. Optimize the attributes AI platforms already use for differentiation.

Market Position Mapping

Create a quarterly visualization plotting properties on two dimensions: Citation Rate (horizontal axis) and Positioning Quality (vertical axis).

High Citation plus High Quality equals Market Leaders. These properties dominate AI discovery through comprehensive optimization. Your goal: defend position if here, or reach this quadrant.

High Citation plus Low Quality equals High Visibility with Poor Positioning. These properties appear frequently with undifferentiated descriptions. Opportunity: improve content quality and positioning strategy from Chapter 6.

Low Citation plus High Quality equals Underexposed Quality. These properties receive favorable descriptions when mentioned with insufficient visibility. Opportunity: expand citation networks following Chapter 7 guidance.

Low Citation plus Low Quality equals Competitive Vulnerability. These properties lack both visibility and favorable positioning. Required: comprehensive optimization following the appropriate Chapter 9 roadmap.

Track property movements across quadrants quarterly. Movement toward the upper-right quadrant signals competitive advantage. Movement toward the lower-left signals increasing disadvantage.

Strategic Response Framework

Your competitive position determines your response. Four scenarios require four different approaches.

Leader Response

Properties trailing market leaders by 20 or more points require sustained investment for competitive repositioning. Full citation networks spanning Tier 1 through Tier 3 sources require 18 to 24 months to build (Chapter 7). Tier 3 foundations develop within 3 to 6 months, Tier 2 authority within 12 to 18 months, and Tier 1 placements within 18 to 24 months of sustained effort. An alternative strategy focuses on niche dominance rather than broad market leadership. Identify traveler segments competitors serve poorly and build authority in those niches. Independent properties in Tier 1 markets pursuing broad market leadership waste resources on unachievable objectives. The market tier framework in Chapter 7 identifies where niche focus delivers sustainable results.

Peer Response

Properties within 10 points of competitors require tactical optimization addressing specific component gaps. Compare component scores to reveal where the gap concentrates. The six-month roadmap in Chapter 9 achieves competitive parity through focused effort. Achievable timeline: 6 to 12 months.

Emerging Threat Response

Competitors showing rapid improvement (10 or more points of quarterly gain) demand investigation. Execute a detailed content analysis comparing your property to the rapidly improving competitor. Review their recent citation acquisitions. Test platform-specific performance to reveal where gains occurred. Sustained improvement over two consecutive quarters requires a competitive response. A single-quarter spike may represent one-time citation acquisition or algorithmic fluctuation that does not require urgent action.

Declining Competitor Response

Competitors showing decline create opportunity. Analyze which traveler segments the declining competitor serves. Evaluate whether capturing their market share aligns with your positioning. Chapter 9 provides roadmap acceleration guidance. Properties observing sustained competitive decline should consider compressed timelines where resources permit.

Quarterly Competitive Intelligence Report

Document all competitive analysis in quarterly reports. These reports maintain institutional knowledge that survives personnel changes. Chapter 10 emphasizes the importance of process documentation.

Report structure: Executive summary covering competitive landscape changes this quarter with three key findings and three strategic recommendations. Detailed scorecards showing all competitors with component scores, overall scores, and quarter-over-quarter changes. Trend analysis showing competitive movements over 12 months. Prioritized lists of competitive vulnerabilities and opportunities ranked by impact and resource requirements. Three to five specific strategic recommendations with resource requirements, expected impact, and implementation timeline.

Competitive intelligence reports inform the quarterly strategic reviews from the Chapter 10 governance framework.

APPENDIX E

OPERATIONAL TEMPLATES AND STANDARDS

Chapter 10 explains organizational integration, requiring standardized processes to prevent capability decay. This appendix provides the operational standards that govern monthly reporting, citation management, schema maintenance, content updates, and AI-assisted content production. Editable templates, spreadsheets, and checklists for each process are available for download at www. vivanderadvisors.com/AI-Visibility.

Monthly Visibility Score Reporting

The monthly report captures your Visibility Score, component breakdown, platform-specific performance, accuracy issues, trend analysis, and next-month priorities. Distribute the report 48 hours before the monthly coordination meeting described in Chapter 10.

The report should include: overall Visibility Score with month-over-month change, maturity level assessment, all five component scores with previous-month comparisons, per-platform mention counts and accuracy issues for ChatGPT, Gemini, Perplexity, and Claude, category performance across Broad Discovery, Location-Based, Amenity-Focused, and Use Case queries, an accuracy issue summary organized by information type (location, contact, hours, amenities, policies, pricing) with correction priorities, a three-month trend line showing direction and rate of change, optimization actions completed this month with hours invested, and next-month priorities with assignments and resource requirements.

The downloadable template includes pre-formatted fields for all components. Properties at Reactive and Structured maturity levels can simplify the report to the component scores, top three accuracy issues, and next-month priorities. The full report structure becomes valuable at Integrated and Optimized levels where governance requires detailed documentation.

Citation Tracking and Quarterly Audits

Maintain a master citation spreadsheet documenting every platform where your property appears. For each source, record: citation source name and URL, authority tier (1 through 4 per Chapter 7), citation type (review platform, directory, media, blog, OTA), NAP accuracy status (name, address, phone each marked accurate, needs correction, or unclaimed), profile completeness percentage, claim status and login credentials location, last updated date, and next review date with assignment.

Run a quarterly citation audit in four phases.

Phase 1, Identification: Search Google and Bing for hotel name variations. Check Tier 3 platforms (TripAdvisor, Yelp, Google Maps), OTAs (Booking, Expedia), and social platforms (Facebook, LinkedIn). Document every URL found.

Phase 2, Consistency Analysis: Create a master spreadsheet of all sources. Identify NAP variations (abbreviations, formatting differences, outdated addresses). Determine the "Gold Standard" format for your property name, address, and phone number. Flag every citation deviating from that standard.

Phase 3, Prioritization: Correct Tier 1 media citations first. Then high-traffic Tier 3 sources (Google Business Profile, major OTAs). Then lower-traffic Tier 3 sources.

Phase 4, Execution: Submit update requests through platform dashboards. Contact platforms requiring manual updates. Document submission dates. Set a reminder to verify changes in 30 days.

Chapter 7 explains the citation tier framework and NAP consistency requirements that this audit enforces.

Schema Maintenance Standards

Execute schema validation during the first week of each month. The process covers three areas.

Technical validation: Test all pages with schema implementation using Google Rich Results Test and Schema.org Validator. View page source to manually verify JSON-LD formatting. Check for common syntax errors (missing commas, unclosed brackets, incorrect quote types). If you implemented the llms.txt file described in Chapter 6, verify its accessibility and confirm all links point to current priority pages.

Accuracy verification: Compare every schema value against current operational information. Check-in and check-out times. Pet policy. Parking details and pricing. Amenity hours and schedules. Room descriptions and inventory. Pricing ranges reflecting current rates. Aggregate rating and review count matching current totals. Document any discrepancies and correct them the same week.

Operational change integration: When policies, hours, amenities, pricing, or room inventory change during the month, update the affected schema within 48 hours. Do not wait for the monthly validation cycle. Stale schema creates the hallucination risk described throughout this book. Chapter 6 provides schema implementation guidance. Appendix B provides the implementation specifications.

Content Update Standards

Every content update, whether a policy change, a new amenity description, or an expanded FAQ, should pass two quality gates before publication: the AI Optimization Checklist and the Meta Tag Retrieval Check.

AI Optimization Checklist

Review new content against Chapter 6 standards before publishing.

Answer-first structure implemented. The first sentence of every section answers the question a traveler would ask. Details follow the answer, not precede it.

Trust density verified. The first paragraph includes the property name and at least three quantified data points: numbers, distances, prices, or capacities. AI retrieval systems evaluate the opening sentences to decide whether the page contains useful information. Front-load the facts.

Quantified information throughout. Distances in miles or walking minutes. Costs in dollars. Hours in specific times. Capacities in guest counts. Vague language ("conveniently located," "competitively priced") provides nothing an AI system can extract or cite.

Question-based organization used where appropriate. Sections structured around the questions travelers ask, not the categories your marketing team prefers.

Complete details addressing follow-up questions. If you state the pool is heated, include the temperature, the hours, and the seasonal availability. Incomplete answers send the AI to a competitor whose page provides the missing detail.

Natural language avoiding marketing-heavy tone. AI systems trained on informational content deprioritize promotional language. Write as if describing the property to a knowledgeable friend, not selling it to a stranger.

Related FAQ entries created or updated. Every content change should produce or update at least one FAQ entry with the answer-first structure.

FAQ content rendered as static text. Not hidden in accordions, tabs, or click-to-expand elements. AI crawlers cannot interact with JavaScript toggles. Content behind interactive elements is invisible to retrieval.

Schema markup updated to reflect new information. If the content change affects any field in your schema (pricing, hours, policies, amenities), update the schema before or simultaneously with the content publication.

Meta Tag Retrieval Check

Chapter 6's Agentic Click section explains that AI systems decide whether to read your page based on the title tag and meta description. Apply these checks to every page update.

Title tag includes the property name and the specific page topic. A title reading "Our Amenities" tells the AI nothing. A title reading "Pet Policy, Parking Rates, and Pool Hours at The Meridian Hotel Downtown" tells the AI exactly what the page contains.

Title tag avoids generic labels. "About Us," "Our Services," and "Welcome" are invisible to retrieval systems scanning for specific answers.

Meta description delivers the answer rather than promising it. Wrong: "Learn about our pet-friendly accommodations at The Meridian. Right: "Dogs and cats welcome up to 50 lbs, $35 nightly fee, ground-floor rooms, advance booking required." The wrong version gives the AI no reason to retrieve the page. The right version gives the AI a citable fact before it opens the page.

Meta description contains at least two extractable facts: numbers, policies, prices, or capacities.

Meta description avoids teaser language. "Learn about," "Discover," and "Click to find out" are human-click tactics that fail with AI retrieval. AI systems do not experience curiosity. They evaluate information density.

LinkedIn published a content optimization checklist for AI search visibility that covers thirteen action areas. The list overlaps significantly with the standards described in this appendix, validating the approach from a major platform's perspective. Their checklist includes items this book addresses in depth: answer-block introductions, descriptive heading structure, FAQ and Article schema, descriptive alt text, embedded video content, "last updated" dates, and meta descriptions that answer the primary query. It also includes items worth incorporating into your own quality gates: using natural-language URL slugs matching the page topic, adding transcripts with VideoObject schema for video content, and embedding relevant diagrams or videos to reinforce the topic for AI extraction. Properties seeking a quick-reference companion to the detailed standards in this appendix can review LinkedIn's guide alongside Chapter 6.

Year-Specific Freshness Signals

When updating content, include an explicit year-context statement near the top of the updated section. Example: "For 2026, The Meridian has upgraded the fitness center with Peloton bikes and expanded pool hours to 6 AM through 11 PM." AI platforms interpret these statements as freshness signals during retrieval. Place them where retrieval systems encounter them early in the content chunk.

AI Context File (Brand Core)

Upload this file to any AI writing session before asking it to draft content for your property. This prevents hallucinated details and maintains voice consistency across AI-assisted content production.

The file should contain: property name (exact legal and marketing names), full address, property type, star rating, room count, 10 critical facts that must appear accurately in all content (your non-negotiable details covering signature amenities, location advantages, pricing boundaries, and policy specifics), brand voice guidelines (tone, preferred vocabulary, and a "do not say" list), primary bridge entities from Chapter 6 that the property connects to, and current rate range with the instruction to never quote rates outside the range without verification.

Update this file whenever operational details change. Include a "Last Updated" and "Next Review Due" date at the bottom. This file supports the Information Accuracy component of the Visibility Score (Chapter 8). Inaccurate AI-generated content creates the hallucination risk described throughout this book. This file is your defense against it.

APPENDIX F
GLOSSARY

This is the vocabulary of the new era. Use these terms to explain the problem to your owners and the solution to your teams.

How to Use This Glossary

This glossary is organized by strategic function rather than alphabetically. This structure allows you to find related concepts quickly during implementation.

- **AI Discovery Terms:** Concepts explaining how the new search landscape functions (e.g., *Answer Spiral, Zero-Click Search*).
- **Technical Terms:** The vocabulary you need for IT and developer conversations (e.g., *JSON-LD, Schema.org*).
- **Measurement Terms:** The definitions required to calculate your Visibility Score (e.g., *Citation Rate, Platform Spread*).

- **Organizational Terms:** The roles and processes for governance (e.g., *AI Visibility Manager*).
- **Citation & Market Tiers:** The specific hierarchies used to classify sources and markets.

AI Discovery Terms

AEO

(Answer Engine Optimization) Optimization focused specifically on earning citations in AI-generated answers. AEO represents one of several emerging subspecialties, alongside GEO, that address different aspects of AI visibility. Chapter 5 discusses where AEO fits within the broader optimization environment.

Agentic Click

The decision an AI system makes about whether to retrieve and read a web page based on its title tag and meta description. Unlike human clicks driven by curiosity, agentic clicks are driven by information density assessment. Pages with vague or promotional metadata get skipped. Pages with specific, fact-rich metadata get retrieved. Chapter 6 details optimization for the agentic click.

AI Agent

An AI system capable of executing multi-step tasks autonomously on behalf of a user, including researching options, comparing prices, and completing transactions. In hospitality, AI agents represent the trajectory toward autonomous booking where the traveler delegates the entire research-to-reservation process to an AI system. The Epilogue explores this trajectory and its implications for visibility infrastructure.

AI Discovery

Process where travelers find hotels through an AI platform recommendation rather than traditional search engines, OTAs, or direct navigation. Discovery happens when AI systems mention properties in responses to travel queries. As traditional search engines integrate AI-generated answers, the boundary between search and AI discovery continues to blur.

AI Overviews

Google's implementation of AI-generated answers appearing at the top of search results. Formerly known as SGE (Search Generative Experience). AI Overviews synthesize information from multiple search results into a single snapshot, often pushing traditional organic links below the fold.

AI Mode

Google's dedicated conversational search experience, distinct from AI Overviews. AI Mode enables multi-turn, question-and-answer interactions within Google Search. In January 2026, Google upgraded AI Mode to Gemini 3, merged it with AI Overviews so that tapping "Show more" flows directly into AI Mode, and introduced Personal Intelligence that tailors results to individual user history. Data shows 75% of AI Mode sessions end without an external click. Chapter 1 introduces the convergence of AI Overviews and AI Mode.

AI Visibility Platform

A category of third-party tools that monitor how brands appear across AI-generated answers. These platforms typically track brand mentions, citation sources, competitive share of voice, sentiment analysis, and AI bot crawl activity across multiple AI engines. The category is evolving rapidly, with capabilities and market participants changing frequently. Chapter 8 recommends evaluating these tools against the Visibility Score framework to determine which signals are reliable enough to supplement manual testing.

Alligator Mouth Effect

The widening gap between search impressions (stable or rising) and clicks (declining) that occurs when AI Overviews answer queries directly. The two lines on a Search Console graph spread apart over time like opening jaws. Properties tracking only rankings or impressions miss the structural erosion this pattern reveals. Chapter 1 introduces the concept.

Answer Engine

An AI platform providing direct answers to queries without sending users to external websites. ChatGPT and Perplexity exemplify answer engines. Traditional search engines like Google showed ranked lists of websites. Answer engines synthesize information and deliver complete responses.

Answer Spiral

Non-linear discovery pattern where travelers ask questions, receive answers, refine queries, then ask again. Each answer generates new questions. The spiral continues until the booking decision.

Bing Webmaster Tools AI Performance

Microsoft's dashboard reporting how website content appears as cited sources across Microsoft Copilot, Bing AI-generated summaries, and select partner integrations. Metrics include total citations, average cited pages per day, grounding queries, and page-level citation activity. Because Bing provides the search infrastructure powering ChatGPT, citation data reflects activity across the broader Microsoft and OpenAI ecosystem. Chapter 2 introduces the dashboard as a measurement signal. Appendix C integrates it into the monthly testing protocol.

Bridge Entity

A well-known landmark, event, institution, or attraction used in content to create a semantic link between your property and a high-authority concept the AI already recognizes. Convention centers, stadiums, cultural districts, and annual festivals all function as bridge entities. Chapter 6 details the strategy for claiming bridge entity associations through content and citation networks.

Chrome Auto Browse

Google Chrome's agentic browsing capability announced in January 2026, where the browser autonomously navigates websites on behalf of users to complete tasks. Chrome Auto Browse extends the agentic click concept beyond AI search platforms to the browser itself. Properties whose pages rely on JavaScript interactivity or fail rendering accessibility tests risk exclusion from Chrome's autonomous navigation.

Citation

Any mention of your property on external websites, platforms, or publications. Citations include review platform listings, booking site profiles, news articles, blog posts, and directory entries. AI systems reference these citations when formulating recommendations. The quantity, quality, and consistency of citations determine AI trust.

Citation Network

A collection of interconnected mentions, references, and links establishing property authority across the web. Strong citation networks include diverse sources spanning review platforms, authoritative publications, industry media, and booking channels. Networks compound over time as new citations reference existing ones.

Co-Citation

The pattern where two or more properties appear together in the same AI response to a query. Co-citation frequency reveals how AI platforms group competitors. Tracking co-citation patterns over time shows whether your optimization work shifts the competitive associations AI systems make.

Content Differentiation

The practice of creating website content that provides specific, quantified, property-level detail rather than generic descriptions common across competing hotels. AI platforms select sources offering the most complete and distinctive answers. A page describing "spacious rooms with great views" loses to a page stating "42 square meter corner rooms facing the harbor, floor-to-ceiling windows on two walls, blackout curtains, Nespresso machine." Chapter 3 and Chapter 6 detail the content differentiation strategy.

Co-Occurrence

A pattern where your property gets mentioned alongside specific terms, locations, or competitors. When multiple sources mention your hotel as "pet-friendly" or "near convention center," AI systems learn these associations. Co-occurrence patterns shape how AI platforms categorize and recommend properties.

Directional Evidence

Data that indicates a consistent trend without providing statistically precise attribution. AI visibility measurement operates on directional evidence because traditional attribution models cannot track AI-mediated discovery pathways. The term acknowledges measurement limitations while affirming the validity of consistent patterns across multiple data sources.

Discovery Layer

Systems and platforms mediating how travelers find hotels. The discovery layer evolved from search engines to AI platforms between 2023 and 2025. Properties optimize for the discovery layer by building visibility across the platforms travelers actually use.

GEO

(Generative Engine Optimization) Optimization targeting how large language models synthesize information across sources when constructing answers. GEO addresses the retrieval and synthesis process rather than traditional ranking. This book uses GEO as the preferred term throughout, as AEO and GEO are used interchangeably across the industry. Chapter 5 explains the distinction from traditional SEO and why the underlying mechanics require different measurement and strategy.

Google Business Profile (GBP)

Google's free business listing platform, formerly Google My Business. GBP data feeds directly into Gemini's recommendations and appears in Google Maps, Google Search, and AI Overviews. For hospitality properties, GBP functions as the single most influential Tier 3 citation source. Inaccurate or incomplete GBP data creates hallucination risk across every Google-connected AI surface.

Hallucination

AI generation of plausible yet incorrect information. A system might claim that your property offers airport shuttle service when it does not. Hallucinations occur when training data contains gaps, when retrieved sources conflict, or when schema and citation information across platforms is inconsistent.

Multimodal Search

Search queries using inputs beyond text, including images (Google Lens), voice, and video. A traveler pointing their phone camera at a building to identify nearby hotels is conducting a multimodal search. AI platforms increasingly support multimodal inputs, expanding discovery beyond typed queries.

NAP Consistency

Maintaining an identical Name, Address, Phone format across all online citations. Consistency enables entity recognition. Variations confuse AI platforms and weaken authority signals.

OTA (Online Travel Agency)

Third-party booking platform such as Expedia, Booking.com, or Hotels.com that sells hotel rooms in exchange for commission, typically 15 to 25 percent of the booking value. OTAs function as both distribution channels and high-authority citation sources for AI platforms. The Prologue and Chapter 1 detail the financial dynamics of OTA dependency.

Primary Bias

The statistical preference of AI models for large, established brands due to their dominance in historical training data. Marriott, Hilton, and other major chains appear so frequently across the web that AI models develop a built-in familiarity advantage before any optimization begins. Independent properties must overcome Primary Bias through superior content specificity and targeted citation networks.

Prompt

A question or query submitted to an AI platform triggering response generation.

Retrieval Mechanism

Method AI platforms use to gather information when responding to queries. ChatGPT combines training data with real-time web search, triggering background searches in 59% of local-intent queries (Chapter 4). Perplexity performs real-time web searches for every query. Gemini blends its Google search index with proprietary data. Understanding retrieval mechanisms informs platform-specific optimization strategies.

Semantic Dilution

The degradation of AI retrieval confidence that occurs when multiple versions of the same information exist across your pages or platforms. Instead of building one strong embedding representing your property, the AI creates several weaker, competing embeddings. Google reconciles these conflicts through its indexing logic over time. AI retrieval systems do not. They average the conflicting signals, producing lower-confidence representations that reduce your likelihood of citation. Consistent NAP information, unified policy statements, and single-source content management prevent semantic dilution.

Visibility Score

Measurement framework quantifying AI presence across platforms through five weighted components. Citation Rate measures mention frequency. Platform Spread assesses balance across systems. Positioning Quality evaluates prominence and favorability. Information Accuracy tracks correctness. Competitive Context compares performance against competitors. Scores range from 0 to 100 points, mapping to maturity levels.

Walled Garden

A platform ecosystem (like Instagram, TikTok, or an OTA) designed to keep users and data inside its boundaries. Walled gardens do not pass authority signals to the open web, meaning popularity inside a walled garden (e.g., Instagram followers) does not translate to visibility in AI search engines.

Zero-Click Search

Query where users receive satisfactory answers without clicking any external links. Zero-click searches represent discovery happening before properties can track engagement, often resulting in a loss of website traffic. In local search contexts (Google Maps), zero-click actions like phone calls or direction requests may still drive offline conversions.

Technical Implementation Terms

@id Property

Schema.org identifier creating a unique reference, enabling connections between schema objects. Hotels use @id properties that link the Hotel schema to the Address and Review schemas. The @id format follows URL patterns: "https://yourhotel.com/#hotel" identifies the hotel entity, while "https://yourhotel.com/#address" identifies the address entity.

AggregateRating

Schema type summarizing review scores across multiple reviews. AggregateRating includes ratingValue (average score), reviewCount (total reviews), bestRating (maximum possible rating), and worstRating (minimum possible rating). This structured data helps AI systems understand guest satisfaction levels.

Alt Text

Descriptive text for images enabling AI understanding of visual content. Effective alt text describes image content specifically without keyword stuffing. Alt text appears when images fail to load and supports accessibility.

Canonical Truth

In the context of AI visibility, the authoritative single source of accurate property information. Your website serves as the canonical truth for AI systems attempting to understand your hotel. When multiple sources conflict, canonical truth provides definitive answers. Single-source content management prevents inconsistencies undermining authority. Note: this differs from the technical SEO term "canonical tag" (rel=canonical), which addresses duplicate content.

Entity Recognition

AI system identification of distinct entities (businesses, locations, people) across mentions. Consistent NAP information enables entity recognition. Variations prevent systems from recognizing that multiple references identify identical properties.

Embeddings

The conversion of text into mathematical coordinates that allow AI systems to measure the semantic relationship between concepts rather than matching keywords. When an AI model processes your content, it converts words into numerical vectors occupying positions in a multi-dimensional space. Concepts that are semantically related cluster together. This is the mechanical basis for why specificity and co-occurrence matter more than keyword repetition.

FAQ Schema

Structured data format mapping questions to answers, enabling direct AI extraction. The FAQ schema uses Question and Answer types within FAQPage containers. Each question includes specific text that travelers ask. Each answer provides complete information addressing the question. This format aligns perfectly with AI discovery patterns.

Fraggle

A specific passage or fragment of a web page that an AI system extracts and presents as a standalone answer, independent of the rest of the page. AI platforms retrieve fraggles rather than full pages, selecting the most relevant text block for each query. Content structured with answer-first formatting and clear heading hierarchies produces better fraggles.

Hotel Schema

Structured data type for accommodation properties, including operational details and amenities. Hotel schema documents name, address, phone, website, hours, policies, facilities, and services. Complete implementation enables AI systems to extract comprehensive property information.

JSON-LD

JavaScript Object Notation for Linked Data. The preferred format for schema markup implementation. JSON-LD appears in script tags within the page's HTML, separate from the visible content. This separation enables structured data management without affecting page design. The format proves easier to implement and maintain than older approaches.

Knowledge Graph

A structured database storing information as entities (people, places, businesses) and the verified relationships between them. Google's Knowledge Graph powers factual AI answers by maintaining a confident record of entity attributes drawn from schema markup, citations, and business listings. When your sources agree, the record strengthens. When they conflict, the record degrades.

LLM

(Large Language Model) An AI system trained on vast amounts of text data to understand and generate human language. ChatGPT, Gemini, Claude, and Perplexity are all powered by large language models. LLMs process your content by converting it into mathematical representations (embeddings) and evaluating relevance to traveler queries through pattern matching rather than keyword matching.

LLMS.TXT

An emerging technical convention where a simple markdown file is placed in a website's root directory to guide AI crawlers. Unlike formal standards (like Schema.org), this is an experimental method designed to provide AI models with a clean, text-only map of priority content, stripping away navigation code and design elements. It functions as a "courtesy file" to help models process site information more efficiently.

LocalBusiness

Schema type for local business entities applicable to hotels. Hotels use dual typing, combining Hotel and LocalBusiness. This combination maximizes compatibility across AI systems looking for either type when gathering business information.

LocationFeatureSpecification

Schema type detailing specific amenity characteristics. LocationFeatureSpecification documents amenity names, availability status, hours, restrictions, and fees. Detailed specifications enable AI systems to answer specific questions about facilities.

Model Context Protocol (MCP)

An open standard that enables AI platforms to connect with external applications and data sources through structured interfaces. In hospitality, MCP allows AI systems like ChatGPT to access hotel availability, rates, and inventory data directly, enabling travelers to search properties and view details within AI conversations. Emerging MCP-based aggregation services function similarly to channel managers, connecting individual properties to AI platforms without requiring custom integrations for each platform.

Product Schema

Schema type for bookable units (room types), including specifications and pricing. Product schema enables AI systems to compare room options. Implementation includes descriptions, images, pricing, capacity, and amenities.

Query Fan-Out

The background process where an AI model breaks a single user prompt (e.g., "Best hotels in Austin for families") into multiple distinct search queries (e.g., "Austin family hotels," "Austin hotels with kids clubs," "Austin hotel safety reviews") to gather comprehensive data before synthesizing an answer. This explains why optimizing for single keywords is no longer sufficient.

Reader Mode

Browser feature displaying simplified page content without complex styling or JavaScript. Reader mode test reveals whether AI crawlers can access your content. Pages that fail the reader mode test are likely to fail AI accessibility.

Rendering Accessibility

Whether AI crawlers can access and process your web page content. Pages built with heavy JavaScript frameworks, client-side rendering, or interactive elements such as accordions and tabs may appear functional to human visitors yet remain invisible to AI systems. The reader mode test provides a quick proxy for rendering accessibility. Chapter 6 details the technical requirements. Appendix C includes rendering accessibility in the pre-test checklist.

Retrieval-Augmented Generation (RAG)

The process by which AI models query external sources in real time before generating an answer, rather than relying solely on their training data. When a traveler asks an AI platform for hotel recommendations, the model does not answer from memory alone. It runs background searches, retrieves current content from the web, and synthesizes that retrieved information into its response. RAG is the mechanical reason why SEO fundamentals remain essential for AI visibility. If your content does not appear in the retrieval results, the AI cannot include your property in its answer, regardless of what the model learned during training. The Query Fan-Out process described in Chapter 6 operates within this retrieval architecture.

Schema.org

Collaborative project defining a structured data vocabulary for the web. Schema.org provides specifications for marking up content, enabling machine understanding. Major search engines and AI platforms support Schema.org vocabularies.

Semantic HTML

HTML using elements conveying content meaning (headings, lists, tables) rather than only visual presentation. Semantic markup helps AI systems understand content organization and relative importance.

Server-Side Rendering

Generating complete HTML on the server before sending it to the browser. Server-side rendering ensures that content is accessible to crawlers. Modern frameworks support server-side rendering while maintaining dynamic functionality for human visitors.

Trust Density

The concentration of verifiable facts in the opening sentences of a content section. AI retrieval systems evaluate the first paragraph to determine whether a page contains extractable information. High trust density means the opening includes the property name and at least three quantified data points such as distances, prices, hours, or capacities. Low trust density (vague language, marketing copy, welcome messages) signals to AI systems that the page lacks citable content.

Universal Commerce Protocol (UCP)

An emerging open standard designed to enable AI agents to discover products, compare options, and complete purchases through structured machine-readable interfaces. UCP would allow AI systems to interact directly with hotel booking engines without navigating human-designed websites. The Epilogue discusses its potential implications for hospitality.

Measurement Terms

Baseline Measurement

Initial Visibility Score measurement establishing the starting point for comparison. Baseline measurement documents current performance across all five components before optimization begins. All future progress measures against the baseline.

Citation Rate

Percentage of tested queries where the property is mentioned. The Citation Rate component is weighted at 30% in the overall score. Calculate as (Total mentions divided by 80 tests) multiplied by 100.

Competitive Context

Visibility relative to direct competitors. The Competitive Context component is weighted at 10% in the overall score. Calculate as (Your Citation Rate divided by Competitor Average Citation Rate) multiplied by 100, capped at 150.

Component Score

Individual score for Citation Rate, Platform Spread, Positioning Quality, Information Accuracy, or Competitive Context. Five component scores combine to produce the Overall Visibility Score.

Information Accuracy

The correctness of the property details AI systems provide. The Information Accuracy component is weighted at 15% in the overall score. Score accuracy across six information types: location, contact, hours, amenities, policies, and pricing.

Maturity Level

Classification of AI visibility capability based on Overall Visibility Score. Five levels: Invisible (0 to 19), Reactive (20 to 39), Structured (40 to 59), Integrated (60 to 79), Optimized (80 to 100). Each level indicates different operational capabilities and resource requirements.

Mention

An AI platform's inclusion of your property in a response to a query. Mentions vary in quality from first position with a detailed description to fifth position with minimal reference. Each mention receives a position score and a quality score.

Mention Trap

The condition where a property achieves a high Citation Rate (AI platforms name it frequently) with low Positioning Quality (descriptions are generic or unfavorable). The AI knows the property exists without advocating for it. Chapter 7 introduces the distinction between mentions and recommendations. Escaping the mention trap requires content differentiation following Chapter 6 and citation authority building following Chapter 7.

Overall Visibility Score

Weighted sum of five component scores ranging from 0 to 100 points. Formula: (Citation Rate multiplied by 0.30) plus (Platform Spread multiplied by 0.25) plus (Positioning Quality multiplied by 0.20) plus (Information Accuracy multiplied by 0.15) plus (Competitive Context multiplied by 0.10).

Platform Spread

Balance of performance across AI platforms. The Platform Spread component accounts for 25% of the overall score. Scoring: 4 platforms equals 100 points, 3 platforms equals 75 points, 2 platforms equals 50 points, 1 platform equals 25 points, 0 platforms equals 0 points.

Positioning Quality

Prominence and favorability of mentions. The quality component is weighted at 20% in the overall score. Score each mention for position (first through fifth) and description quality (detailed positive through minimal). Average all mention scores, then multiply by 2, capped at 100.

Prompt Library

Standardized collection of test queries enabling consistent monthly measurement. Chapter 8 provides the core 20-prompt library across 4 categories: Broad Discovery, Location-Based, Amenity-Focused, and Use Case. Appendix C expands the available prompts to 10 per category and adds a fifth category, Multi-Criteria Compound Queries, while maintaining the 20-prompt monthly test set.

Share of Search

Branded search volume for your property expressed as a percentage of total branded search volume across your competitive set. Measured through Google Trends and tools like Semrush. Share of Search serves as a proxy for brand awareness and correlates with AI recommendation frequency due to Primary Bias. Chapter 2 introduces the methodology. Appendix D integrates it into competitive intelligence.

Organizational Terms

AI Visibility Manager

Role with explicit accountability for AI visibility performance. Manager coordinates team activities, executes measurement, analyzes results, identifies priorities, and reports to leadership. The role requires 15 to 40 hours per week, depending on property size and maturity level.

Governance Framework

Structures and processes ensuring sustained execution and strategic alignment. Framework includes monthly operational reviews, quarterly strategic reviews, annual planning, clear role assignments, decision-making authority, and escalation procedures.

Infrastructure Mindset

The strategic reframing of marketing investment from "campaigns" (short-term, direct ROI) to "infrastructure" (long-term, essential utility). Similar to paying for electricity or roads, AI visibility is treated as a necessary cost of doing business to ensure discoverability, even when direct attribution is impossible.

Monthly Operational Review

Regular meeting addressing tactical coordination and issue resolution. Operational reviews occur monthly and cover performance updates, initiative progress, blockers, resource needs, and next month's priorities. Duration 45 to 60 minutes. Participants include a manager, technical specialist, content lead, and operations representative.

Process Documentation

Written procedures ensuring execution consistency despite personnel changes. Documentation covers monthly testing procedures, schema maintenance workflows, content update standards, citation monitoring, and review response protocols. Store centrally with version control.

Quarterly Strategic Review

Periodic meeting addressing performance analysis and resource allocation. Strategic reviews occur quarterly and cover full performance analysis, competitive positioning, initiative effectiveness, resource allocation, and platform evolution response. Duration 90 to 120 minutes. Participants include the manager, director, IT director, general manager, and revenue manager.

Citation Tier Terms

Tier 1 Sources

The highest authority sources establishing unquestionable credibility. Tier 1 includes major news publications (*New York Times, Wall Street Journal*), national travel magazines (*Travel + Leisure, Condé Nast Traveler*), and authoritative reference sources (Wikipedia for entities that meet notability criteria). AI systems treat Tier 1 sources as ground truth. Tier 1 citations prove difficult to obtain yet provide significant visibility advantages.

Tier 2 Sources

Strong authority sources more accessible than Tier 1 sources. Tier 2 includes regional media outlets, trade publications (Hotel Business, Lodging Magazine), and authoritative travel blogs with substantial readership. Tier 2 sources provide the best return on investment for most hotels. Properties can secure Tier 2 placements through relationship development and strategic storytelling.

Tier 3 Sources

Baseline presence platforms establishing foundational legitimacy. Tier 3 includes review platforms (TripAdvisor, Google), booking sites (Expedia, Booking.com), business directories (Bing Places, Yellow Pages), and local listings (chamber of commerce, tourism boards). Every property requires a complete Tier 3 foundation. Tier 3 citations prove easy to obtain through claiming and optimization.

Tier 4 Sources

Minimal authority sources contributing negligible trust signals. Tier 4 includes user-generated platforms without editorial standards, low-quality directories, link farms, and content aggregators. Tier 4 citations provide minimal value. Properties should avoid investing resources in pursuing Tier 4 placements.

Market Tier Terms

Major Metro Markets

Major metropolitan centers, including New York City, Los Angeles, San Francisco, Miami, Las Vegas, Chicago, Boston, and Washington, DC. These markets share characteristics, creating intense competitive pressure. Major hotel brands dominate discovery through massive citation networks, substantial marketing budgets, and established algorithmic momentum.

Regional Hub Markets

Regional hubs and secondary metros, including Austin, Nashville, Portland, Denver, Charleston, Savannah, Santa Fe, and Asheville.

These markets enable independent competition. Hotel brand presence remains significant yet less overwhelming than major metro markets.

Emerging Markets

Smaller cities, specialized resort destinations, rural tourism areas, and emerging destinations. Limited hotel brand penetration means independents often represent primary lodging options. Low competitive intensity enables rapid establishment of visibility. First-mover advantages prove particularly durable.

APPENDIX G

QUICK START GUIDE

This quick assessment differs from the Visibility Score framework in Chapter 8. The Visibility Score requires monthly testing across AI platforms and produces precise competitive benchmarking. This assessment provides immediate self-evaluation using questions you can answer right now without testing. Use this assessment to determine your starting point. Use the Chapter 8 framework for ongoing measurement. The score ranges below use broader bands than the five maturity levels in Chapter 5, grouping properties into four action-oriented categories rather than five capability tiers. When this assessment directs you to a Chapter 9 roadmap, treat that as your recommended starting point. Once you complete the full Visibility Score testing from Chapter 8, use those results to confirm or adjust your roadmap selection. This assessment applies to any discovery-dependent business. Replace "hotel" with your business type, "traveler" with your customer, "property" with your business, and "booking" with your conversion action. The diagnostic questions measure the same capabilities regardless of industry.

This assessment reveals two critical questions: Can customers actually find and trust your business through AI platforms, and do you have the capabilities to maintain and improve that findability? You can be accidentally findable without sustainable processes. Or you can have great processes while remaining invisible. Both situations require different fixes.

Why This Matters: The Prologue documents that 69% of global searches now end without a click, and AI-generated answers appear at the top of results for the majority of hotel queries. When a traveler asks ChatGPT or Gemini, "best hotels in [your city]," does your property appear? This 11-question assessment tells you where you stand and what to fix first.

PART A: ARE YOU FINDABLE? (50 points possible)

These questions measure whether AI platforms can actually discover, understand, and recommend your property.

Question 1: Can AI systems access and read your website? (10 points)

Two checks. First, open any page on your website in Chrome, Edge, Safari, or Firefox Reader Mode. Does all your content display properly? Second, visit yourdomain.com/robots.txt. Do you see lines blocking GPTBot, OAI-SearchBot, ClaudeBot, PerplexityBot, CCBot, or Google-Extended?

- **10 points:** Content fully visible in Reader Mode AND no AI crawler blocks in robots.txt.

- **5 points:** Content visible in Reader Mode BUT robots.txt blocks one or more AI crawlers. OR content partially broken in Reader Mode with no crawler blocks.

- **0 points:** Content fails Reader Mode AND/OR robots.txt blocks major AI crawlers.

- *Why this matters:* Chapter 6 explains that AI systems cannot execute JavaScript like human browsers. If your content requires JavaScript to display, AI platforms cannot see it. Blocking AI crawlers in robots.txt locks the door entirely. You cannot improve visibility while preventing the systems from reading your site.

Question 2: Does your content signal that it is current? (5 points)

Look at your FAQ page, policies page, or website footer. Is the current year (2026) explicitly mentioned in the text or in a "last updated" date?

- **5 points:** Current year visible in page content or update dates.
- **0 points:** No dates visible or most recent dates show prior year or earlier.
- *Why this matters:* AI models struggle with temporal accuracy. Explicit dates act as anchors telling the AI "this is current information," boosting your authority over competitors with undated content. Chapter 6's content architecture emphasizes freshness signals as retrieval advantages.

Question 3: Do you have structured data telling AI what you offer? (15 points)

Go to Google's Rich Results Test (search for it). Paste the URL of your most popular room type page, not your homepage. Does it detect 'Hotel,' 'Product,' or 'LocalBusiness' schema? *(Alternative: View Page Source and search for 'application/ld+json'.)*

- **15 points:** Schema markup on homepage, room pages, and amenity pages.
- **7 points:** Schema on homepage only.
- **0 points:** No schema found.

- *Why this matters:* Chapter 6 details how schema markup transforms your website into a database that AI systems can query reliably. AI agents often land on specific room or amenity pages, not your homepage. Testing only the homepage misses the pages where booking decisions happen.

Question 4: Is your information the same everywhere? (10 points)

Check your exact business name, address, and phone number on your website and Google Business Profile first. Then check TripAdvisor and two major booking sites.

- **10 points:** Identical on your website and Google Business Profile.
- **5 points:** Website and GBP match, but variations exist on TripAdvisor or booking sites.
- **0 points:** Website and GBP do not match, or different information appears across sources (wrong street, old phone).
- *Why this matters:* Chapter 7 explains how inconsistent citations confuse AI systems' entity recognition. Your website and Google Business Profile form the foundation. If those two agree, you have addressed the highest-priority consistency requirement. Secondary platforms matter, but the Website-GBP match drives the majority of entity recognition signals.

Question 5: Do AI platforms know you exist? (10 points)

Ask ChatGPT, Gemini, AND Claude: "Best hotels in [your specific neighborhood]." Do you appear in at least two of the three responses?

- **10 points:** Your property mentioned on two or more platforms.

- **5 points:** Your property mentioned on one platform only.
- **0 points:** Your property not mentioned on any platform.
- *Why this matters:* Chapter 8's Platform Spread component measures cross-platform presence. Appearing on ChatGPT but not Gemini may indicate your data exists in older training sets but is not being retrieved through real-time search. Testing multiple platforms reveals whether your visibility is robust or fragile.

PART A TOTAL: _______ / 50 points

PART B: CAN YOU SUSTAIN AND IMPROVE? (50 points possible)

These questions measure whether you have the operational capabilities to maintain findability and respond to competitive threats.

Question 6: Do you know if travelers can find you? (10 points)

In the past 30 days, have you tested whether your property appears when travelers ask AI platforms for hotel recommendations?

- **10 points:** Yes, tested within the past 30 days.
- **3 points:** Tested once, but more than 30 days ago.
- **0 points:** Never tested.
- *Why this matters:* Chapter 8 shows that systematic measurement reveals problems within weeks of emergence. Waiting until occupancy drops means competitors have already captured market share.

Question 7: Does someone own this responsibility? (10 points)

Can you name a specific person at your property who is account-able for monitoring and improving your property's visibility on AI platforms?

- **10 points:** Specific person with explicit responsibility in job description.
- **5 points:** Shared responsibility across the marketing team.
- **0 points:** No one specifically owns this.
- *Why this matters:* Chapter 10 shows that without explicit ownership, AI visibility becomes "everyone's job," meaning it becomes no one's priority. Capabilities decay within months.

Question 8: Have you fixed problems you discovered? (5 points)

If you have tested AI findability and found problems (wrong information, not appearing, bad descriptions), did you take action to fix them within 30 days?

- **5 points:** Yes, fixed problems systematically.
- **2 points:** Discussed fixing, but have not implemented.
- **0 points:** Have not tested yet OR found problems but did not fix.
- *Why this matters:* Chapter 5's maturity model distinguishes between "Reactive" properties that discover problems and "Structured" properties that fix them through systematic processes.

Question 9: Is your Google Business Profile actually complete? (10 points)

Check your Google Business Profile. Do you have: 20+ high-quality photos uploaded, complete information in every available field, responses to reviews from the past 60 days, regular posts (minimum monthly), and an active booking link or price feed connected to your profile?

- **10 points:** All five elements present.
- **5 points:** Three or four elements present.
- **0 points:** Two or fewer elements.
- *Why this matters:* Chapter 7 identifies Google Business Profile as your single most critical citation source. Gemini draws directly from GBP data. An incomplete profile signals to AI platforms that you do not maintain current information. A connected booking link or price feed enables the transactional capability the Epilogue describes as the next phase of AI discovery.

Question 10: Do you have FAQ content covering essential topics in the right format? (10 points)

Count the number of questions on your website structured as clear question-answer pairs. Confirm they cover these required topics at minimum: check-in/check-out times, pet policy with specific fees, parking details and cost, cancellation policy with timeframes. Confirm the FAQ content is displayed as static text on the page, not hidden inside accordions or click-to-expand elements.

- **10 points:** 30+ question-answer pairs covering all four required topics, displayed as static text.
- **5 points:** 10-29 question-answer pairs OR missing one or more required topics OR displayed in accordions.
- **0 points:** Fewer than 10 question-answer pairs.

- *Why this matters:* Chapter 6 explains how FAQ structure directly feeds AI-generated answers. Marketing paragraphs do not get extracted. Direct question-answer pairs do. Accordion elements that hide text from crawlers defeat the purpose. The four required topics represent the highest-stakes facts where AI hallucination causes immediate guest frustration.

Question 11: Can someone else do this work if you leave? (5 points)

If your marketing manager left tomorrow, does written documentation exist enabling a replacement to continue your AI visibility work within two weeks?

- **5 points:** Thorough documented processes.
- **2 points:** Some informal notes or emails.
- **0 points:** No documentation exists.
- *Why this matters:* Chapter 10 emphasizes that process documentation protects capabilities through personnel changes. Undocumented tribal knowledge leaves six months later when people leave.

PART B TOTAL: _______ / 50 points

YOUR READINESS ASSESSMENT

Add Part A + Part B for your total score: _______ / 100 points

0-29 POINTS: FOUNDATION CRISIS

What this means: You are not findable on AI platforms, AND you lack the processes to systematically improve. Travelers who ask AI for recommendations never discover your property.

Your three actions this week:

1. **Discover the problem (2 hours):** Test the prompt from Question 5 on ChatGPT, Gemini, and Claude. Screenshot what appears (or what does not appear).
2. **Fix your most visible problem (3 hours):** Complete your Google Business Profile OR create a basic FAQ page with 10 question-answer pairs.
3. **Assign ownership (1 hour):** Identify one person who will own AI findability. Schedule 30 minutes weekly on their calendar for testing.

Your roadmap: Chapter 9's 90-Day Foundation Sprint.

30-59 POINTS: PARTIAL FINDABILITY

What this means: You have either (A) accidental findability without processes to sustain it, or (B) good processes while remaining invisible.

Your three actions this week:

1. **Identify your specific scenario (1 hour):** Look at your Part A vs Part B scores. Are you findable but disorganized? Or organized but invisible?

2. **Fix your biggest single gap (3 hours)**: If Part A is lower, implement basic homepage schema. If Part B is lower, establish a weekly testing routine.
3. **Plan your systematic build (2 hours)**: Review Chapter 9's Six-Month Comprehensive Build. Map your first 30 days of tasks.

60–79 POINTS: COMPETITIVE POSITIONING

What this means: You are findable AND you have processes to sustain it. The question becomes whether you are gaining ground or losing ground relative to competitors. Your roadmap: Chapter 9's 12-Month Market Leadership Path.

Your three actions this week:

1. **Competitive intelligence (3 hours):** Select 10 prompts from your 20-prompt library and test them for your property and your three closest competitors.
2. **Identify your next capability tier (2 hours):** Audit your Tier 2 citations (regional media). Identify the single most valuable citation you could pursue.
3. **Expand content differentiation (4 hours):** Identify 10 questions travelers ask that competitors do not answer comprehensively.

80-100 POINTS: OPERATIONAL EXCELLENCE

What this means: You have achieved both findability and sustainable processes. AI platforms consistently mention you with favorable positioning.

Your three actions this week:

1. **Audit for decay (2 hours):** Retest the fundamentals: schema validation, reader mode, information consistency.
2. **Competitive intelligence (3 hours):** Test whether your competitors have closed the gap in the past 90 days.
3. **Explore content innovation (3 hours):** Identify one content format competitors have not adopted and prototype it.

RESOURCE CONSTRAINTS

The book provides detailed frameworks requiring substantial resources. If you lack dedicated team members or a substantial budget:

- **Start with shared foundations:** Technical accessibility (Q1-3), Consistency (Q4), GBP (Q9), Basic FAQs (Q10).
- **Defer platform-specific tactics: Chapter 9** explains sequencing optimization when resources constrain simultaneous work.
- **Extend timelines:** A 12-month roadmap executed over eighteen months delivers better results than a rushed implementation.

FINAL NOTE

Discovery has moved to AI platforms. This assessment reveals whether travelers can find you and whether you can sustain and improve that findability.

Begin today. Complete three actions this week. The properties that build visibility infrastructure now will carry advantages that late movers cannot shortcut.

ABOUT THE AUTHOR

After graduate school, I spent five years at Andersen Consulting and its successor firm Accenture, building internet strategy for enterprise financial services clients before most companies had a website. That experience established a principle I carried through every role that followed: organizational resistance kills more technology initiatives than the technology itself.

I then spent twenty years in hospitality leading digital marketing and technology strategy through senior roles at Starwood Hotels and Resorts, Wyndham Worldwide, Dolce Hotels, Club Quarters Hotels, and The Hotels Network. Across those roles, I built and led the teams responsible for search optimization, paid media, distribution strategy, and direct booking programs. Every transformation followed the same pattern: early signals dismissed by incumbents, a compression period where laggards scrambled, and a new baseline that rewarded the properties who moved first. I have watched this cycle repeat with mobile, social media, direct booking, and now AI-mediated discovery.

What I Do Now

I founded Vivander Advisors to help hotels and organizations across industries navigate the AI visibility transformation. I deliver 25 to 30 keynote presentations annually at conferences worldwide. I lead workshops for hotel groups on AI strategy, AI literacy, digital transformation, and the future of work. I write regular columns for Hospitality Upgrade on AI adoption and its operational implications for the industry.

I serve as Co-Chair of the Hospitality AI Council at HFTP (Hospitality Financial and Technology Professionals), a working committee of technology executives and consultants publishing original AI research and guidance for the global hospitality industry. At the Kellogg School of Management at Northwestern University, I Co-Lead the Product Data Strategy and Analytics program, teaching data-driven decision-making to executive-level students. My industry board work includes the Global Foundation Board at HSMAI (Hospitality Sales and Marketing Association International) and the presidency of the largest HSMAI chapter in New York City.

HSMAI selected me as one of the Top 25 Extraordinary Minds in Sales, Marketing, and Revenue Optimization in 2020. International Hospitality Institute recognized me as a Top 100 Digital Thought Leader in Hospitality in 2026. My marketing campaigns have won multiple HSMAI Adrian Awards, including the highest Platinum recognition for innovative social media work and Gold recognition for website excellence.

I have written two previous books on AI adoption. *Too Many Hats, Too Little Time* teaches professionals how to build virtual advisory teams using AI personas as executive specialists. *The AI Literacy Playbook for Hoteliers* provides operational guidance for integrating AI tools into daily hotel workflows. Both address the practical realities of implementation in resource-constrained environments.

I hold an MA in Business Communications from Northwestern University, a BA in Literature from the University of Michigan, and professional certifications including Project Management Professional (PMP), Certified Hotel Digital Marketing Professional, and Certified Revenue Management Executive.

What Makes This Book Different

I write for practitioners facing real constraints rather than theorists imagining ideal conditions. The frameworks in this book acknowledge measurement limitations. They provide pragmatic guidance for properties with limited resources. They segment recommendations by risk level and market tier. They address organizational resistance explicitly because I have lived through that resistance across three decades of technology transformation.

Connect with Michael

Michael J. Goldrich provides keynote speaking, workshops, and advisory services for hotel groups and organizations across industries navigating the AI transformation.

Website: www.vivanderadvisors.com
LinkedIn: www.linkedin.com/in/michaelgoldrich/

CITATIONS

Accor. (2026, January 29). Accor leads hospitality innovation with the launch of its ALL Accor app in ChatGPT. https://press.accor.com/accor-leads-hospitality-innovation-with-the-launch-of-its-all-accor-app-in-chatgpt/

Adegbola, A. (2026, February 26). ChatGPT ads expand as more brands and trigger patterns emerge. *Search Engine Land.* https://searchengineland.com/acceleration-in-chatgpt-ad-activity-spotted-470346

Advanced Web Ranking. (2024, July 1). AI Overview study. https://www.advancedwebranking.com/blog/ai-overview-study

Aggarwal, A. (2026). Generative engine optimization: The next frontier of search Milestone Inc. https://www.milestoneinternet.com/generative-engine-optimization

Agius, N. (2026, January 29). How to optimize for AI search: 12 proven LLM visibility tactics. Search Engine Land. https://searchengineland.com/optimize-ai-search-llm-visibility-tactics-468106

Ahrefs. (2025, April 17). AI Overviews reduce clicks by 34.5% (300k-keyword study). https://ahrefs.com/blog/ai-overviews-reduce-clicks/

Ahrefs. (2025). 90+ AI SEO statistics for 2025. https://ahrefs.com/blog/ai-seo-statistics/

Bandarra, A. C. (2026, February 10). WebMCP is available for early preview. Chrome for Developers. https://developer.chrome.com/blog/webmcp-epp

Bliss, B. (2026, January 14). How UCP could erase your customer journey data. Propellic. https://www.propellic.com/blog/how-ucp-could-erase-your-customer-journey-data

Busby, L. (2026, February 6). Why content that ranks can still fail AI retrieval. Search Engine Land. https://searchengineland.com/content-ranks-fail-ai-retrieval-468301

Business of Apps. (2025). Facebook revenue and usage statistics. https://www.businessofapps.com/data/facebook-statistics/

CampaignLive. (2025, September). 'The weather is changing': How much should publishers fret about Google AI Overviews. https://www.campaignlive.com/article/the-weather-changing-publishers-fret-google-ai-overviews/1933229

Cloudbeds. (2025, July 23). The data – The signals behind hotel AI recommendations. https://www.cloudbeds.com/hotel-ai-recommendations/data/

Conductor. (2025, December). The 2026 AEO / GEO Benchmarks Report. https://www.conductor.com/academy/aeo-geo-benchmarks-report/

Datos, A Semrush Company. (2025). State of Search Q3 2025: Behaviors, trends, and clicks across the US & Europe. https://datos.live/report/state-of-search-q3-2025/

Datos, A Semrush Company. (2026). State of Search Q4 2025: Behaviors, trends, and clicks across the US & Europe. https://datos.live/report/state-of-search-q4-2025/

de Rosent, T. (2025). Airline lost the AI search battle to its rivals. Medium. https://medium.com/@tim_62250/case-study-how-a-leading-global-airline-lost-the-ai-search-battle-to-its-rivals-a9c29b8934f8

Digiday. (2023, October 4). Publishers reckon with declining Facebook referral traffic as the platform pulls away from news. https://digiday.com/media/publishers-reckon-with-declining-facebook-referral-traffic-as-the-platform-pulls-away-from-news/

Digiday. (2025, July 10). AI platforms are driving more traffic, but not enough to offset zero-click search. https://digiday.com/media/in-graphic-detail-ai-platforms-are-driving-more-traffic-but-not-enough-to-offset-zero-click-search/

Digiday. (2025, August 15). Google AI Overviews linked to 25% drop in publisher referral traffic. https://digiday.com/media/google-ai-overviews-linked-to-25-drop-in-publisher-referral-traffic-new-data-shows/

Digital Third Coast. (2025, December). How Google Search is changing [January 2026 update]. https://www.digitalthirdcoast.com/blog/ai-mode-use-trends

DMG Media. (2025, July 10). Submission to the UK CMA on AI Overviews' impact [PDF]. https://assets.publishing.service.gov.uk/media/68a5aa50a6acbbc7fb96a3b2/DMG_Media.pdf

Eight Oh Two. (2026). 2026 AI search behavior study. https://eightohtwo.com/2026-ai-search-behavior-study/

eMarketer. (2025, August). Google AI Overviews decrease referral traffic as much as 25%. https://www.emarketer.com/content/google-ai-overviews-decrease-referral-traffic-much-25

European Central Station – 36KR. (2025, October 13). Google product vice president: It's not about piling on features, but teaching AI to understand humans. https://eu.36kr.com/en/p/3506866650864001

Fishkin, R. (2025). Exactly what to measure with lift based marketing investments. SparkToro. https://sparktoro.com/blog/exactly-what-to-measure-with-lift-based-marketing-investments/

Fishkin, R., & Gumshoe.ai. (2026, January). New research: AIs are highly inconsistent when recommending brands

or products. *SparkToro*. https://sparktoro.com/blog/
new-research-ais-are-highly-inconsistent-when-
recommending-brands-or-products-marketers-should-
take-care-when-tracking-ai-visibility/

Fox, L. & Hines, M. (2025, June). How hotels should
be thinking about their visibility on AI platforms.
PhocusWire. https://www.phocuswire.com/
cloudbeds-ai-hotel-search-results-study

Frase.io. (2025, November 17). Are FAQ schemas important
for AI search, GEO & AEO? https://www.frase.io/blog/
faq-schema-ai-search-geo-aeo

Goodwin, D. (2025, October 13). Google's Robby
Stein on AI Mode, GEO, and the future of search.
Search Engine Land. https://searchengineland.com/
google-robby-stein-ai-mode-geo-future-search-463271

Google. (2025, October). New AI-powered features help
you connect with web content in Search and Discover.
The Keyword. https://blog.google/products/search/
ai-features-web-content/

Google (2026, February) Q4 earnings call: Remarks from our
CEO https://blog.google/company-news/inside-google/
message-ceo/alphabet-earnings-q4-2025

Google. (2026, January). AI Mode in Google Search and AI
Overviews get Gemini upgrades. The Keyword. https://
blog.google/products-and-platforms/products/search/
ai-mode-ai-overviews-updates/

Google Developers. Test and debug your structured data with
the Rich Results Test. Google Search Central. https://
search.google.com/test/rich-results

Google Developers. (2025). Structured data guidelines for AI
Overviews. https://developers.google.com/search/docs/
appearance/ai-overviews

Haigler, N., & Chan, G. (2025, June 3). Case study: 6
learnings, 1 site – How traffic from ChatGPT converts.
Seer Interactive. https://www.seerinteractive.com/insights/

case-study-6-learnings-about-how-traffic-from-chatgpt-converts

Holland, A. (2025, October 14). How to know if GEO is working. Search Engine Land. https://searchengineland.com/geo-working-463278

Hotel Technology News Staff. (2025, July 3). Research: OTAs dominate as primary source in AI-powered hotel discovery. Hotel Technology News. https://hoteltechnologynews.com/2025/07/research-otas-dominate-as-primary-source-in-ai-powered-hotel-discovery/

HotelRank. (2025). GPT-5 OTA Bias Report — Comparative Insights. https://hotelrank.ai/case-studies/ota-bias-gpt5-models

HSMAI Commercial Strategy Conference. (2025). Marriott case study: Fixing cannibalization with GENAI. https://asia.hsmai.org/2025/09/22/beyond-google-how-hotels-can-win-in-the-age-of-ai-search/

Indig, K. (2026, February 16). The science of how AI pays attention. *Growth Memo*. https://www.growth-memo.com/p/the-science-of-how-ai-pays-attention

Insider Intelligence / eMarketer. (2020, July 9). The Majority of Americans' Mobile Time Spent Takes Place in Apps. https://www.emarketer.com/content/the-majority-of-americans-mobile-time-spent-takes-place-in-apps

Instagram. (2023, May 31). Instagram ranking explained. https://about.instagram.com/blog/announcements/instagram-ranking-explained

Instagram Creators. (n.d.). See how Instagram algorithms can work for you. https://creators.instagram.com/grow/algorithms-and-ranking

King, M. (2025). The AI Search Manual. iPullRank. https://ipullrank.com/ai-search-manual

Krause, F. (2022, August 10). iOS privacy: Instagram and Facebook can track anything you do on any website

in their in-app browser. https://krausefx.com/blog/
ios-privacy-instagram-and-facebook-can-track-anything-
you-do-on-any-website-in-their-in-app-browser

Krause, F. (2022, August 18). Announcing
InAppBrowser.com: See what JavaScript runs
in in-app browsers. https://krausefx.com/blog/
announcing-inappbrowsercom-see-what-javascript-commands-
get-executed-in-an-in-app-browser

Lazuk, E. (2025, January 28). Google's search quality rater
guidelines (2025): Lowest-quality section insights. https://
ethanlazuk.com/blog/sqrg-lowest-quality-section/

Li, A. (2026, January 27). Google AI Overviews get Gemini
3 upgrade, seamless AI Mode transfer. 9to5Google.
https://9to5google.com/2026/01/27/gemini-3-ai-overviews/

LinkedIn. (2025). How to optimize your owned content for
AI search. LinkedIn Marketing Solutions. https://business.
linkedin.com/marketing-solutions/blog

Long, C. (2025, October 14). New data study: What queries
is ChatGPT using behind the scenes. Nectiv. https://
nectivdigital.com/new-data-study-what-queries-is-
chatgpt-using-behind-the-scenes

McCurdy, W (2025, October). Wikipedia:
AI-generated summaries are hurting our traffic.
PC Magazine. https://www.pcmag.com/news/
wikipedia-ai-generated-summaries-are-hurting-our-traffic

McKinsey & Company. (2025, October 16). New front door to
the internet: Winning in the age of AI search. https://www.
mckinsey.com/capabilities/growth-marketing-and-sales/
our-insights/new-front-door-to-the-internet-
winning-in-the-age-of-ai-search

Mercury Technology Solutions. (2025). How QQS
became the cited hospitality consultant in AI
search. https://mtsoln.com/blog/case-study-721/
how-qqs-became-the-cited-hospitality-
consultant-in-ai-search-3849

Meta. (2018, January 11). News Feed FYI: Bringing people closer together. https://about.fb.com/news/2018/01/news-feed-fyi-bringing-people-closer-together/

Meta. (2023, June 29). How AI influences what you see on Facebook and Instagram. https://ai.meta.com/blog/how-ai-powers-experiences-facebook-instagram-system-cards/

Microsoft. (2025, October). Optimizing your content for inclusion in AI search answers. Microsoft Advertising Blog. https://about.ads.microsoft.com/en/blog/post/october-2025/optimizing-your-content-for-inclusion-in-ai-search-answers

Microsoft. (2026, February). Bing Webmaster Guidelines. Microsoft. https://www.bing.com/webmasters/help/webmaster-guidelines-30fba23a

Microsoft Bing Webmaster Tools Blog. (2026, February). Introducing AI Performance in Bing Webmaster Tools public preview. https://blogs.bing.com/webmaster/February-2026/Introducing-AI-Performance-in-Bing-Webmaster-Tools-Public-Preview

Miller, M. (2025, October 15). Why AI still runs on search – and SEO still runs the show. Search Engine Land. https://searchengineland.com/why-ai-still-runs-on-search-and-seo-still-runs-the-show-463325

Montti, R. (2025, October 15). Google answers what to do for AEO/GEO. Search Engine Journal. https://www.searchenginejournal.com/google-answers-what-to-do-for-aeo-geo/558322/

Montti, R. (2025, October 17). Google says what content gets clicked on AI Overviews. Search Engine Journal. https://www.searchenginejournal.com/google-ai-overviews-clicks/558608/

Newman. N. (2026). Journalism, media and technology trends and predictions 2026. Reuters Institute for the Study of Journalism. https://reutersinstitute.politics.ox.ac.uk/

journalism-media-and-technology-trends-and-predictions-2026

Originality.ai. (2024). Can Google detect and does it penalize AI content? (Manual actions study). https://originality.ai/can-google-detect-penalize-ai-content

Originality.ai. (2025, October). Amount of AI Content in Google Search Results – Ongoing Study. https://originality.ai/ai-content-in-google-search-results

Pew Research Center. (2025, May 23). What web browsing data tells us about how AI appears online. https://www.pewresearch.org/data-labs/2025/05/23/what-web-browsing-data-tells-us-about-how-ai-appears-online/

Pew Research Center. (2025, July 22). Google users are less likely to click on links when an AI summary appears in the results. https://www.pewresearch.org/short-reads/2025/07/22/google-users-are-less-likely-to-click-on-links-when-an-ai-summary-appears-in-the-results/

Pew Research Center. (2025, October 1). Americans have mixed feelings about AI summaries in search results. https://www.pewresearch.org/short-reads/2025/10/01/americans-have-mixed-feelings-about-ai-summaries-in-search-results/

Position Digital. (2026, February). 100+ AI SEO statistics for 2026. https://www.position.digital/blog/ai-seo-statistics/

Punturo, B. (2026, February 3). How ChatGPT sources the web. Profound. https://www.tryprofound.com/blog/chatgpt-citation-sources

Punturo, B. & Rajpal, S. (2026, February 9). How ChatGPT cites social media. Profound. https://www.tryprofound.com/blog/chatgpt-reddit-youtube-citations

Ray, L. (2025, November 12). GEO, AEO, LLMO: Separating fact from fiction & how to win in AI search [Video]. YouTube. https://www.youtube.com/watch?v=2nJkT8zOzcM

Reuters. (2025, September 24). Meta CEO Zuckerberg says Instagram has grown to 3 billion monthly active users. https://www.reuters.com/business/meta-ceo-zuckerberg-says-instagram-has-grown-3-billion-monthly-active-users-2025-09-24/

Safari Digital. (2026, January). 16 AI Overview (AIO) statistics worth knowing in 2026. https://www.safaridigital.com.au/blog/ai-overview-aio-statistics/

Schema.org. Hotel. https://schema.org/Hotel

Search Engine Land. (2024). Nearly 60% of Google searches end without a click (2024 zero-click search study). https://searchengineland.com/google-search-zero-click-study-2024-443869

Search Engine Land. (2025, April 9). Google quality raters now assess whether content is AI-generated; Automated or AI content may earn a lowest rating. https://searchengineland.com/google-quality-raters-content-ai-generated-454161

Search Engine Land. (2025, April 21). Google AI Overviews are hurting click-through rates (Ahrefs / Amsive). https://searchengineland.com/google-ai-overviews-hurt-click-through-rates-454428

Search Engine Roundtable. (2025, July 3). Zero-click searches rose from 56% to 69% YoY after AI Overviews (report coverage). https://www.seroundtable.com/Similarweb-google-zero-click-search-growth-39706.html

Search Engine Land. (2025). Measuring AI visibility and GEO performance: Hard truths. https://searchengineland.com/measuring-ai-visibility-geo-performance-hard-truths-467197

Similarweb. (2025). AI referral traffic winners by industry. https://www.Similarweb.com/blog/insights/ai-news/ai-referral-traffic-winners/

Siu, E. (2026, January 12). Real GEO optimization case studies with proven results. Single Grain. https://www.singlegrain.com/search-everywhere-optimization/real-geo-optimization-case-studies/

Skai. (2022, October). Why walled gardens are a marketer's best bet. https://skai.io/wp-content/uploads/2022/10/Walled-Garden-Survey-report.pdf

Southern, M (2025, September). Google AI Overviews Impact on Publishers & How to Adapt into 2026. Search Engine Journal. https://www.searchenginejournal.com/impact-of-ai-overviews-how-publishers-need-to-adapt/556843/

Southern, M. G. (2026, February). Bing adds GEO to official guidelines, expands AI abuse definitions. *Search Engine Journal*. https://www.searchenginejournal.com/bing-adds-geo-to-official-guidelines-expands-ai-abuse-definitions/

SparkToro. (2024). 2024 zero-click search study: For every 1,000 U.S. Google searches, only 360 clicks reach the open web. https://sparktoro.com/blog/2024-zero-click-search-study-for-every-1000-us-google-searches-only-374-clicks-go-to-the-open-web-in-the-eu-its-360/

Starkov, M. (2025, June 2). Food for thought: Is traditional search dead? HITEC.org. https://www.hitec.org/news/4127473/food-for-thought-is-traditional-search-dead

Steinberger, P. (2026). OpenClaw: Open-source personal AI agent. https://openclaw.ai/

Stoy, L. (2025, December 12). How AI search platforms expand queries with fan-out and why it skews intent. iPullRank. https://ipullrank.com/expanding-queries-with-fanout

Tank. (2025, October). The Google AI search shift report. https://tank.co.uk/the-google-ai-search-shift-report

The Guardian. (2018, January 11). Facebook overhauls News Feed in favor of 'meaningful social interactions'. https://www.theguardian.com/technology/2018/jan/11/facebook-news-feed-algorithm-overhaul-mark-zuckerberg

The Guardian. (2025, July). AI summaries cause 'devastating' drop in audiences, online news media told. https://www.theguardian.com/technology/2025/jul/24/

ai-summaries-causing-devastating-drop-in-online-news-audiences-study-finds

The Washington Post. (2025, October 7). How TikTok keeps its users scrolling for hours a day. https://www.washingtonpost.com/wellness/interactive/2025/tiktok-addiction-algorithm-scrolling-mental-health/

Tirdao, E. (2025, September). Mentioned but unlinked: How ChatGPT diverts airline clicks. PROS. https://pros.com/learn/blog/mentioned-unlinked-chatgpt-diverts-airline-clicks

Visibility Labs. (2026). ChatGPT traffic converts 31% better than non-branded organic search: 94 ecommerce sites analyzed. https://visibilitylabs.ai/chatgpt-vs-organic-search-conversion-rates/

WinBuzzer. (2026, February 6). Google's efficiency breakthrough proves its search is thriving, not dying. https://winbuzzer.com/2026/02/06/google-efficiency-breakthrough-search-thriving-ai-xcxwbn/

Wordtracker. (2024). Nearly 60% of searches on Google are zero-click. https://www.wordtracker.com/blog/seo/nearly-60-percent-of-searches-on-google-are-zero-click

Wyndham Hotels & Resorts. (2026). 2026 Hotel Owner Trends Report. Conducted by Wakefield Research among 325 hotel owners and property developers. https://development.wyndhamhotels.com/2026-hotel-owner-trends-report/

Wynter. (2026). How B2B SaaS CMOs buy software in 2026. https://wynter.com/post/how-b2b-saas-cmos-buy-software-in-2026

Yext. Case study: SIXT partners with Yext for online visibility and reputation management. https://www.yext.com/customers/sixt